The
Beauties
and the
Beasts

THE BEAUTIES

AND THE BEASTS

The Mob in Show Business

by
HANK MESSICK

David McKay Company, Inc.
New York

THE BEAUTIES AND THE BEASTS

COPYRIGHT © 1973 BY HANK MESSICK

LIBRARY OF CONGRESS CATALOG CARD NUMBER: 73-84068
ISBN: 0-679-50424-9
MANUFACTURED IN THE UNITED STATES OF AMERICA

To
Steve Allen,
who bears no responsibility, and to
Susan and Lois,
who do.

Foreword

Consider this synopsis as presented in words a gangster might employ:

There's this doll, see. Real young. Her old man's a big wheel in Hollywood and a real bastard. She's in love with this younger cat. He's what you call a tycoon too, like her old man, but square as heaven. That's why she likes him. The contrast. Anyhow, things get rough. The old bastard puts the squeeze to the square Joe. Gets him by the balls but good. Well, he may be square, but he knows his way around. When he gets enough of the crap, he has a talk with some of the boys. They "do a deal," as the Limeys say, to knock the old fart off.

Naturally, the good jerk needs an alibi, so they arrange to make the hit while he's flying east. Back then they didn't have no jets, see. The trip took like forever. Up and down, up and down, delivering the mail. And you can guess what happens. The good guy gets to thinking. Just like that the rub-out becomes a big moral thing. He decides the game just ain't worth a killing. So he looks at his watch and figures there's still time to call it off. Makes up his mind to phone long-distance from the next airport and cancel the contract.

Anyhow, he's sitting there feeling real virtuous or something when the plane hits a mountain and every bastard on board gets creamed. Naturally, the contract don't get canceled, and the hit comes off on schedule. It's all a little tough on the doll, I guess, losing her old man *and* her boyfriend too. Makes you wonder what it's all about. Seems sort of meaningless. But hell, what doesn't? When you stop to think about it, that is.

Does this mini-sketch sound familiar when stripped to the basics? It should. For in essence it is the plot of F. Scott Fitzgerald's unfinished epic of Hollywood in the 1930s, *The Last Tycoon*, which the late Edmund Wilson called Fitzgerald's "most mature piece of work."

Fitzgerald has been the subject of much sentimental nonsense by an intelligentsia which still finds stimulating that period when movies were silent and gangsters were folk heroes. Along with Ernest Hemingway and Dorothy Parker, he was and remains a symbol of the "Lost Generation," that self-centered group of juvenile delinquents who came on stage at a time when it was possible to believe that all wars were won, all challenges met. He was lucky to die at just the right moment, unlike Hemingway and Parker, and the cult has continued to grow as succeeding generations look wistfully backward in an innocence born of ignorance.

In their concern with building and cultivating a literary legend, few critics have devoted much time to Fitzgerald the reporter. That Jay Gatsby was a bootlegger is obvious to any reader of *The Great Gatsby*, and some have even acknowledged that one character was based on a real personality, Arnold Rothstein, the first mastermind of organized crime. But the critics have been more concerned with the polo players, the flat-chested flappers, the idle and aimless rich. Similarly, while Wilson can note that Fitzgerald intended in *The Last Tycoon* to "exploit the element of racketeering and gangsterism" in Hollywood, emphasis has always been placed on other qualities. Philip French, no friend of the movie industry, was bolder than most when he wrote that Fitzgerald, "a romantic to the last, saw his hero as the dying representative of a vital tradition."

Perhaps he did, and for those concerned with the legend of Fitzgerald there are scores of works analyzing every facet of his personality — every facet, that is, but the one with which we are here concerned: Fitzgerald the reporter. Indeed one could, if necessary, go a long way toward proving that Fitzgerald's fiction was only as good as his facts. When he ceased to be a good reporter, he fell flat in his fiction. As with every other writer, he was most effective when dealing with characters and situations drawn from personal experience. *The Last Tycoon*, unfinished as it is, can be called "mature" only because it was concerned with a Hollywood Fitzgerald knew only too well — a Hollywood controlled by gangsters.

For what was the "vital tradition" his last tycoon fought to save? Nothing less than art for art's sake in the motion-picture business. Under the pressure of gangsters, art was being abandoned in favor of fast-buck productions designed to appeal to the largest common denominator of society.

In the Twenties, for which Fitzgerald had been considered a spokesman, the gangster became accustomed to big money and luxury. Almost incidentally he put his foot in the stage door during a "nightclub era" spawned by bootleg booze. With the coming of legal liquor, the development of "talkies" made the motion-picture business a major target. And as always, when the gangster goes into business, art takes second billing to the fast buck.

This process noted by Fitzgerald continued long after the death of his last tycoon. Nightclubs boomed once more, with the economic heart being the casino instead of the speakeasy. The coming of television permitted even tighter control as the old "star system" died and a new breed of money men established conglomerates. Just ahead looms the potential bonanza of pay television. As Ezra Goodman, one of the more objective students of show business, has put it: "Movies and TV hope to be married, after which the happy bride and groom plan to raise a large family of slot machines."

It is perhaps ironic that F. Scott Fitzgerald, the sentimental symbol of the Lost Generation, should have been one of the few writers of the Thirties to discover what was happening in Hollywood. It is perhaps even more ironic that his legion of admirers should fail to note that in his last book "Fitz," at last, found a cause. Ironic but hardly surprising, for to acknowledge Fitzgerald as a reporter is also to ask why no one caught up the fallen banner and carried on the fight.

If there's hypocrisy in this failure it is hypocrisy that flows naturally from a society which finds the tragic figure more acceptable than the heroic. We can identify with him more easily. "No one," said Groucho Marx, "is completely unhappy at the failure of his best friend." Certainly, few citizens are truly shocked when a public idol proves to have a hollow core. Some politicians never achieve popularity until the public discerns a humanizing streak of larceny in them.

So why discourse upon the obvious? Suffice it in the pages following to show that the most "mature" stories of sex and crime are those that, like *The Last Tycoon*, are based on fact. Hopefully the reader realizes what veteran journalist Quincy Howe was said to know — "that things are rarely what they seem and even more rarely what they're said to be." If such insight is lacking, prepare, then, to find some surprises waiting down these mean streets.

HANK MESSICK

Peace River, Arcadia

Contents

Because it is sometimes so unbelievable,
the truth often escapes being known.

—Heraclitus

PART I
Gigolos and Gorillas

In covering the nightclubs I found myself enmeshed in the underworld without quite realizing what was taking place.
—EARL WILSON

. . . the Hollywood of the 1930's in which the studios were run by pirates, semi-illiterates, amoral immigrants, men who indulged in corruption, blackmail, sex orgies, nepotism, men who made exorbitant profits, bought beautiful women for bit parts, discarded them for younger favorites and trafficked with the most despicable segments of the underworld.
—LLOYD SHEARER

I'm going to marry a blind man.
— FANNY BRICE

1

Fanny and Her Man

Follies of 1917, Florenz Ziegfeld's new show, was the talk of New York. It featured two new comedians everyone agreed had promise: Will Rogers and Eddie Cantor. No one wise to the ways of show business, however, assumed they were responsible for all the newspaper-generated excitement. By the nature of things, a woman had to be involved.

The clue was the behavior of William Randolph Hearst, the middle-aged, long-married lord of a newspaper empire. This tough, often ruthless man had been smitten by the charms of a girl more than thirty years his junior who kicked nightly in the chorus line. For eight weeks Hearst appeared to watch her, reserving the same two seats each night, one to sit in, the other for his hat. And the Hearst press made Marion Cecilia Davies, daughter of Brooklyn politician Bernard Douras, into a star.

Marion was, all agreed, very lovely even though she stuttered. Hearst considered her a princess, and for her he would build by the ocean in California a castle called San Simeon. It would have two nippled towers, more than a hundred rooms, and be fitted with art treasures from a thousand castles in Europe. His personal suite would have a bed once owned by Cardinal Richelieu and gold-plated bathroom fixtures.

At the beginning, however, Hearst was too proud of Marion to shut her away in a castle. He wanted the whole world to admire her beauty and talent. Since the *Ziegfeld Follies* offered too small a stage, Marion had to appear in movies where millions could see and applaud. To achieve that goal Hearst formed Cosmopolitan Pictures. When its New York studios burned in 1924, he moved the company to Hollywood. On the studio lot of Metro-Goldwyn-Mayer, with whom Cosmopolitan had a working agreement, he built a fourteen-room bungalow to serve Marion as a dressing room. And to emphasize that his mistress was pure in heart, Hearst placed a statue of the madonna above the front door. This gesture annoyed Dorothy Parker, who wrote:

> Upon my honor,
> I saw a Madonna
> Standing in a niche,
> Above the door
> Of a prominent whore
> Of a prominent son of a bitch.

All of which, while romantic, was of little interest then or later to the reigning Ziegfeld star of 1917. A tall, plain Jane with that quality of friendliness always ascribed to the girl next door, Fanny Brice had great comic talent. She could be happy for Marion, but her own love life came first. After two years in prison, Nicky was coming home. What's more, he had promised to marry her.

Conventional morality has never been a private problem for many show business personalities. There are no qualms about working with killers, serving as shills in illegal gambling casinos, or sleeping around as fancy or career dictates. And seldom does the public object — unless someone makes an issue out of it for immoral reasons of his own. In any event, all who had known of Fanny's affair knew she always *wanted* to marry her lover.

A few who knew Fanny intimately guessed that more than love was involved. From childhood she had been obsessed with the desire to be needed. To have something to give, she would steal if necessary. Perhaps she assumed that her looks, her personality weren't enough — that her only chance of being wanted was to make herself useful. This basic insecurity remained long after talent made her a star. In those days she was called noble. Today she would be called sick.

The affair, which had been going on since 1913, began in Baltimore when Fanny, on tour with the *Follies*, met the charming Jules W. Arnstein, whom everyone knew as Nicky. Tall, suave, he had learned his Continental manners while working as a card shark on transatlantic liners. Wealthy persons going to Europe for a little culture were often a dull lot, and more than one bored passenger felt the money lost to Nicky a small price to pay for his entertaining charm.

Little wonder, then, that when the sophisticated Nicky invited funny Fanny to his room for a drink she was flattered. All doubts faded when she visited his bathroom and noticed his seven toothbrushes, gold-backed, in individual leather cases. In bed, Nicky proved as efficient as his manner had promised, leaving Fanny in such a state that she could only note that his pajamas were of twill silk — the real thing — as compared to "that shiny pimp silk."

So when he agreed to return to New York with her, she could scarcely believe her good fortune. She saw the disdain with which he greeted her comfortable apartment only as additional proof of his high quality. And when next day he went to Gimbels and selected new furnishings, she was unhappy only because she lacked the $10,000 with which to pay the bill. Magnanimously, Nicky arranged for her to pay in monthly installments. Her admiration for his *savoir-faire* increased.

A skilled and sophisticated lover is fine for a time, but one day a woman in love begins to think of children. And in the early part of this century, at least, marriage was a necessary preliminary.

Nicky, of course, was prepared. When Fanny brought up the subject, he very gently explained that he was already married, the father of a daughter. For his daughter's sake, he didn't want to get a divorce. After all, he was a gentleman.

Ah yes, a gentleman. And, frankly speaking, Nicky's honor wouldn't permit him to continue to accept money from a woman he couldn't marry. Only his love for her had made him stoop so low. The only thing to do, he had decided, was to make a clean break. He would go to England, where he had many friends and business opportunities.

Where love is concerned, women and gangsters will believe anything. Confronted with the loss of her man, she put aside her dream of family. When Nicky nobly refused to reconsider, she abandoned her career and boarded the boat with him. Eventually, when none of Nicky's big projects paid off in cash, she went back to work. The British found her as entertaining as their American cousins had, and soon Fanny was making enough money for Nicky to live in the style his sensitive sensibilities demanded.

Those months in England were happy ones. If Fanny's arms ached for babies, she concealed her hurt in the best "laughing on the outside" tradition of show biz. Then the outbreak of war and the resulting economic restrictions drove the couple back to the States. Regaining her position as a headliner at the Palace was no problem for Fanny. And she was able to demand and receive bigger salaries. The money was needed, for Nicky was always on the verge of making a million and had to have capital as well as walk-around money. Somehow his big deals never came off, but Fanny shared his optimism. Meanwhile, life was gay, exciting.

One night after the show, Fanny accompanied Nicky to a brownstone house on West Forty-sixth Street. It was a gambling joint, plush enough but not exceptional. Basically it was a male hangout, lacking that Continental elegance women of fashion inspire. Even the food was masculine — a cold buffet, hard liquor. Since Fanny was hungry, she fashioned a sandwich of smoked salmon and rullepølse on rye bread. She was washing it down with a whisky and soda when Nicky appeared with a stranger in tow. Despite his attempt to be casual, Fanny sensed he was feeling proud of himself.

"Dear," he said, "permit me to present the whitest white man of them all, Arnold Rothstein."

The slim, handsome man took her hand, pressed it slightly, held it only long enough for her to realize his skin was cold. She stared into his eyes, large and soft and brown. Against the pallor of his cheeks, they seemed intense. A woman could lose herself in those eyes, Fanny thought as she murmured her sincere if standard formula that was at once a promise and a challenge: "Any friend of Nicky's is a friend of mine."

"Nicky and I have been friends for a long time," said Rothstein. "I've looked forward to meeting you. Nicky's a splendid fellow, but sometimes I think he's a bit selfish."

"Only where marks are concerned," said Nicky, smiling a little.

"That's what I mean," replied Rothstein. He bowed slightly. "Excuse me; I've got to get back to the game."

"What the hell was that all about?" asked Fanny Brice as Rothstein disappeared into the cluster of men around a poker table. "He practically called me a sucker. Is that what your friends think of me?"

Nicky's eyes were angry, but he laughed easily. She had misunderstood. Arnold was referring to an episode that had happened back in the old days, back before he settled down. It was ancient history.

Ordinarily Fanny was content to assume that all events prior to her fateful meeting with Nicky in Baltimore were unimportant, but something in the soft eyes of Arnold Rothstein had disturbed her. She wanted details. Reluctantly Nicky Arnstein supplied them.

It began when two self-made millionaires from the sticks came to town in search of culture and good clean fun. At one of the art galleries they visited they encountered Arnstein, who impressed them immensely with his polished air and knowledge of all things artistic. He soon made it plain, of course, that New York was not a true cultural center. Only in Europe could a civilized man find food for his soul. If only he had the time, what fun it would be to introduce his new friends to the old masters. Business was such a bother.

Inevitably the two millionaires from mid-America were able to persuade Arnstein to be their guide. At their insistence he booked passage to Europe.

Rothstein watched Nicky's progress along with other Broadway con men. At the time, 1910, he was still in the process of building the bankroll that would eventually make him the most powerful man in New York, and he desperately wanted a big score. Arnstein, equally hungry, refused to steer the two marks to Rothstein's poker game, but Arnold was not a man to admit defeat. He too bought a ticket to Europe and en route there offered Arnstein ten thousand dollars for the privilege of sitting in on the inevitable poker game. The offer was declined. Rothstein was forced to watch as the millionaires were clipped for a hundred thousand. When the ship docked he didn't get off the boat.

"Of course," Nicky told Fanny, "Arnold has come a long way since then. Since he started handling lay-off bets, a hundred grand is chickenfeed. That's why he likes to rib me about not sharing the marks."

Less than a month later, Nicky was arrested. He was charged with being involved with the notorious Gondorf brothers in a wiretapping swindle that allegedly made him many thousands. That allegation alone made the whole affair absurd, Nicky told his stunned mistress. If he had made so much dough, where was it? And why had it been necessary for him to borrow from her?

So Fanny pawned her jewels to bail him out and pay his lawyers. But the lawyers lacked pull, or perhaps ability. On June 28, 1915, Nicky was sentenced to three years in prison. Gracefully accepting the inevitable while asserting his innocence, he went off to Sing Sing. Fanny visited him every week and sent food packages every other day. This display of devotion touched the prisoner, who was feeling somewhat melancholy about life in general. He agreed to get a divorce and marry Fanny as soon as he got out of prison. Love, if not virtue, had triumphed, Fanny decided.

Paroled with some regret after two years, Nicky came back to New York to make an honest woman out of Fanny. True to his word he married her. Indeed, he married her twice. A second ceremony was necessary three months after the first one when Fanny discovered that Nicky's divorce wasn't yet final. Was the slippery Arnstein trying to pull a fast one? No one even suggested such a possibility.

Fanny celebrated her new respectability by moving to an apartment on Central Park West. And shortly thereafter she became pregnant. Somehow it seemed so logical. Of course, an addition to the family meant added expense. An apartment was no longer sufficient. So, guided by Nicky, in whose taste she had infinite confidence, she purchased an estate at Huntington on Long Island. Nicky personally supervised the reconstruction of the stables, where the stalls were lined with mahogany as befitted a country gentleman who always traveled first class or not at all.

The birth of a daughter, while wonderful, did little to

change Fanny's routine. She worked as long as possible — into the seventh month — before the baby arrived, and she returned to the stage immediately afterward. For money was needed. Nicky was away a lot, involved in vague, mysterious deals that Fanny no longer believed would ever pay off. She herself was the breadwinner, but far from feeling bitter about it she considered herself lucky to have the talent to make the money to finance life with Nicky. Marion Davies might have won the affection of one of the country's richest men, but Fanny would not have changed places with her for an instant. Let Marion be a princess and live in a castle; Fanny had Prince Charming all for herself. And a sweet little baby to boot. So what if Hearst's love for Marion had destroyed his political ambitions? For love of her, Nicky had given up his career as an international con man. And, after all, wasn't politics just a glorified confidence game?

Frances Brice Arnstein was six months, ten days old when the happy dream her mother had created evaporated like a crapshooter's hot streak. Fanny came home from the Palace to find Nicky shaving off the mustache of which he was so proud. He was dressed in a shapeless suit, as unstylish as it was cheap. Nicky, obviously in haste and terrified, took time to be gentle. He kissed her lightly, pressed a newspaper into her hand. "I'll be in touch," he said and was almost running as the front door closed behind him.

Fanny Brice sat down slowly and opened yesterday's newspaper. Nick's name was there in big black type. He was, the story said, the mastermind of a ring of thieves which over a two-year period had stolen five million dollars of highly negotiable Liberty Bonds.

"Mastermind?" said Fanny. "Nicky couldn't mastermind a light bulb into a socket."

It was a remark she was to make again and again, to friends in confidence and to reporters for publication. Loyal Fanny, trying to help her husband by belittling his abilities? So her friends assumed, but they were only partly right. The process of disillusionment had begun. It would continue slowly, oh so slowly, as reality crept like a cat burglar into the barricaded recesses of the girl-woman's heart.

In attempting to help Nicky, Fanny sought information about the crime of which he was accused. In the process she learned a lot more than she bargained for.

It had begun in 1918, even before the shooting stopped in Europe. For many months patriotic Americans had bought Liberty Bonds to contribute to the war effort. As negotiable as currency, the bonds were in constant use as collateral in stock-market deals. Messengers from brokerage houses would be dispatched to pick up an envelope containing bonds worth thousands of dollars. No guards were provided, for, after all, the brokerage houses were insured by bonding companies. To hold up a messenger, and perhaps slug him to delay the alarm, required no great professional skill. Any punk could do it. The problem was in knowing who to rob and what to do with the loot. It was only after dozens of robberies and the disappearance of millions of dollars' worth of bonds that the police concluded that a mastermind was at work.

Fanny thought about Arnold Rothstein.

In the four years since Nicky had introduced Rothstein to his wife, the pasty-faced gambler had become a living legend as the man "who dwells in doorways." He was "the man uptown," the "Big Bankroll," the loner with friends in Tammany Hall and the State House in Albany where Al Smith dreamed of higher office. Since the 1919 World Series it had been whispered that, incredible as it sounded, the games had been fixed and that Rothstein had fixed them. A few months later, Bancroft Johnson, president of the American League, would make a formal accusation.

So it wasn't suprising that when the word "mastermind" was mentioned in connection with the bond thefts, the name Rothstein should come to Fanny's mind and to the attention of the police. The problem — as it would be with the World Series caper, with the rumrunning business, with narcotics smuggling, and a dozen other rackets — was finding hard evidence on which to base an arrest. Only the naive would dream about getting a conviction. The Dominic Henry incident proved that.

On January 19, 1919, New York police raided a floating crap game but made the mistake of knocking on the door without identifying themselves. The response was a volley of shots that wounded three cops. The gamblers fired almost automatically, assuming the visitors were robbers. The shooting stopped when the cops corrected the error. Twenty men were found in the room but no guns. On a fire escape outside, however, was Arnold Rothstein. And he had a gun. As a man who carried thousands of dollars, he needed a gun and had a permit to prove it.

Everyone agreed the shooting was all a mistake, but Inspector Dominic Henry — an honest cop — thought it set a bad precedent. Shooting a policeman in pursuit of his duties was a felony, and Henry wanted the law enforced. Charges of felonious assault were brought against Rothstein — and promptly dismissed. The affair was over until William Randolph Hearst saw in the affair a chance to embarrass Tammany Hall and Al Smith — the organization and the man who had blocked his political ambitions by threatening to expose his romance with Marion Davies. The Hearst paper in New York, the *American,* raised new charges. It hinted broadly that Rothstein had bribed someone. A grand-jury probe was launched, led by a district attorney friendly to Tammany. Inspector Henry, still trying to do his duty, gave an affidavit.

In due time the grand jury issued a report clearing Rothstein. It also issued an indictment charging Inspector Henry with perjury. What's more, a trial jury convicted him, and years passed before he won vindication. The accuser had become the accused. It was technique corrupt officials would use again and again in years to come. No better way of displaying power, and confusing do-gooders, could be found.

So when the grapevine whispered that Rothstein was the mastermind behind the bond thefts, police shrugged cynically and waited. A break came on February 6, 1920, when police got lucky and charged Joe Gluck and six other men with stealing $2,500 in securities. Someone, somewhere, slipped up, and Gluck was not bailed out as he expected to be. After sitting forgotten for ten days, he decided to talk. There was a mastermind, Gluck said, and he was known as "Mr. Arnold."

All available pictures of Rothstein were collected and shown to Gluck. He shook his head. No, the "Mr. Arnold" he had seen was more of a gent — tall, slender, with a rakish mustache and an air of refinement. Police sifted their files for men of that general description. They came up with several, one of which was Nicky Arnstein. And it was then that someone remembered that Nicky on occasion had called himself "Jules Arnold."

When Gluck instantly identified Nicky, there were mixed emotions in official circles. Pleasure at the prospect of at least officially solving the bond thefts was mingled with a strange feeling that once again Arnold Rothstein had outwitted them. The case against Nicky had developed a little too smoothly. It was almost too easy. Moreover, it didn't seem to be Nicky's kind of caper — too complicated in detail, too many people, too much violence. Nicky was an artist who used charm, not a blackjack, and who operated alone.

While police wondered if Rothstein was using Arnstein as a patsy, Fanny Brice waited for Nicky to get in touch. When word came at last, it was by way of W. C. Fields, the drunken juggler who made it big as a comic in the *Ziegfeld Follies of 1915*. Nicky was in a "safe" city in Ohio, which, as everyone knew, was a "safe" state. "Safe" in this context meant that appropriate officials were corrupt and would protect local gangsters and their friends from other areas. Indeed, the "Ohio Gang" was even then preparing to make Warren G. Harding the next President of the United States in an almost successful effort to make the entire country "safe" for their friends. And Nicky Arnstein, the man taking the rap for Arnold Rothstein, was a friend.

Fields, who was a friend of everyone, made it plain he didn't want to continue as a go-between. If Fanny would go to the Opera Cafe at such and such a time, Nicky would call her and make his own arrangements for the future. The establishment was a gambling joint much patronized by show-business second raters.

Nicky called on schedule. He sounded bored. Fanny needn't worry. He was in Cleveland under the protection of Ed Strong. Surely she remembered Ed. A fine fellow with a lot of influence, the Arnold Rothstein of Cleveland, no less. Speaking of Arnold, Fanny should contact Bill Fallon and retain him as counsel. Bill would fix things fast.

Fallon, soon to be famous as "The Great Mouthpiece," was Rothstein's attorney. A flamboyant character, Fallon left the fine points of the law to his partner, Eugene McGee, while he put on acts for trial juries. For a time he was very successful, and Rothstein paid him well. In the end love and the bottle betrayed him.

Fanny was familiar with Fallon's reputation. Ed Strong was another matter. An Irish playboy politician, he had a tenuous claim to show-business loyalties; his law partner, Fred Desberg, was a theatrical promoter and agent in Ohio for Loew's Inc., the giant theater chain which soon would create Metro-Goldwyn-Mayer who would make movies for Loew's to show. Fanny didn't know it, but Arnold Rothstein was a major stockholder in Loew's, having been tipped off by his good friend, Joe Schenck. In years to come Schenck would become the Arnold Rothstein of the entertainment world, a money man who would loom large in Hollywood. Strong, too, had a piece of the action with Loew's. As a close friend and business associate of Cleveland's Sammy Haas, Strong would watch the birth of the Cleveland Syndicate, that amazing "combination" which over the years would operate plush casinos from Havana to Las Vegas and provide employment for the top names of the entertainment world. Part of the Strong–Haas technique was to be on good terms with personalities of both political parties. Thus Strong was close to Maurice Maschke, for years the Republican boss of Cleveland and, with Samuel Ungerleider, the stockbroker who handled President Harding's secret account.

How deeply Strong was involved with Rothstein in the disposition of the stolen Liberty Bonds has never been made clear, but the subsequent trials and hearings left little doubt that he was an important part of the operation. In a deposition taken June 4, 1920, in New York, Strong admitted that he promised Fanny Brice he would put up bail for Nicky if she would keep his name a secret. Fanny did. In her biography, Rothstein is credited. Strong also acknowledged disposing of stolen Liberty Bonds but denied knowing they were stolen.

The working alliance between New York and Cleveland as symbolized by Rothstein and Strong was to continue in the next two decades and ultimately to become a vital part of the underpinning of the national crime syndicate and would pay immense dividends.

But of this, past and future, Fanny Brice knew nothing and cared less. Her man was in trouble and needed all the friends he could get — gangster or philanthropist or both. As Nicky had instructed, she went to Fallon, not knowing that both Strong and Rothstein had prepared the way, and Fallon took her to meet the man who paid his bills. Rothstein still looked like a fugitive from sunshine — which he was — but his brown eyes were sincere as he told Fanny how much he admired her "guts." Courage was something he had come to expect from women in show business. His wife, the former Carolyn Greene, was playing a small part in *The Chorus Lady* when he met her in 1907, and Carolyn would never forgive him if he didn't help Fanny. Once again Fanny suspected a double meaning in Rothstein's words, and oh so subtle undertone of contempt. But it wasn't something she wanted to think about. Later, maybe, when Nicky was free again, there would be time to put everything into perspective.

Fallon began negotiations with the district attorney. Nicky, after all, didn't like the living standards in New York jails. He was willing to surrender if assured of prompt release on bail. The district attorney thought bail of $100,000 would be appropriate for a mastermind of crime. Fallon offered $50,000.

While the lawyers argued, Fanny continued to have clandestine long-distance telephone conversations with Nicky, who was bearing up bravely. Indeed, Fanny got the notion he was enjoying the publicity. For the first time in years he was no longer Mr. Fanny Brice. But the game was dangerous. Police, hoping to break up the charade, began following Fanny. It became necessary to find new telephone locations. Eventually she settled on the office of a brassiere factory owned by one of Rothstein's friends. For Miss Brice to visit such an establishment at frequent intervals may have caused some comment in the police locker room, but obviously it was too delicate a matter to investigate.

Meanwhile, Fallon reached agreement that Nicky's bail would be $60,000. In Cleveland, Strong collected Liberty Bonds worth that amount and sent them to Rothstein, who gave them to Fanny. And on March 16, some three weeks after Nicky fled, Rothstein tipped his friend, Herbert Bayard Swope, editor of the New York *World*, that Nick would give himself up next day. Swope and his wife had been best man and maid of honor at Rothstein's wedding, so the gambler owed the journalist a favor. If Swope would assign a reporter to stick close to Fallon, he'd get the scoop. And, not incidentally, Rothstein would be sure the story would stick to the official facts and not wander off into speculation that Nicky was a tall guy for the real "Mr. Arnold." A friendly press is as important to gangsters as it is to politicians and movie stars.

Chance and Fallon's sense of theatrics combined to make the World's scoop even better than planned. Fanny, Fallon, and the reporter got together with the urbane fugitive on upper Broadway and, after a brief reunion, started downtown to the district attorney's office. On Fifth Avenue they were halted by the annual St. Patrick's Day parade, the big event of the year for the Irishmen of New York's finest. Sensing his opportunity, Fallon slipped in line with the aid of a friendly cop, and the car containing the alleged mastermind of crime moved triumphantly past the reviewing stand, where the Police Commissioner, among other dignitaries, saluted.

Arraignment followed. The judge, perhaps annoyed by the high spirits of the prisoner and his attorney, unexpectedly fixed bail at $100,000. This left Fallon $40,000 short. Nicky was forced to wait in jail while someone hurried to Rothstein for additional money. Fallon took Fanny, the reporter, and an interested insurance executive to a nearby speakeasy where the waiting time could be put to profitable use. While the lawyer toasted the beautiful and talented wife of his client, someone stole her new Cadillac from its parking space out front. Fallon was indignant when the theft was discovered, and he insisted the bartender get word to the crooks to return it.

"Tell it to the cops," said the bartender scornfully.

The reporter, Donald Henderson Clarke, took it upon himself to do what Fallon was too proud to do — mention the name of Arnold Rothstein. When the bartender heard the Caddy belonged to a friend of "A.R.," as the gambler was popularly known, he rushed to the telephone. Within fifteen minutes the car was back, and Monk Eastman, leader of the toughest gang in New York City, apologized profusely, assuring Fanny her car had not been damaged.

Had Fanny needed proof that Nicky's friends were big in crime, the swift return of her car would have supplied it. Even the irrepressible Fallon was silenced, drinking quietly until a messenger returned with $40,000 worth of − what else? − Liberty Bonds. Nicky was sprung, and Fanny took him home to Long Island in the liberated Cadillac. Nine months later when a son was born, she named him William, after the attorney.

Three weeks after the baby was born, Fanny returned to work. Ziegfeld had a new song for her written by Channing Pollock from a French tune, *"Mon Homme."* She was delighted, and the song became her trademark. The public was well aware of her love for Nicky and found the lyrics properly sentimental:

> It's cost me a lot
> But there's one thing I've got
> It's my man

Nicky was later to claim that the song made him look bad and hurt his case, but for Fanny it was at once an apology and a challenge.

With Fallon directing the defense, considerable delay was obtained. On his attorney's instructions, Nicky politely but firmly refused to answer the prosecution's questions. The judge held him in contempt of court. Fallon carried an appeal to the Supreme Court of the United States and won a victory much appreciated in the years that followed, by gangsters as well as honest citizens. The justices ruled that a man could legally claim the protection of the Fifth Amendment to the Constitution and refuse to answer questions that might tend to incriminate or degrade him.

Important as the decision was, it was secondary to the

question of guilt or innocence, and eventually the case came to trial. Despite Fallon's decision not to permit Nicky to testify and thus expose himself to cross-examination, the jury could not agree on a verdict. A second trial was ordered. But then came disaster. Fallon fell in love with Gertrude Vanderbilt and began acting, as Nicky put it, "like a schoolboy." Perhaps in an effort to improve his image, or, more likely, because he simply lost interest, he dropped the Arnstein case completely. His partner, Gene McGee, tried to carry on, but McGee lacked Fallon's way with a jury. The second trial ended in a conviction. Nicky got the maximum of two years, but even in his disappointment he could be thankful that Fallon had earlier forced the case into federal court. Under New York law, the maximum sentence was twenty-five years.

Arnstein went off to prison, and Fanny's rendition of "My Man" now carried enough pathos to make anyone cry. No performance was complete without the song. As admiration for her courage and loyalty rose higher and higher, there was a corresponding decrease in respect for the imprisoned Nicky. Was Fanny getting a personal revenge? It seemed so to the proud Arnstein when his request that she drop the song from her act was ignored.

Times were changing. Much had happened since Fanny became an instant sensation singing "Lovie Joe" in the *Ziegfeld Follies of 1910*. Change accelerated in 1920 with the coming of Prohibition. The old cabarets soon passed out of business, their operators too old or too honest to adjust to new conditions. The speakeasy took their place and soon developed from a hole in the wall into a nightclub. Since the key to success, a supply of booze, was controlled by gangsters, the nightclubs of the era became the property of the bootlegger. As Stanley Walker, former city editor of the New York *Herald Tribune*, put it in 1933 as he looked back: "At its best the nightclub, in all sense, was a poor imitation of the old-time spacious, clean-aired cabaret; at its worse it was horrible — a hangout for thugs, cadets, porch-climbers, pickpockets, half-wits, jewel thieves, professional maimers, yeggmen, ex-convicts and, in its later days, adepts at kidnapping or the 'snatch racket.' "

Nightclubs served as fronts for gangsters as well as outlets for their bootleg booze. More important, however, were their value as public-relations vehicles to win tolerance from indulgent citizens and equally "liberal" officials. The willingness of the public to pay the tab, however outrageous, for the privilege of getting smashed while watching a line of synchronized pudenda from ringside tables had been established with the introduction of cover charges. Now, as the quality of the liquor varied wildly from "the real McCoy" just off the boat to pure rotgut, the big spenders kept coming. Being "taken" was, somehow, part of the fun. If nothing else, it seemed to *prove* you had money to waste, and in an economic period when everyone expected to be rich tomorrow *seeming* to be a big shot was all-important. In 1909 Texas Guinan's act consisted of tossing flowers from a basket suspended from the ceiling and singing "Pansies Bring Thoughts of You." Now she was hostess at the El Fey Club and greeted customers with "Hello, suckers." Did it bother Texas, or her customers, that El Fey was owned by Larry Fay, a racketeer financed by Arnold Rothstein? Certainly Ruby Stevens didn't care. Ruby was an entertainer at El Fey, but soon she would be a shining star of motion pictures, the dearly beloved Barbara Stanwyck. Fay would be gunned down before that happened, bumped off in the gold and ivory "Hall of Mirrors" of the Club Napoleon, where a glass of ale cost one dollar. In such surroundings, who recalled that the dead man had engineered a racket that had added pennies to the cost of a quart of milk in New York City?

Fay was not unique in coming to Rothstein for money. Anne Nichols went to Rothstein for the $25,000 she needed to keep her new play running just a little longer. She offered him 50 percent of the play, but Rothstein gambled only when the odds could be controlled. He turned down the offer in favor of a straight 10 percent interest. As a result he made only $3,000 instead of half a million when the play, *Abie's Irish Rose,* ran for five years on Broadway. "Dandy Phil" Kastel financed his "bucket shops" — where high-pressure salesmen sold phony stocks, with money from "A.R." Soon Kastel would be a partner of Meyer Lansky and Frank Costello and operate the fabulous Beverly Club, with its illegal casino, outside New Orleans and, later, the Tropicana on the Strip outside Las Vegas. Leading stars of the entertainment world were happy to be booked into either.

Irving Wexler, more famous as Waxey Gordon, began rum-running for Rothstein and went on to become independent when Rothstein decided the business was too much for one man to control. Eventually Wexler would be imprisoned for income-tax evasion.

Entertainers are not unique, of course, in their willingness to co-exist with crime. A New York newspaper in 1931 was shocked when it got possession of an intelligence memorandum that concerned Owney "the Killer" Madden's successful effort to get his Park Avenue Club suitably decorated.

Tall and lean, with sleek black hair, bright blue eyes, and a face "like a falcon," Madden looked like a modern buccaneer in Bond Street clothing. Born in England, he was one of the few WASPs to achieve success in organized crime. His nickname was won as a youth while heading a pre-Prohibition gang, the Gophers. Graduate school was Sing Sing, where he served eight years on a murder rap. Released in 1923, he made millions out of the bootleg business and invested the loot in everything from nightclubs to a string of world-champion boxers.

The newspaper's memo listed twenty-three downtown nightclubs owned by Madden and his associates. For the most lavish of them all, Joseph Urban, the leading architect and theatrical designer of the day, was paid $50,000 to give it class. Urban had decorated the Austrian building at the St. Louis Exposition and served for four years as art decorator of the Boston Opera Company. Later he designed the stage settings for the first *Ziegfeld Follies* and subsequently the Ziegfeld Theatre itself. (Which perhaps explains how he came to Madden's attention.) Utilizing his talents for Killer Madden apparently no more disturbed Urban than working for Larry Fay bothered Ruby Stevens. Eventually, Madden would leave New York for Hot Springs, Arkansas, where he would marry the postmaster's daughter and live next door to the police chief while he ruled a miniature gambling empire for more than thirty years. Hot Springs became a "safe" town, a hideout for gangsters, playboys, and politicians.

Organized crime had its beginning in that age of ignorance known as the Roaring Twenties. Rothstein in New York had his counterpart in every major city. Few matched his power or his versatility, but each in his own way laid the foundations on which others would build empires. Charles "King" Solomon in Boston, Ed Strong in Cleveland, John Torrio in Chicago were pioneers in their own cities and in building interstate relationships which, in the very near future, would become that loose but lasting alliance known variously today as the Outfit, the Combination, the Syndicate.

In a society where Maddens, Waxey Gordons, Rothsteins, and assorted other gangsters flourish, an honest man sometimes has little choice. Fallon, who could have been a success in many fields, turned to the bottle to reconcile his contempt for Rothstein with the necessity — as he saw it — of accepting his dirty money. His drinking increased when his pursuit of the lovely Miss Vanderbilt proved fruitless. His troubles mounted when the Hearst newspapers, still trying to smear Tammany Hall and Al Smith, investigated the bucket-shop activities of Dandy Phil Kastel and Arnold Rothstein. Fallon was successful in getting them off the hook, but in the process he slipped up and was himself indicted for bribing a juror.

Fallon was drunk when the indictment was returned, so he hid for a week while drying himself out. Once semi-sober, he surrendered. Rothstein put up the usual quota of Liberty Bonds for bail, and Fallon announced he would defend himself. The case against him looked unbeatable. The bribed juror was ready to testify he had been bribed. In evidence was the check Fallon, in a moment of mental lapse, had given him. There were even reliable witnesses to the discussion. The presiding judge remarked: "Fallon has his back to the wall."

Inspired by the odds against him, and well aware of current moral and political prejudices, Fallon fought back. In his opening statement he told the jury he was the victim of a gigantic conspiracy conceived and organized by William Randolph Hearst. Hearst was a man of mystery, unbelievably rich and immensely powerful. A man accused of fomenting the Spanish-American War would be capable of subverting the courts of New York to destroy an attorney — if he so desired. But why would he so desire? Fallon let the suspense build during the trial, and then, in his closing statement, he gave what purported to be the answer. Placing his hand over his breast pocket, he declared. "I have here the actual birth certificates of illegitimate children of a motion-picture actress."

No need to name the actress. There had been whispers about Hearst and Marion Davies since the *Follies of 1917*. But so long as they remained whispers no one was hurt. To imply in open court that proof of an illicit relationship between the married millionaire and the unmarried actress existed was to change naughty rumor into ugly fact. Victorian hypocrisy was offended.

Such was the magic of Fallon, the courtroom actor, that he convinced the jurors that he did indeed have the evidence of which he spoke. And once that premise was accepted it was easy enough to believe that Hearst would move heaven, earth, and the judicial system to discredit him.

The jury found him not guilty. Fallon thanked the jurors, then turned to Nat Ferber, the reporter who had broken the bucket-shop story. "Nat," said Fallon loudly, "I promise you I'll never bribe another juror."

Anything that followed would have been anti-climatic, and Fallon was wise enough to die. His partner, McGee, was disbarred and tried on charges of receiving stolen Liberty Bonds. Fanny Brice, ever loyal, testified on McGee's behalf, and he was acquitted. The syndicate sent him to work with Phil Kastel in New Orleans, where he became just another faceless man of crime.

At 10:53 A.M. on November 6, 1928, as Herbert Hoover was elected President to continue "Republican prosperity," Arnold Rothstein died of a bullet wound inflicted thirty-six hours earlier. Had he lived until the polls closed, he would have won $570,000 in election bets.

Two years later Paramount Pictures based a movie on the life of Rothstein. Called *Street of Chance,* it starred William Powell, Kay Francis, and Jean Arthur. Shortly after making it, B.P. Schulberg, head of production, was fired. His friends blamed Louis B. Mayer, boss of MGM, the company controlled by Loew's, Inc., in which Rothstein had invested. Schulberg told his son that when he died his son was to cremate the body, put the ashes in a box and have a messenger blow them into Mayer's face. The son, Budd, didn't obey, but he did write a best-selling novel about Hollywood, *What Makes Sammy Run,* which annoyed Mayer immensely.

Rothstein's murder remains unsolved today, but the investigation into his death uncovered links with judges which, in turn, brought about the Seabury Commission. The Seabury probe put the heat on Tammany Hall and eventually forced Governor Roosevelt to discredit and humiliate New York's playboy mayor, "Beau James" Walker.

William Randolph Hearst in his castle at San Simeon considered this a victory after a long campaign. Princess Marion,
for whose sake he had sacrificed his own ambitions to be
President, was avenged. Now Hearst, in good conscience,
could support Roosevelt over Al Smith for the Democratic
nomination in 1932 and, much to Louis B. Mayer's horror,
back him over Herbert Hoover as well.

All of which meant nothing to Fanny Brice.

A year before Rothstein's death, Fanny's marriage to Nicky
Arnstein ended. Released from prison in 1926, a sullen Nicky
came home to a cool welcome. Because the old spell was
broken, Fanny was no longer a "mark." Baffled but still
hoping for a miracle, Nicky went to Chicago to work in a
casino where rich widows would appreciate his charm. After
thinking about it for a few months, Fanny secured a divorce.

But even as Rothstein's death did not end his influence,
neither did Fanny's divorce close the books on Nicky. Sixteen months later, on February 9, 1929, she married Billy
Rose, an up-and-coming theatrical producer. It was her way
of telling Nicky she was putting the past behind her. He
responded on October 18, 1929, by marrying a divorcee.

Determined not to be "Mr. Fanny Brice," Rose struggled to
make it on his own. Fanny helped with advice. Once when he
needed money badly, she sent him to Waxey Gordon, one of
Rothstein's partners, who paid Billy $5,000 for two skits to
be used in a new musical Waxey was sponsoring. When it
flopped in spite of the skits, Waxey sent for Rose and
demanded his money back. Billy said he would tell Fanny
that the great Waxey Gordon was a cheapskate who wouldn't
keep a bargain. Rather than lose Fanny's respect, Waxey let
Rose keep the money.

That marriage ended in 1938 when a now successful Rose
fell in love with his swimming star, Eleanor Holm. Along with
Johnny Weissmuller and Morton Downey, Eleanor would star

next year in "Billy Rose's Aquacade," the greatest attraction at the New York World's Fair. In its first year it earned the man who a decade earlier had worked for gangsters a net profit of one million dollars. Meanwhile, Fanny moved to Hollywood, where for the next few years she won millions of new fans as radio's ubiquitous "Baby Snooks."

Fanny Brice was to hear once more from Nicky Arnstein. At age seventy, with his third wife newly dead, he appealed to Fanny to try again. Kindly but firmly she refused. Nicky had not changed, she decided.

On May 29, 1951, Fanny died of a cerebral hemorrhage. In less than three months the death of William Randolph Hearst was announced. He was eighty-eight. Marion Davies was not invited to the press lord's funeral. Ten weeks later she got married at El Rancho Vegas, a Las Vegas casino. Some said her husband looked like Hearst as a young man. She wore dark blue slacks and a blue sweater and listed her age as forty-five. It was, she said, her first marriage.

2

*Cut and Re-Cut
with Joe E. Lewis*

David O. Selznick once told his writers he couldn't understand why motion-picture people should revise a classic book
or play and substitute things of their own creation. He
learned the value of following the original story line when he
produced *Gone with the Wind* and included Rhett Butler's
most famous line: "My dear, I don't give a damn." But
Selznick was unique. Few producers could resist the tempta-
tion to improve on a masterpiece. "A form of ego," Selznick
called it.

Ego, however, was not the problem in 1955 when Frank
Sinatra decided he wanted to make a movie out of *The Joker
Is Wild*, a biography of the great nightclub comedian Joe E.
Lewis, written by Art Cohn.

In a hard-hitting introduction, Cohn noted that the book
pulled no punches. "When truth and friendship were at
odds," he said, "I chose truth in the name of friendship."

The only concession, he added, was to publisher Bennett Cerf in the selection of the title. Cohn concluded: "It is Joe's life. It is Cerf's title. It is my book."

But it was to be Sinatra's movie.

Crime casts a long shadow. Many who became rich during Prohibition lived on for decades and achieved great influence in many fields. Show business is only one of them. So consider:

Frank Sinatra, who played Joe E. Lewis in the movie, was a friend of Joseph Fischetti. Fischetti and his two brothers, Rocco and Charley, were cousins of "Scarface Al" Capone and worked for his gang. Capone's favorite killer, a colleague of the Fischetti brothers, was Machinegun Jack McGurn. McGurn's boys cut the throat of Joe E. Lewis on November 9, 1927. Just a matter of show business, the business there's no business like.

There was, of course, a woman. A nice girl, a pretty girl. In show business to make a living while she found a man, she lived with Joe E. Lewis for a while. Joe, the son of Abraham Klewan, was an up-and-coming young singer in Chicago. But Jack McGurn, born Vincent Gebardi, had already arrived. McGurn at sixteen was already a killer engaged in a vendetta to revenge his father, an alky cooker who died after selling two gallons of rotgut to the wrong people. So great was McGurn's skill with the Thompson submachinegun, and so great his pleasure in using it, that Capone singled him out for special status and very special assignments. Moreover, in the fashion of the day, he was a "sheik," sleek and handsome, dark and dapper in a way Joe could never be. When Machinegun Jack crooked his finger, the girl went willingly. Joe was philosophical. Love was something to sing about. Friendship made no demands. Quickly he found another friend to warm his bed.

In any case, it was time to change jobs. For a year Joe had been packing them in at the speakeasy-casino known as the

Green Mill. His salary had climbed to $650 a week. Not bad, but popularity was something to cash in on. The New Rendezvous Cafe offered him a thousand a week, plus a cut of the gambling profits. Joe E. Lewis cared less that both gambling and bootleg liquor were illegal. He accepted the world as he found it and claimed the privilege of non-involvement so typical of show-business personalities, then and now. "I'm not a hoodlum — I'm an entertainer," he insisted. But McGurn, who was a hoodlum and proud of it, didn't agree.

McGurn owned a "piece" of the Green Mill. What's more, the New Rendezvous belonged to the rival Bugs Moran gang. To let one's top drawing card go over to the enemy was bad business — personally and corporately. In a friendly fashion he pointed out these facts to Joe, who was hungry — and naive. He grinned widely when Jack told him, "You'll never live to open."

And so two healthy young men were at odds. One of the two had to back down. While the girl both men had bedded watched. McGurn, who had taken the girl away from Joe, would lose face if Lewis defied him successfully. He would be less of a man. Joe, on the other hand, would be less than a man if he permitted Jack to take his girl *and* his new job away. It was all very basic, silly, and human.

The girl called, pleaded with Joe to come to her apartment. Fearing a trap, he refused. McGurn, he well knew, would not have refused had the situation been reversed. But Joe, as he kept insisting, was under no compulsion to swagger. He was an entertainer, not a hoodlum.

A Chicago police captain, a frequent visitor to the Green Mill while Joe sang there, tried to talk sense to his friend. "You can't buck the Outfit," said the cop, and weary experience sounded in his voice. "Not unless you're Arnold Rothstein."

The reference was simple. In 1916 Arch and Edgar Selwyn

had gone into business with Sam Goldfish. Borrowing from both names, they formed the Goldwyn Picture Corporation. Goldfish liked the new name so well he substituted it for his own. Shortly thereafter, the company merged with others and became the middle part of Metro-Goldwyn-Mayer. Control of MGM belonged to Loew's, Inc. A major stockholder in Loew's, as has been noted, was Rothstein. When the Selwyn boys encountered labor trouble at theaters they owned and were building in Chicago, they asked "A.R." for help. Rothstein sent a message to Chicago: "What you're doing to them, you're doing to me." The troubles stopped.

But Joe E. Lewis was not Selwyn, and he had no Rothstein to whom he could appeal. He was an entertainer, not a business executive.

Rumors that Lewis's opening at the New Rendezvous might star Machinegun Jack circulated through Chicago. It was hardly necessary for the club to supplement the attraction with "twelve (12) unadorned daughters of Eve." On the night the joint opened there wasn't even standing room. Among those standing, however, were a number of plainclothesmen, assigned by Joe's cop friend to protect the operators of one illegal establishment from the operators of a rival illegal establishment. Aiding in this civic duty were a number of gunmen sent over by Bugs Moran. Joe, who was an entertainer, not a hoodlum, carried a pistol in the pocket of his white jacket.

No action. At least none involving gunplay. The casino and the bar did big business, however. The customers, after all, had to do something to blunt the edge of tension. Waiting for murder was exciting entertainment, and when a busboy dropped a tray in the middle of Joe's second song, it only emphasized the potential.

A week went by. The New Rendezvous continued to do a land-office business, and the Green Mill was dying fast. Joe had difficulty concealing his growing glee. He had faced down the toughest killer in Chicago. The next time the girl invited him to her apartment he'd accept.

At 5:00 A.M. on the seventh day, Joe and the New Rendez-vous manager were happily walking to Joe's hotel when McGurn, accompanied by two bodyguards, got out of a car and stopped for a chat. He was reasonable. Joe had made his point, he noted. By opening on schedule, Joe had demon-strated he had balls. Now it was time to cut the comedy and come back to the Green Mill.

Joe refused.

Jack smiled gently. He offered his hand.

Joe shook it.

Jack got into his car and left.

In his room Joe counted his roll. It was thick with his pay for one week. It represented big-time show business. No doubt about it — Joe E. Lewis had arrived. He went to bed. He slept.

Five hours later there was a knock on the door. Struggling out of a deep slumber, Joe got out of bed and unlocked the door. Three men brushed in. Still groggy, Joe closed the door. One of the men asked a favor: "Don't yell."

They clobbered Joe from behind. And then one of the men stuck a knife into Joe's jaw and ripped downward.

It was all very impersonal, a matter of business. Show business.

Joe bled like a stuck pig. Blood came from a skull fracture, from the cut throat, from wounds that left his right arm paralyzed. The knife that severed his vocal cords missed his jugular vein by a minute fraction of an inch.

But he was alive. Somehow he got to the telephone. He could hear the operator ask for his number, but, strange, she couldn't hear him. Matter of fact, he couldn't hear himself. His lips moved but no sound came. Slowly, painfully, he crawled out into the hall. A maid came along, spotted the bloody body on the floor — and fainted. He reached the elevator but couldn't lift his left hand to the button. Some-how he pulled his feet under him, arched his back, and got his head up to the button. He pressed; the buzzer sounded. And Joe passed out.

The elevator man found him. The police rushed Joe to a nearby hospital without waiting for an ambulance. Dr. Daniel Orth, the only surgeon available, went to work. Seven hours passed before he finished. Miraculously, his patient was still alive when the operation ended. He was placed in a private room. Bugs Moran, Capone's chief rival, assigned two top gunmen to guard the room. He might talk if he lived. Well, not exactly talk. Finger. He might finger the men who cut him. Realizing this possibility, McGurn would try again, given half a chance. And who could trust the cops to stop him?

But the precautions seemed unnecessary when Joe regained consciousness. He couldn't talk. More, his brain was dam-aged. From his bed he could see the sun shining through the window, but to think "the sun is shining" was impossible without words. He had no word for "sun," no word for "shining."

He was almost a vegetable.

In the best tradition of gangster movies as yet unmade by Pat O'Brien and James Cagney, it was a Catholic priest who with patience and compassion saved the Jewish boy. Father J.A. Heitzer, an English teacher at Notre Dame, came to the hospital to see his sick sister who happened to be in the room next to Joe. Hearing from her about Joe's troubles, the priest determined to help the stricken entertainer.

Each Sunday Father Heitzer came with his large signs, each bearing a letter of the alphabet. Slowly, painstakingly, he taught his student how to make the appropriate sound — or an approximation. From letters to words they went, and the pace increased as Joe's memory came alive. Soon his brain was sending signals of impatience as hand and lips progressed less rapidly.

Just before Christmas, Joe's police friend brought in one of McGurn's punks for Joe to identify. The cops knew he was one of the men involved in assaulting Joe, but they needed his confirmation to file charges. The patient recognized the hood, but he gave no sign. The gunmen of Bugs Moran watched impassively. The cops were disgusted. If Joe wasn't a hoodlum as he had so often claimed, why didn't he act like a good citizen? As long as men believed in private vendetta over legal process, the Mob would rule Chicago.

Six days later the punk was shot to death in an alley. Within a month his two accomplices were murdered by unknown persons. Bullets found McGurn but only wounded him. He would live to get revenge on the day of St. Valentine.

Eleven weeks after Joe E. Lewis's throat was cut, he reopened at the New Rendezvous. It was his own idea. Word had reached him that the girl — his girl, McGurn's girl — was working in a two-dollar crib in the Levee, the notorious redlight district of Chicago. McGurn had put her there to make clear to her and to the world his contempt. By her presence she had converted a business squabble into a test of manhood, a test the hot-blooded soldier of Al Capone had lost. That Lewis subsequently had his throat cut made no difference. Only by humiliating the woman, making her into the cheapest of whores, could he feel again that quality of *omerta* — manliness so dear to the sons of Sicily. There was only one way for Lewis to strike back; he had to reopen at the New Rendezvous. Rage demanded it, but fear and pride reinforced the decision.

The announcement that Joe E. Lewis would return to show business was in and of itself a matter of show business. Perhaps because they refuse to become emotionally or intellectually involved in so many social and moral issues, show-business personalities love opportunities to prove to the Damon Runyons of the world that beneath their thick hides of cynicism beat hearts of gold. Joe's comeback would be such an occasion. Within an hour of the announcement the Rendezvous was sold out. Sophie Tucker led the show-business group and Bugs Moran the gangsters.

His head bandaged, his right arm crippled, his voice the croak of a frog, Joe delivered his lines and was applauded. He knew what he wanted to say; the audience could only guess at the punch lines. As high drama it was great; as entertainment it was absurd. Despite the cheers, the encores, at the end his pride was gone.

But there was plenty of liquor. Drunk enough, Joe would try to perform. By the end of three weeks the curious had seen and heard enough. They quit coming. Joe was given a ticket to Miami, where more of the curious waited. Back in Chicago a testimonial dinner was arranged, the first of many for Lewis over the years. Top show-business personalities gave of their talent: Sophie Tucker, Tom Mix, Hoot Gibson, Al Jolson. The benefit raised $14,000 for Joe. He was supposed to invest it in a solid business — a haberdashery store. Everyone knew that but Joe. He got drunk and handed most of the money to a stranger.

But show business is loyal. Jolson took him out to Holly-wood and let him loaf for months. The rest did him good. And then one night at the Plantation Club Fatty Arbuckle invited him to sing. The crowd applauded in a patently un-spontaneous demonstration. But Joe was convinced — he sang — and the ovation he received delighted him. Already he was on the way back.

New York for three weeks, and then back to the Green Mill — under new management, of course — at $1,000 a month and a piece of the action. And then one day at the Capone-owned dog track in the Capone-owned suburb of Cicero, he came face to face with Machinegun Jack McGurn. With Jack was Charley Fischetti. The two man stared into each other's eyes. It was a moment Joe had dreamed about. And when

Jack dropped his gaze and walked away, Joe felt triumphant. He had won.

With his feud settled, to his satisfaction, at least, Joe could concentrate on something important — getting stoned. One session ended in an argument with Frank Gusenberg, a Bugs Moran gunman who had served as a bodyguard while Joe was in the hospital. The next day Joe went looking for Frank, hoping to make peace with him. He was ten minutes too late in arriving at the garage where Gusenberg hung out. McGurn had been there first and had mowed down seven men in the belief that Capone's chief rival was one of them. Bugs Moran had also been delayed, but Frank and Pete Gusenberg were among the dead. It was February 14, 1929. Capone was in Miami Beach when the killings occurred. And shortly thereafter he let himself be picked up in Philadelphia for carrying a concealed weapon. He spent a few comfortable months in jail, safe from the vengeance of Moran.

Joe E. Lewis, still living off his friends and his fame as "the man the Mob couldn't kill, " floated around. He even visited Europe, where Chicago gangsters were held in high regard; they were convincing proof that America was uncivilized.

Eventually Joe got back to Chicago shortly after Al the hoodlum got home from Philadelphia. Scarface One called in Scarface Two and there was a long discussion. The upshot was that Scarface Two (Lewis) left town for New York, where he bought — that's the official story — the Chateau Madrid on West Fifty-fourth Street. Show-business tradition was observed as all the "Names" in town showed up. The gangsters tossed thousand-dollar bills around like confetti, and the entertainers — Al Jolson, George Jessel, Jack Benny, Jimmy Durante — cracked jokes, sang, and drank rotgut supplied by the hoods. It was a gala evening.

Before long Joe was "adopted" by a rather self-satisfied character who, at times, insisted he was Jesus Christ. Most people called him Dutch Schultz, but his real name was

Arthur Flegenheimer. He had been a rather run-of-the-still bootlegger and beer baron, notable only for his temper and petty greed, but suddenly he had blossomed. It happened a year or two before, and a lot of people were still wondering. Overnight, it seemed, Dutch developed both confidence and power and became something of a man about town as well.

It was some years before the truth became known. Dutch had simply become a junior partner of Johnny Torrio, the mentor of Al Capone. A New Yorker, Torrio had gone to Chicago to work for his uncle back in the days when the white-slave trade was big business. Displaying remarkable ability, Johnny gradually took over. When his uncle failed to appreciate the possibilities of Prohibition, Torrio had him killed and became boss in name as well as fact. Meanwhile he imported Capone from New York and, after testing him, taught him the business. For Torrio, a quiet, home-loving man, crime was a business, and gang wars were exercises in futility. Unable to make peace in Chicago, he turned the organization over to his protégé Capone and took a long cruise to Hawaii. Returning to New York in 1928, he had talked rival rumrunners into joining together in an alliance known as the "Big Seven." In 1929 Torrio had proposed a national organization, and a preliminary meeting was held at Atlantic City. It was while returning from this meeting that Capone had been jailed in Philadelphia. Torrio believed prospects were good for eventual cooperation, but he preferred to work in the shadows. One of the tools he selected to front for him was Schultz. After years of experience in Chicago with such individualists as Dion O'Bannion, Hymie Weiss, and Bugs Moran, Dutch presented no particular problem.

And so it was that Joe E. Lewis, the entertainer who couldn't entertain, became Johnny Torrio's roving goodwill ambassador, moving from New York to Chicago to Miami to

Hollywood to Cleveland to New Orleans as the situation demanded. While Torrio, aided by such men as Meyer Lansky, Lucky Luciano, Moe Dalitz, and Hyman Abrams, laid the foundation of the national crime syndicate to be, Lewis served as shill, courier, court jester, and peacemaker.

Again and again he made the rounds, playing the joints big and small, cracking jokes, sharpening his wits and his timing. Slowly his voice improved, in volume and in clarity. He was evolving into a nightclub comic. Insults and vulgarity became his thing, acceptable because he played drunk while performing. Usually he was drunk.

Indicative of his new status was his last meeting in 1935 with Machinegun Jack McGurn. Joe was in a bar hoisting a few with his friends before his impending departure for Hollywood. McGurn came in. Eight years had passed since the New Rendezvous affair. McGurn held out his hand. Joe took it. They were big boys now. Or were they?

Jack had a favor to ask. If Joe ran into George Raft out in Hollywood, he would spit in Raft's eye.

Why? Raft and McGurn were old buddies. They had played golf together. So why the beef?

Why? Because Raft had turned actor. That was all right, maybe. The movie people usually gave the boys a square shake. But in his last movie Raft had played a cop. A cop for God's sake. Some people will do anything for money.

Of course McGurn was a hoodlum, not an entertainer. An uncomplicated man. A few months later, on the seventh anniversary of the St. Valentine's Day Massacre, someone gunned him down in a bowling alley. Using a submachinegun, of course. From Alcatraz, Capone ordered white rosebuds placed on his coffin.

The old order, the time of the speakeasy, was passing; the Casino Era had begun. A new breed had emerged, and the bribe replaced the bullet. But show business remained important. Men like Joe E. Lewis, George Raft, and, yes, Frank Sinatra had entrée everywhere and a special status that permitted them to be slobs.

At first glance the choice by Sinatra of Sinatra to play his fellow slob, Lewis, in a movie seemed a good one. Both had known the Fischetti brothers.

But the truth could not be filmed. Too many illusions would crumble. Show business would suffer. Mob business would suffer. No, if a movie was made, it had to be made right. Which is why Sinatra, reading Art Cohn's book in galleys, decided to buy the movie rights.

The movie began in Chicago in 1927. Two "cafe owners" were competing for the talents of Sinatra-Lewis. Their real names weren't used nor the names of their joints. Machine-gun Jack McGurn wasn't mentioned. Heaven forbid! But the intelligent viewer could get the idea that things weren't exactly tame in the Windy City.

There were some fake dramatics — funeral wreaths deliv-ered, etc. — before "Coogan," the rival "cafe owner," got around personally to cutting Sinatra-Lewis's windpipes. Someone conveniently bumped off "Coogan," so he could be forgotten. Sinatra-Lewis recovered, but he found he couldn't sing. He got on a train for New York and, in a flash, ten years passed.

No need to mention Capone, Torrio, Schultz, Madden, Luciano, Costello. No need to report the rise of the syndi-cate. Not even any need to tell the story of a brave if amoral man, slowly fighting his way back.

No need. Suddenly, one bright day, two of Sinatra-Lewis's friends who have been looking for him for a decade get lucky and find him. He puts on an act, of course. God's in his heaven and all that. But they sense something is wrong. They check up. Frankie-Joe is playing second banana in a third-rate burlesque show.

Show business to the rescue. Sophie Tucker, playing herself, gives the has-been a chance on her am-now success. The boys have it all figured out, you see. All he needs is a change, a little confidence, and he'll sing again. Apparently he hasn't had enough faith in himself to try for ten years.

He tries. Surprise! He can't sing. But the show must go on, don't you know, so he croaks some bitter jokes and he's suddenly a comedian.

Of course it's a hard adjustment to make and takes a lot of sympathy. He finds plenty in Letty, a rich gal he runs into backstage.

But why go on? From there on out the movie degenerates into soap opera. He loves Letty, but she's too good for him. Finally when he gets up his courage to propose, he discovers she got tired of waiting and married someone else – from her world, of course. Wham, another body blow! But you can't keep a good man down. Can You? He finds a girl from his world. They marry, yet the bluebird of happiness eludes them. He can't give up his bottle, his buddies, his love of gambling. She won't give up her own career. So, alas, these nice but star-crossed lovers stumble on, laughing on the outside, crying on the inside, and bringing joy to a cruel and heartless world.

There is no mention, of course, that the clubs Sinatra-Lewis plays – the Beverly in New Orleans, the Mounds in Cleveland, the Riviera in New Jersey, the Beverly Hills in Newport, the Clover in Hollywood, the Chez Paree in Chicago, the Colonial Inn north of Miami, the Club Continental in Miami – were illegal gambling joints. No mention that the syndicate operated them and corrupted state and local governments to do so. No mention, no implication. The movie is a fairy story for children, one of a long and continuing series of self-serving productions.

A few months before his death on June 4, 1971, the boys got together to give Joe E. Lewis another testimonial dinner. This one took place at the Riviera in Las Vegas, and everyone that was anyone — from the related worlds of crime, show business, and politics — was there to get drunk with Joe one last time. Everyone but Frank Sinatra, that is.

Frankie and Dean Martin had been scheduled to host the affair, but a few days earlier Sinatra lost a fight, and teeth, when he was denied credit at a Las Vegas pleasure palace. Martin came up with the best line: "Frank was an unwanted child," he said. "Now he's wanted in five states. But you have to give Frank credit — or he'll bust up your joint."

Joe E. Lewis had no comment. He got drunk early in the proceedings and passed out cold. Perhaps he was bored.

*They preached of the good, noble and
beautiful, and they themselves fostered in their
lives and works the evil, the
ignoble, the ugly.*
—EZRA GOODMAN

3

Who Killed
Harlow's Husband?

The girl was everything the picture promised, decided Abner
Zwillman. More, maybe. But her act was lousy.

She knew it too.

He watched from the wings as polite applause straggled up
from the half-filled theater and the curtain fell. There would
be no encores. The Philadelphia audience was impatient for
the movie.

She was coming toward them, and he could see tears streak-
ing her makeup. Her left hand cupped her right breast, cud-
dling it as if it were alive. Over and over she was repeating;
"Fuck them, fuck them, fuck them."

Nig Rosen chuckled. "Sure you don't want me to stick
around? This dame is sore."

Zwillman smiled, his eyes on her hair. "No, thanks, Nig.
Tell Meyer I'll call him tomorrow."

"Right," said Rosen. "See yuh."

Zwillman kept looking at that hair. It had fascinated him from the first. Not blond, not white, but in between. And a lot of it, brushed back and up to form an electric cloud, almost a halo. Was it real? Would it be soft?

There was just a whiff of odor, an acrid blend of stale sweat and cheap perfume, as she brushed by him. He watched her walk away down the corridor toward her dressing room. Hell, even her walk was sexy. She undulated, but somehow it was unlearned, unpracticed. Hell, any stripper could rotate her hips. With this dame it was as natural as breathing.

He waited until she vanished into the room, then slowly counted to fifty before moving down the hall. The door opened easily. She had taken off the awful red dress — who the devil had picked it? — and was sitting naked in front of a mirror. Not moving, just staring at herself. As the reflection of the tall man in the Palm Beach suit abruptly appeared, she shifted her gaze but not her head. He had dark brown hair, she noted, and big shoulders.

"Who the hell are you?" she asked in a high, nasal voice. "And who invited you?"

He studied her face in the mirror. It wasn't angry, outraged, or, for that matter, very interested. Frustrated, maybe. As their eyes met in the glass, she licked her full lower lip.

"The name is Long, " said Zwillman. "Abe Long. I invited myself. I'm one of your fans."

She turned on the bench to face him. Her hands were in her lap, casual-like, not trying to conceal anything.

"You're a liar, Longie. I don't have any fans. All I've got is a bunch of guys trying to screw me any way they can."

No muscle moved on her face, but tears formed in the corner of both eyes.

"I don't blame them," said the man who thereafter would be known as "Longie," "but I can wait." He crossed the room in two strides and snatched a blue dress from a hanger on the wall. "Cover it up, huh?"

There was suprise in her glance and then perhaps a touch of amusement. Without a word she took the dress, pulled it over her head and squirmed it into place.

"No underwear?"

"Nah, who needs it?"

He lighted a cigarette and looked around the shabby room.

"What's the poop? I heard Hughes spent millions on your movie, but he's treating you like Apple Mary. Is he broke?"

Jean Harlow turned back to the dressing table and began making up her face.

"Don't be stupid, Longie. Billie Dove didn't want me in town. People were talking. So he agreed to send me on this tour to promote the movie. I thought it was a big deal. God, was I a sucker."

"Whatta you mean?"

"Do you have to ask? Strictly second rate all the way: act, wardrobe, publicity. To top it off, it's costing me money. That's the big joke. Handsome Howard's getting richer while I get deeper in debt."

Again she was ready to cry. From an inner pocket Zwillman produced a flat silver pint flask. He unscrewed the cap and passed it to her.

"Cognac," he warned. "It's strong stuff."

She tilted the flask, tasted its contents. "Um, good. Baby likes that. You must know a good bootlegger."

"The best."

She drank deeply, gasped, began to cough and then to laugh. He took the flask from her shaking hand, recapped it, and put it back in his pocket. She pulled him down to the bench beside her.

"Thanks, Longie. That hit the spot."

"How come you're going into debt with the money they're paying you?"

She sighed. It was such a mess. The theaters were paying $3,500 a week for her personal. appearances, and naturally she had thought she'd get the money. Six weeks was $21,000 and it sure looked good. So she'd invited Mama to come along, and, of course, Mama had to have the little Wop — well, she was married to him — and he had to stop at the best hotels and have room service all the time. It was only after the tour began that she found the money went to Caddo Corporation — Howard Hughes's outfit — and she was going to get only $250, which was her regular contract salary. So instead of getting rich like she thought, she'd have to borrow from her agent just to finish the tour. Wouldn't matter so much if the tour was making her a big star, but the way things were going it'd break her instead, which is probably just what the little sneak Billie Dove wanted.

Jean was sobbing most convincingly before she finished the tale. Zwillman, no stranger to stress, was convinced the tears were sincere. She was close to hysteria. He held her tightly for a time, letting his hand play through that wonderful hair. Soft, like spun silver might be — or platinum. When she had recovered he put her gently aside and went to the door. The manager appeared within seconds. Jean watched as Longie talked to the nervous little man, his voice low and hard. Then he pulled out a roll of bills and peeled off several. The manager nodded, clutched the money, and ran.

Zwillman put the roll away and turned to the girl. "That'll get the ball rolling," he said. "Now let's get some food."

"I'm starved."

They went by cab to a glittering nightclub. Jean, accustomed to the drugstores of Kansas City and the sleezy dives of Hollywood, was properly impressed by the vast dining room and the even larger gambling casino at the rear. Her escort, she noted, got the kind of treatment Louis B. Mayer received at MGM. Service was swift and the food delicious. She ate greedily. Zwillman pretended to eat but was more concerned with getting information. He was particularly interested in her stepfather, Marino Bello.

"He's a phony, but he's got Mama fooled. She thinks he's an Italian nobleman. Half the time he's bragging about his family estates in Sicily and then he turns right around and brags about how he's a buddy of Johnny Torrio and Al Capone. One thing's certain — Mama thinks he's God's gift to women, so the little jerk must have something."

"How does he treat you?"

She stopped chewing for a second. "He's always trying to paw me and hints how much he could do for me if I'd let him, but that's as far as it's gone."

"Does he really know Capone?"

"I don't know. I doubt it. He likes to swish around in a cape. He's even got this little sword cane. Tries to act like Doug Fairbanks, but he doesn't have the build. If he saw real blood he'd faint."

Zwillman chuckled. "I know the type. Now what can you tell me about Hughes? Is he off his rocker?"

"No, Longie, but he's a sucker. Always gotta be the man in charge, if you know what I mean. Everything's gotta be his way regardless of how much it costs or how silly it is. Four men got killed in his stupid planes, and he almost killed me before I got that boudoir scene to suit him." Her voice became slightly stilted. " 'Excuse me while I slip into something more comfortable.' " She groaned. "I said that so many times it got to be funny. Everybody laughed but Howard."

"Some people say he's a genius."

"Some people would say anything. Take my word for it, Longie, he's a sucker. Get him in something too big for him and you could take him for plenty, 'cause he'd never admit he couldn't handle it."

"I'll make a note of that," said Longie Zwillman.

A waiter hurried up and whispered in Zwillman's ear. He put down his napkin.

"Excuse me a minute," he said. "There's somebody I gotta talk to."

She watched as the waiter crossed the room to return with a fat little man with a red face and a red rose in his buttonhole. Zwillman met him at a small table. They sat down. The stranger glanced once at Jean, nodded at intervals, got up suddenly, and scurried away. The interview had taken less than two minutes.

"What was that all about if you don't mind my asking?"

"About you, Harlean." Longie lighted a cigarette and smiled at her astonishment. "We're in business. By tomorrow we'll have a team of writers working on your material, a new master of ceremonies, and some new clothes. We'll write off the rest of this week and concentrate on getting ready for Brooklyn. You'll be a big hit. With the build-up the flacks will give you, even Billie Dove would be a hit."

She didn't speak. Just looked at him. He grinned at her through the smoke.

"Longie?"

"Yes, Harlean?"

"How did you know my name?"

"I checked up."

"Why?"

"I told you — I'm one of your fans."

"Is that all?"

He pressed her hand. "Right now it is. Later . . ."

"Yes?"

"Hell, who knows? Later I may be in jail. Let's have a drink. The booze here is pretty good if I do say so. What we used to call 'the real McCoy' before McCoy decided the business was becoming a racket and quit."

The booze was good. Jean quit trying to understand and got cheerfully stewed. The rest of the evening became a hazy memory. When next morning she awoke in her hotel room, she didn't believe it. Then the telephone rang, and a man who said he was her new tour manager rattled off a list of appointments and a messenger brought two dozen white gardenias to the door. No card came with the flowers.

The next few days were busy ones.

The flacks, or someone, did their work well. Loew's Metropolitan Theater in Brooklyn was full an hour before curtain time, and people were still fighting to get in. The show, completely revised, opened on a darkened stage. A spotlight cut through the blackness and centered on Jean. Her dress was white and it shimmered in the light — shimmered like her hair. Low-cut, tight-fitting, the dress emphasized the thrusting breasts and sinuous thighs.

And now the little voice, strong with its nasal undercurrents, began fifteen minutes of patter. A team of the best writers in the business had fashioned that monologue, tailoring it to her personality, and during long rehearsals in Philadelphia she had mastered every innuendo, every naughty implication.

The laughter grew with every joke, and the applause at the end was enthusiastic. And when flushed and triumphant she left the stage, the reporters were waiting with predictable questions. They were so predictable that her versatile writers had provided bright and mildly shocking answers in advance. That some of the questions had been planted never occurred to Jean. But one question, at least, was not, and her reply was her own.

"What do you say to critics who say you can't act?"

"If audiences like you, you don't have to be an actress."

The hard-boiled gentlemen of the press burst into applause — putting themselves on record then and there. After the next, and anticipated, question — "Do you think a woman ought to forgive an unfaithful husband?" — there was even louder applause when she replied, "I can't imagine that happening to me."

Neither could the reporters.

The photographers were still demanding "one more" when the theater manager hustled the Fourth Estate from the flower-filled dressing room. Jean, exalted and tingling with excitement, was sorry to see them go. Suddenly she was afraid of being alone — afraid the dream might vanish without live props.

But one live prop remained.

He arose from a corner of the room where, completely unnoticed, he had watched the press conference. Jean's eyes opened wide at the sight of him, and then, impulsively, she ran to meet him with arms outstretched.

"Longie," she said. "My fan."

"First, last, and always," said the gangster.

To understand the role of the gangster in the development of the motion-picture industry, one should look at its history.

In 1895 a machine was developed to project film onto a screen. "Nickelodeons" sprang up in a thousand stores, and soon there was a steadily growing demand for more and better film.

The business developed rapidly — and ruthlessly. The "film exchange" came into existence as a sort of middle man to buy or lease films from producers and rent them to the owners of the nickelodeons. Inevitably the owners rebelled when the middle men sought monopolistic power over quality and prices. Rival film exchanges were formed, and out of the many a few survived. Marcus Loew, a furrier, put together the largest chain of nickelodeon theaters and, by eliminating the middle man completely, dealt directly with the producers. Such power was not easily achieved, and pitched battles, rivaling the newspaper circulation wars of the period, were frequent. Just as many future gangsters learned the commercial possibilities of violence in the newspaper struggles, so did others learn to break windows and heads for theater-chain owners. In both cases it was free enterprise at its most uncontrolled, although the principals if asked would talk at length about freedom of speech and creativity.

Yet more consolidation was necessary before investors could feel secure. To be certain of stable profit, the theater owners needed control over the number and content of the films they displayed. That meant a voice in the production of movies. Again muscle as well as money was employed to break down resistance, and the movie studios soon became "production units" of the theater chains. Marcus Loew, aided by Nick and Joe Schenck, led the way. Several small companies were combined to produce the giant of the industry, Metro-Goldwyn-Mayer.

That the theater chains with their huge volume of cash business could, when they wanted to, control the studios was a fact not lost on some younger men who had arrived too late to get in at the beginning. For the moment, however, they had their own way to quick wealth. Illegal liquor was the gimmick of *their* generation, and it provided more cash than they could spend. Some of it they invested in the movies, which gave them entree to the developing amoral society on the West Coast — so convenient to Mexico should the need to lay low arise. Indeed, some sociologists have rated the proximity of Mexico as being at least as important as the California sunlight in the development of the movie industry.

The *nouveau riche* are always nervous, and the first lords of the movies were no exception. Eager to avoid criticism, they sought to conform, and for guidance they looked quite naturally to the seat of government. The Great Red Scare of 1919 was an opportunity for these new Americans to demonstrate their patriotism and disassociate themselves from all radical ideas. So there was a flood of propaganda films dedicated to celebrating the virtues of the American Way. Typical was Joe Schenck's production of *The New Moon*. It had the added advantage, from Schenck's point of view, of starring his wife, Norma Talmadge. Other films were designed to persuade restless labor to turn deaf ears to the siren songs of union organizers and put its trust in paternal capitalism.

As the alleged threat of revolution faded with the coming of the Twenties and prosperity, the movie makers were in complete agreement with Republican leaders that "the business of the country is business." Something of a paradox developed, however, in that old-fashioned sentimentality existed side by side with the new aspirations of the business age. Where morality is concerned, big business is always conservative, paying lip service to what it calls "the old values." But in this case, the old values had to be shown in a new setting, where a fast-buck life of conspicuous consumption was desirable.

This paradox, or, to use a better word, hypocrisy, was well illustrated in the rules piously promulgated by the Hays Office. The Hays Office itself was part of the general climate of the times. Following Arnold Rothstein's experiments with the 1919 World Series, organized baseball successfully headed off federal controls by hiring a respected jurist, Kenesaw Mountain Landis, to be "Czar" of the national "sport." So when a series of messy scandals involving sex, drugs, and fat men hit Hollywood in 1921, the moguls looked around for a "Czar" who would convince the public that Main Street, U.S.A., ran through Babylon West. Rather ironically they turned to President Harding's Cabinet.

Postmaster General Will Hays was a shrewd politician, but he *looked* the part of a kindly Hoosier, so he was offered the $100,000 job. Who could refuse such a chance to save society from itself while getting well paid for the chore? In his maiden speech to the Los Angeles Chamber of Commerce, Hays promised that all would be for the best. "This industry must have," he thundered, "toward the sacred thing, the mind of a child, toward that clean virgin thing, that unmarked slate, the same responsibility, the same care about the impressions made upon it, that the best clergyman or the most inspired teacher of youth would have."

A few years later when Congressional investigations disclosed the corruption of the Harding Administration, Hays was forced to leave "that unmarked slate" unguarded while he testified how he helped his good friend Harry Sinclair dispose of some of the loot from Teapot Dome. Sinclair "loaned" him $260,000 in "hot" Liberty Bonds, which Hays peddled to various prominent Republicans. Senator T. H. Caraway was quite bitter about the Czar of all the Movies, calling him "a fence who knew that certain goods were stolen and was trying to help the thief find a market for them . . ."

But no one really cared. Hays went back to Hollywood to make sure "impure love" was never presented as "attractive and beautiful." Impure love was officially defined as "the love which society has always regarded as wrong and which has been banned by divine law." Presumably the emotion which sometimes caused President Harding and Nan Britton to couple in a White House cloakroom was "impure love," since Hays would not permit Nan's best-selling book, *The President's Daughter*, to be made into a movie. But Hays saw no harm in movies advertising "brilliant men, beautiful jazz babies, champagne baths, midnight revels, petting parties in the purple dawn," or "neckers, petters, white kisses, red kisses, pleasure-mad daughters, sensation-craving mothers" — no harm at all, so long as virtue triumphed in the end.

That interesting new species, the gangster, could also be shown in the films — subject, of course, to a few rules of piety. The tough guy had to love his mother and be either redeemed by the love of a good girl or else die like an animal. If, in the meantime, he had a lot of fun, lived like a prince, and hurt a lot of people — well, that was necessary for realism. Howard Hughes, who rather liked the life style of gangsters, made *The Racket*, with a lot of help from director Lewis Milestone, and its success encouraged him to attempt the more ambitious *Hell's Angels*, which co-starred, among others, Jean Harlow. But the gangster did not really become popular as a subject for films until a combination of technical and economic events conspired to bring the real-life gangster into the boardrooms of motion-picture companies as a silent partner.

The first of the events was the coming of age of sound. People had been experimenting with synchronized sound for years. David Griffith, the great pioneer who made *Birth of a Nation*, used sound sequences as early as 1921 in *Dream Street*. It was Warner Brothers, however, having less to lose than other studios, who gambled heavily on sound. *The Jazz Singer*, staring Al Jolson, was just a schmaltzy story of a dying rabbi and his long-strayed son, a popular crooner, until Jolson opened his mouth and sang. Public reaction was enthusiastic, and the other studios had no choice but to follow suit. The cost was tremendous, not only for new equipment but for new personnel: sound technicians, directors with stage experience, and actors with suitable voices. Many stars had to be discarded, making room for new ones. Hughes had already sunk more than two million dollars into *Hell's Angels* when Jolson spoke on October 6, 1927, and much of it had to be scrapped. The female lead, Greta Nissen, a popular Norwegian star, had to be dropped — her accent was not that of an English girl — and Harlow, completely unknown, replaced her.

Not all studio executives were as willing to spend money as Hughes, and not all of them had the money to spend. The changeover to sound was just getting under way when the second key event of the era occurred: Black Tuesday, October 29, 1929 — the collapse of the stock market and the onset of the Great Depression. It couldn't have come at a worse time for many studios, as the case of William Fox illustrates.

As head of the Fox Film Corporation, William Fox had built an important studio. By the late 1920s it was turning out a feature a week. Ambitious, Fox began putting together a chain of theaters, following the example of other studio leaders. By 1929 he was ready to gobble up the giant of the industry, Loew's, Inc.

Marcus Loew, founder of the firm, was dead. Nick Schenck was president, and it was Schenck who worked with Fox to sell the company. Fifty million was necessary. Fox raised the money with the help of a bizarre dwarf, A. C. Blumenthal, a former associate of New York's Mayor Jimmy Walker, with contacts in the underworld. The deal went through. A few days later Fox suffered a serious injury when his Rolls-Royce mysteriously crashed into another car. For three months he was inactive, in the hospital, unable to attend to business. He got out just in time for the crash of the stock market. Shares of Fox Film Corporation dropped from a high of $119 to $1, and Fox faced bankruptcy.

To top off Fox's troubles, Louis B. Mayer, production head of MGM, resented Fox's takeover and used his influence with President Hoover to have an anti-trust action brought against Fox. As of March of the next year, Fox had sold his stock in Loew's, Inc., to a group of bankers. But his troubles increased. By 1936 he was bankrupt, and Fox Film was picked up by Nick Schenck's brother and merged with Twentieth Century. Eventually Fox went to prison on a charge of attempting to bribe a judge at his bankruptcy hearing.

Fox Film wasn't the only one hurt by the crash of the market, although its switch from a $9.2 million profit in 1930 to a $5.5 million loss in 1931 was more dramatic than most. RKO, for example, went from a $3.3 million profit in 1930 to a deficit of $5.6 million the following year. Warner Brothers had a $7 million profit in 1930 and a $7.9 million loss in 1931. In 1932 it almost doubled its deficit, going to $14,095,054, but there was also some corporate monkey business involved. And so it went for the entire industry.

The months following the crash were crucial to the development of organized crime. For as cash, credit, and confidence dwindled, as brokers, bankers, and businessman jumped from office windows or went into bankruptcy, the only persons with liquid, unencumbered cash were the big bootleggers. Some had invested in Wall Street, but most of the others had stashed their loot in hiding places safe from the searching eyes of income-tax agents. Loan-sharking, or shylocking, had long been a profitable racket; now, over night, it became a legitimate business. Lots of tycoons and would-be tycoons had to have cash money if their companies were to survive. To get it they were ready to make almost any kind of deal, from paying high interest rates to accepting the gangster as a silent partner. The gangsters, for their part, had more money than they knew what to do with, and the golden stream showed no signs of slackening, so they were happy to accommodate the businessmen. Thereafter, at infrequent intervals, there would be solemn warnings that organized crime was attempting to "infiltrate legitimate business," and newspapers would worry the subject for a few weeks. In reality, the process was a continuing one. It had been going on in a small way for several years, as speakeasies became nightclubs, but after 1929 it became a major factor in the national economy.

So, not unexpectedly, the motion-picture moguls — confronted with an even greater need for cash than other business men — were quick to offer investment possibilities.

Many movie executives had little opportunity to become acquainted with what is sometimes called "the better things." They had no time for, or interest in, literature or the arts. While paying lip service to the values of home and matrimony, they got their kicks out of sharp deals, sex, and gambling. With many, gambling became a disease, and more than one board of directors took steps to curb the excesses of its chairman.

Many examples could be given, but the story of Harry "King" Cohn well illustrates the hypocrisy of the industry

Czar Hays was protecting with his platitudes.

Born on the East Side of Manhattan in 1891, Cohn worked as a pool hustler, sold "hot" furs, and operated a trolley before breaking into show business as a song plugger. His older brother, Jack, meanwhile, studied law and found work with a pioneer film company. After a few years he persuaded his boss to hire Harry. Upon learning the business, the brothers and Joe Brandt formed the C.B.C. (for Cohn, Brandt, and Cohn) Film Sales Company, better known as "Corn, Beef, and Cabbage." Harry was sent west to Hollywood, while Jack and Joe remained in New York to peddle the product. In 1924 the name of the company was changed in an attempt to achieve dignity. It became Columbia Pictures.

The change was made possible by the triumph of love. Back when Harry was a struggling song plugger, he met Rose Barker. Rose was a struggling actress, not beautiful but memorable, and she had a lot of hot-blooded Italian relatives. So Harry looked but did not touch. They went to the New Amsterdam Roof to see Fannie Brice in the "Midnight Frolics," but the affair never got off the ground. Harry went west to make movies, and Rose married a prosperous attorney. The end of story? Not exactly.

On a visit to New York, Harry called up his ex-flame and invited her to lunch. She accepted, and before long he invited her to California to see how film epics were produced. Eventually she agreed. Accompanied by a trusted girl friend, Rose made the trip. Harry treated her like a queen and introduced her to such notables as Rudolph Valentino. Eventually she returned home with no plans to change her name or her place of residence.

The trusted girl friend had other ideas, however. She squealed on Rose. The attorney was a gentleman, and he gave his erring wife several hundred thousand dollars as a divorce settlement. Then he turned around and married the trusted girl friend. Who conned who isn't certain, but, anyway, Rose was free to marry Harry. What's more, she was able to bring a sizable dowry, and it was that dowry which saved Columbia Pictures from sudden death.

Success increased the rivalry between the two Cohn brothers, and it grew bitter over the years. Joe Brandt, the third partner, tired of trying to arbitrate and decided to sell his share of the company. His price was a half million dollars, and whichever brother could raise it first would have control of Columbia.

Jack, being in New York with Brandt, was first to recognize the opportunity. He went to the conventional sources — the bankers. But cash and credit were tight in 1932. No one could help him.

Harry Cohn was more realistic. A heavy gambler — in later years his annual gambling losses reached $400,000 — he knew who had money to spare. He consulted his bookie, who put him in touch with a well-heeled gentleman back east. The money was supplied, Brandt's stock was purchased, and Harry Cohn became president *and* chief of production of Columbia Pictures. That well-heeled gentleman back east was know to Jean Harlow as "Longie."

Jean and Longie Zwillman celebrated the triumph at the Metropolitan he had arranged for her by dining in a private suite at the Waldorf-Astoria. The suite in Manhattan was rented on a yearly basis by the Reinfeld Syndicate, an international organization which supplied at least 50 percent of all the illegal booze delivered along the East Coast, from Boston to Philadelphia. As the organization's superintendent of transportation, Zwillman counted the suite among the many fringe benefits that came with his job.

After dinner and a shot of cognac from the silver flask — it had achieved symbolic status — they went to bed. Jean took the initiative in the spirit of an honest show girl who is willing to *give*, not sell, pleasure to a friend. As she saw it, he had it coming.

But once in bed, Zwillman proved anything but hesitant. Jean, at age nineteen, had known only two men, and one of them was no more than a boy. She had married Chuck three years before because she was bored with school. The one night she had with him was, as far as she was concerned, disappointing. Sex, she decided, was vastly overrated. In Hollywood, where her mother and stepfather took her while the divorce was obtained, she attempted the casting-couch route to stardom. The elderly producer proved to be a bad lover as well as a liar, and her previous opinion of sex was confirmed. It was obvious, however, that men enjoyed it, and she wanted to give Longie the thing — she assumed the only thing — she had that he might want. Her generous motives were soon forgotten. Longie Zwillman was neither a kid nor an old man but a twenty-six-year-old buck in perfect physical condition. Strength and experience, moreover, were tempered with intelligent purpose and affectionate compassion. In his big hands, gentle but strong, the girl's ripe body came alive with excitement. When the climax came, she was screaming exultantly.

A few minutes later as they lay resting, her head on his chest and his hand in her hair, she spoke softly, as much to herself as to him.

"It's so wonderful it's frightening. Now I can understand why Mama is such a fool over Marino."

Zwillman chuckled. "She likes it, huh?"

"She's crazy for it. All he has to do is threaten to leave her and she's down on her knees ready to give him everything she's got or I can make. I'd hate to be that dependent on a man."

"Why?"

"I don't know exactly. Somehow it just don't seem right.

This man-woman thing ought not to be one-sided, if you know what I mean. If it's going to be a sex thing, then the man ought to need her as much as she needs him."

"I don't think you ever have to worry about that, Harlean."

"I'm not so sure, Longie. Right now I guess I feel like Mama. She comes out of the bedroom looking real smug, like a cat that's just lapped up a bowl of thick cream. Purring, almost, as if she was saying to me, her daughter, 'I've got something you can't have.' I thought Mama was crazy, but now I'm not so sure. Is it like that every time, Longie?"

"I guarantee it," he said. "Matter of fact it gets better and better."

"Prove it."

He did.

When she awoke hours later after the deepest sleep of her life, Zwillman was gone. On the table by the bed were white gardenias. This time there was a card, and on it was written in a bold hand: "Tonight."

She smiled. It was going to be a good day.

It was also a good week. By the time Jean moved over to Loew's State Theatre on Broadway, the legend of Harlow, the sex kitten, successor to Theda Bara and Clara Bow, was well established. As usual stories were circulating that men had castrated themselves in Harlow-created frustration, and there were tales that at least one of the four men killed during the making of *Hell's Angels* failed to bail out of his falling plane because he knew his love for Jean was not returned. A report, taken seriously by at least one New York writer, that the Purple Gang of Detroit in convention assembled had voted Jean the girl they would most like to hijack actually originated in the wide bed at the Waldorf. Longie Zwillman had been describing the sometimes lonely life of rumrunners stationed on Rum Row off New York. Sometimes, he explained, syndicate executives arranged for boatloads of prostitutes to come out at intervals. Jean offered to supply what today would be called "pin-up poses," and Longie replied that undoubtedly the rumrunners would vote her the broad they would most like to lay. Concocting a press release to fit the hypothetical occasion took several minutes, but Zwillman felt the story would be more acceptable to the local press if the liquor mob was located in another city. Detroit seemed far enough, and, as he pointed out, the Purple Gang would always be popular with the press because it had such a colorful name. Allied Artists even made a movie by that name.

Jean enjoyed those long, relaxed conversations, the intermissions of what she soon termed their three-act play each night. She had never before experienced that friendly companionship with a male which can come only when sexual challenges are put aside. At such times Longie seemed more like a father than a lover. Once Zwillman confessed he became interested in Jean when he saw her, briefly, in a Laurel and Hardy comedy called *Double Whoopee*. It was a slapstick scene in which a cab door closed on her dress and pulled it off, leaving her standing on the street in her black unmentionables.

"I was too busy looking at your legs to laugh," said Zwillman, "so I sat through it again. The second time I looked at your hair. I was taking too much time seeing the movie, so I asked Joe Schenck to get me a picture. The more I looked at that picture the more your hair fascinated me."

"What about my legs?"

"Adequate, my dear, but not in a class with your hair. When I found out you hailed from K.C., I asked some of the boys to check you out. Guess they thought I was nuts, but they did a good job. Told me the hair was natural anyway. I still didn't believe it. Figured there was only one way to be sure, but that was one bit of research I wanted to do myself."

"As Howard Hughes would say, back to the drawing board."

"Don't you ever get enough?"

"Do you?" She sighed. "Besides, there's so little time. This tour won't last forever."

"I'll get it extended."

Which he did for four more weeks. But finally the future had to be faced. Urgent business required Longie's presence in New Jersey. There was a strong possibility, in fact, that he might have to spend a few months in jail on an old assault-and-battery-with-intent-to-kill charge. Nothing really serious — at least not as serious as murder. Inconvenient as hell, of course, but plans could be made.

The planning session took place one afternoon in the Harding Room of the Hollenden in Cleveland. The hotel, Longie explained, was the headquarters of the so-called "Moe Davis Syndicate," the largest rumrunner on Lake Erie and ally of the Big Seven in the East. Moe Davis was actually Moe Dalitz, and he was one of several men who dropped in to pay his respects to the distinguished visitor. A former laundry operator in Detroit, Dalitz learned the liquor business with the Purple Gang but had broken off to form an enduring partnership with Sam Tucker, Morris Kleinman, and Louis Rothkopf. In years to come that "sort of entity," as Tucker once described it, would operate lavish gambling casinos from Kentucky west to Las Vegas and south to Havana and contribute much, in the process, to the evolution of the entertainment industry.

Dalitz, who always had an eye for pretty women, was reluctant to leave when a brief discussion of liquor problems was completed, but Zwillman hustled him out anyway. He wanted no third set of ears around for his farewells.

Jean had seen Joe Schenck in Hollywood, but he, like his brother, Nick, belonged to the higher levels of studio management. To attract an interest of such men Jean would gladly have stripped in the middle of the Clover Club's Casino or "entertained" Mutia Omooloo in his kraal on the back lot of MGM. How strange it was then to sit relaxed in a luxury hotel far from Hollywood and hear complicated deals discussed that, for all their wide-ranging nature, were solely in the interests of Jean Harlow, Star.

Joe Schenck was an affable, greedy man who at age fifty-three was becoming a bit frustrated. While he had made much money over the years, he lacked the prestige of brother Nick, who three years earlier had become president of Loew's, Inc. Moreover, his marrage to Norma Talmadge was breaking up. He had married her in 1917 as a means of persuading the great star of silent movies to let him make her pictures. Many producers achieved tycoon status by signing up an established star, but few had to go to the altar. Perhaps to compensate, he had become known as "one of the heroic hedonists of Hollywood." On top of that he was a compulsive gambler, equally adept at losing money on horses, cards, or dice. On some days his losses totaled more than $30,000. Naturally, such a pigeon was popular, and Joe called some of the top gangsters in the country his friends. He did favors for them in Hollywood and, in turn, shared in their more legitimate investments.

The basic problem in planning Harlow's future involved Howard Hughes, who held Jean's contract. Had he not been under the influence of Billie Dove, who was insanely jealous, the problem could have been resolved. Both Schenck and Zwillman agreed that Jean should eventually become the property of a major studio that would invest the time and money to make her a major star. But until that happened, Jean should get as many screen credits as possible while she was being promoted unofficially. Every disadvantage can be turned around, said Longie Zwillman. If Hughes wants to make pictures starring Billie Dove, give him the opportunity, but only if he farms out Jean Harlow. Billie would approve of that, wouldn't she?

Schenck thought she'd be happy to see Jean away from

Caddo Corporation. As president of United Artists, he would offer Hughes a five-picture contract for 1931. Howard could star Billie Dove in two of them, say. But, in return, he had to let Jean make five pictures for other studios. That would give a lot of executives a chance to see her and give her a chance to decide where she'd like to settle permanently when the time came.

Zwillman nodded. "I hear Hughes is broke. Where's he going to get the dough to make five pictures?"

"He'll have to borrow like everybody else, I guess."

"Good," said Zwillman. "Maybe I can make something on this end too."

"Save a little," said Schenck. "I may need a favor before long."

"Another one?" But Zwillman smiled. "What is it this time? On second thought, don't tell me. I'll find out soon enough."

Schenck bowed his way out. Zwillman explained an additional fact: Hughes would be able to rent Jean to other studios for as much as $2,000 a week, but she'd receive only $250 under her contract. Still, that could be to her advantage maybe in her efforts to check the expensive tastes of her mother and stepfather. Meanwhile, unbeknownst to them, he'd send her enough money to live as a star should. It would be a loan, of course, to be paid back at her convenience. Then Longie told Jean there was one more person she had to meet.

"Do I have to?" she objected.

"Yeah, Harlean, this is important. Personally and professionally. You'll probably be playing in some gangster movies soon, so you ought to meet one."

She stared speechlessly. Zwillman smiled thinly and picked up the phone. Two minutes later Johnny Roselli walked into the room. A young man still but no youth, he was about five feet eight. Heavy, he carried the weight well. His blue eyes seemed hooded somehow.

Zwillman performed the introductions. There was perhaps five minutes of conversation about the weather, the state of the economy, and the pennant race. Then, at an invisible signal, Roselli shook hands, flashed white teeth, and departed.

"What was that all about?" asked Harlow.

Roselli, explained Zwillman, was Mafia. He was also muscle. A Chicago product, he was on good terms with the Capone Mob but not part of it. The Outfit — Zwillman's word for his organization — had sent Johnny to California as sort of a hoodlum-in-residence. He was available. To his old duties would now be added the task of keeping an eye on Jean Harlow. He would see that no one tried to move in on her. And if she had any problems of an emergency nature, she should call Johnny at a number he would supply.

They retired to a bedroom, where farewells spoke themselves and no explanations were needed. Separation and the uncertainty surrounding Zwillman's court case gave an added flavor to the act of love and once again left the girl-woman frightened.

"Grow up," said Longie Zwillman as he left her. "I'll be in touch."

Back to Hollywood went Harlow, to a busy schedule that left her little time to think. The era of the gangster movie was in full flower now, and "the blond with the big tits" was in demand at every studio. In *Iron Man*, a fight story made by Universal Productions, she played a Broadway moll, and her sexual aura rather than her acting ability interested the reviewers. Then came the classic *Public Enemy* for Warner Brothers, the studio that had begun the cycle the year before with *Little Caesar*. The brothers Warner understood gangsters, having made a lot of money speculating in company stock at a time when it appeared the studio might fold following the crash of the stock market. Moreover, Chicago gangsters served as unofficial consultants, a logical development in that many of the movies made by Warners were variations of the Capone story. On one occasion a group of Army officers were guests during the shooting – and the word is appropriate – of a gangster movie. They were astonished to observe that the machineguns operated without jamming. The company officials explained they couldn't afford jamming, so they hired experts to improve the guns. The Army soon incorporated the changes.

Public Enemy, starring James Cagney, Mae Clark, Joan Blondell, *and* Jean Harlow, was typical of the era. It was, or pretended to be, a morality play: a struggle between a good son and a bad son, with the poor old mother trying to reconcile the two. The Hays Office had to approve. But Cagney as the bad son was handsome, virile, decisive. His "good" brother was something of a sullen prig – although he threw a mean punch when sufficiently aroused by a slight to his mother. And the mother – a slob. Fat and stupid, entirely unappealing. Consequently the viewer almost had to identify with Cagney even though he knew he would come to a bad end. For a nation that was violating Prohibition law with abandon while paying lip service to law and order, this wasn't too hard to do.

Harlow wasn't particularly exciting – or so it seems to those who see the movie on the late, late show today. Several shots of her rear seem intended to explain why gangsters referred to their women as "broads." Perhaps the funniest scene – surpassing even that famous episode when Cagney shoved a grapefruit into Mae Clarke's face – was the murder of the horse. The four-legged beast had tossed a boss gangster to his death while on a canter in the park. Naturally, his loyal associates had to have revenge, so they shot the animal. According to Chicago legend, such an incident really happened, but whether the gangsters took the hint from the movie or vice versa isn't clear. In any case, the screen version takes place off camera. The angry killers enter the stall, shots ring out. Then comes a strange sound of escaping air — a sigh from the dying horse or a fart? At any rate it makes the modern viewer double up with laughter. The noise, whatever it was intended to portray, serves as a commentary on the films of the period — movies that created a public image of the gangster sadly at variance with the real leaders of crime who were fashioning a silent syndicate while such egoists as Capone in Chicago and Dutch Schultz in New York were making headlines. Much the same thing was to happen in the 1970s when, following the success of *The Godfather*, a new era of gangster films concentrated attention on punks with Italian names.

Chicago was again the locale for Jean's next movie, *The Secret Six*, made for MGM. Indicative of progress was her billing ahead of Clark Gable, another star just going into orbit. Then came *Goldie* for the Fox Film Corporation, notable only for the use of the word "tramp" in reference to a woman. The next stop was Columbia Pictures, ruled by "King Cohn," and the picture was *Platinum Blonde*. The title was a public-relations masterpiece, the more so since Jean lost the "hero" to Loretta Young and thus did not deserve top billing let alone the name of the movie. But "platinum blonde" filled a need — it supplied the description for Jean's hair so many men had sought so long. And that completed the process of promotion begun that day in Philadelphia by Longie "Abe Long" Zwillman.

As far as Zwillman was concerned, the timing was perfect. For it was just at this time that Harry Cohn was feuding with his brother, Jack, and needed a half million to get control of the company. Zwillman, who had been following events in Hollywood closely after serving his six months in prison on that assault charge, decided to make Columbia the permanent home of his protégé. Cohn was aggressive, ruthless, and on the make. Jean could grow with the studio, and Zwillman, as a silent partner, would be able always to protect her.

Longie explained all this to Jean during an interlude at the Garden of Allah on Sunset Boulevard. One of the twenty-five bungalows arranged around the pool was leased by "The Outfit." Over the next few years it would be used by such men as Meyer Lansky, Bugsy Siegel, Moe Dalitz, Mickey Cohen, and Frank Costello, but in that early period it was reserved almost exclusively for Zwillman.

Jean, who found her benefactor as exciting as ever, nevertheless had reservations as Longie outlined his program for the immediate future. Prohibition was doomed, he said. Despite what such moguls as Louie Mayer were saying, Roosevelt would beat Hoover and restore legal liquor. Already Zwillman and others in the Outfit were planning the transition. They would go legit. The time might not be too far distant when Longie could emerge as a respectable businessman with interests in, among other things, the movie industry. Maybe then they could even think of going legit in their personal lives as well. Luckily, neither had a spouse to be rid of first. And, believe it or not, Longie had hired a tutor. There was a helluva lot he wanted to learn. Money was power, and of both he had plenty and would get more, but something else was needed if life was to have any meaning. It was one thing to look back and see how far one had come, but it was something else to look forward and see how far there was to go.

Jean sensed vaguely what he was talking about. Already the thrill of eating regularly, of being a headline star, of posing in low-cut gowns on the arms of famous men had begun to wear thin. The desire to be recognized as something more than a sex kitten grew stronger with each picture. When would they give her a role to challenge her ability, let her prove she could act? But why was Columbia the place to begin? It hadn't escaped from Poverty Row. Why not MGM, the home of established stars?

But Jean said nothing. Her fear of being dominated, as her mother was dominated, by a man was growing stronger. It created a certain resentment with Longie's masterful ways. Longie, she told herself, would respect her more if she asserted her independence now and then. Sure, he idealized her now, and that was fine for a lover, but if the affair was ever to become something more, he would have to realize she had a mind as well as a body.

And so it was that Joe Schenck got Jean's cooperation when he decided to pull a corporate double-cross. Schenck, of course, claimed later that he knew nothing of Zwillman's behind-the-scenes action in bailing out Harry Cohn and maintained he was following plans made earlier to find Jean a home with a major studio. Jean, in turn, said that she assumed Schenck was acting with Longie's approval. After all, she had been present when the two men mapped out her professional career. Why didn't one or the other double-check with Zwillman? Well, there was an answer to that too. Charles A. Lindbergh, Jr., had just been kidnapped from his home at Hopewell, New Jersey, and intense "heat" was on all gangsters locally and across the nation. The search for the baby interfered with Zwillman's booze convoys, causing him to offer a $50,000 reward for the kidnapper. From prison, Al Capone offered to solve the case if released, a suggestion the Hearst press thought had great merit. Owney "the Killer" Madden was actually employed by Lindbergh to help recover the baby. All in all it was a hectic time, and Zwillman's attention was diverted from Hollywood. And Schenck had a perfect excuse not to bother Longie with what basically was personal business.

The double-cross consisted of an offer to Jean by Joe Schenck on behalf of his brother, Nick, president of Loew's, Inc., which, of course, was the parent company of MGM. The deal wasn't complicated. Joe Schenck would persuade Howard Hughes to sell Jean's contract, and Nick Schenck would order Louis B. Mayer, production boss of MGM, to buy it.

Quickly, lest Zwillman get wind of it, the deal was made. Jean screwed up her courage and signed a contract binding her to the giant studio for seven years. Her salary was to range from $1,250 a week for the first year to $5,000 a week for the seventh year. There were also the usual fringe benefits: secretary, hairdresser, and personal maid. Shortly thereafter an unusual fringe benefit was offered: a studio executive as a husband, a dapper little man named Paul Berns.

Obviously, the Schenck brothers figured such a marriage might bind Jean a little closer to the studio and perhaps put a barrier between the star and the gangster who had dreamed of going "legit" in both his personal and professional life.

Berns didn't appear on the scene for some time, however, as Jean waited anxiously for Zwillman's reaction to the contract with MGM. That he would be furious she assumed, but she was confident she could convince him of her right to look after her own interests. But there was only silence. Even the monthly envelope containing a single thousand-dollar bill stopped coming. And now to her fear was added loneliness. There was no one to listen to her complaints, to advise, to laugh. She missed her "between-the-acts" conversations with Longie almost as much as she missed his lovemaking. In desperation she called Johnny Roselli. Johnny was polite, bland, and blank, promising only to pass on her message. Still no reaction. She began a mild flirtation with Clark Gable, scheduled to play the male lead in her next picture *Red Dust*. But Gable, big ears and all, wanted to talk about Carole Lombard. He was willing to have some innocent fun, but he was too much like Longie in his desire to idealize women, she decided.

One day while at the studio she met Berns, a bald-headed, harmless-looking little man with a timid mustache. A native of Germany, brought up on the East Side of Manhattan, he was considered one of Irving Thalberg's brighter assistants, and Thalberg was the number-two man at MGM. They talked, and Jean was flattered when he seemed to be soliciting her ideas about serious subjects. When he invited her to lunch she was flattered again. They talked about books and music and the problems of fame. But she was still suspicious. When he asked her to have Sunday dinner at his home she thought her suspicions confirmed. Yet Berns had a reputation for discretion, and what difference did it make? The dinner was lovely, the talk on a high plane, and when the expected pass never came Jean relaxed. Somewhat to her own astonishment she told her host about Zwillman.

Paul listened carefully, asked sympathetic questions, and after deliberation suggested a solution. She should get married. Not to a gangster, of course. That would be fatal to her career. No, she should find someone who would understand her problem, who would stand between her and the underworld, and who would also cherish her for herself while advancing her career.

Before he had finished talking, it was clear to Jean that Berns had a candidate in mind — himself. And suddenly in the quiet of Berns's book-lined study, with cognac warming her stomach as of old, it all made supreme good sense.

There was more talk. Berns assured her that he was broadminded. Both would be free to, as he put it, "find solace elsewhere if necessary," so long as no hint of scandal arose. Moreover, he would force Mama and Marino to stay far away and thus reduce both their emotional and financial drain on Jean. In time, hopefully, she would grow to love him, but, meanwhile, there would be companionship of the mind and spirit.

As Berns talked, the memory of Longie Zwillman rose unbidden in her mind: Longie, tall and strong, moving like a cat across the shabby dressing room; Longie, cold and quiet, giving orders to men who jumped at his command; Longie, solid and safe, planning her future as they lay in bed. How would he react to this?

She put her thoughts aside. Paul, nice as he was, would certainly never dominate her as Longie threatened to. And that was important if ever she was to achieve her true potential as an actress, as an individual. It boiled down to that: Paul would help her, Longie would be an obstacle. She made up her mind.

The announcement of the wedding stunned Hollywood. MGM's facile promotion people were hard put to explain why the platinum-blond bombshell should want to share the life and bed of the mousy little executive who looked more like a frightened waiter than a Don Juan. Interviews with Jean were of little help, but they pounced on her reference to Paul's "capacity for understanding." A little imagination, and soon studio press releases were hailing Berns as "the little father confessor" of Hollywood. All kinds of stars, male and female, old and young, had taken their troubles to Berns and found sympathy and understanding. Jean Harlow alone had captured his heart.

A week after the announcement Jean received a call from Johnny Roselli. A mutual friend was in town and wanted to see her. A car would pick her up that night. She dressed with care, dabbing on plenty of 'Mitsouko,' Longie's favorite perfume. Over her blond hair she wore a red wig, a disguise but also an act of defiance to offset the perfume. While waiting, she found herself wondering if Longie would make love to her. It had been a long, long time. The thought made the nipples of her breast harden, and she went to the kitchen for ice. Rubbing ice across her nipples, she had learned, would calm them down.

The car came on time. The driver was a stranger. He took her to the Garden of Allah and down a dark path to a bungalow. There Zwillman, tall, lean, and dapper, waited with a bottle of Scotch. He was cool, completely composed, and appeared only mildly interested. Jean wasn't fooled, and suddenly she was afraid. She discarded her plan to talk frankly, to explain her fears of male domination and her need for artistic fullfillment. No, she had to find a scapegoat, and the logical person was Joe Schenck. After all, Joe had helped arrange the MGM contract. What could be more natural than that he should move to protect his brother's investment by arranging her marriage with a studio executive? Only Joe knew of Zwillman's interest, of the possibility that the new star might impulsively elope with an ex-convict, a gangster.

How much of her story Longie believed Jean couldn't tell. He asked questions, and eventually she found herself explaining how the marriage to Berns would not interfere with their own affair. And if some day he was able to "go legit," a divorce would be easily arranged. Paul would cooperate, she was certain.

Somehow the mood changed. Longie became more tolerant, almost amused. While relieved, she nevertheless felt slightly annoyed. He was treating her like a child. Didn't he care anymore? Why didn't they adjourn to the bed? Things would be simpler there. Zwillman did not respond. And when she pressed against him and stood on her toes for a kiss at parting, he pushed her gently away. She was outraged.

"Damn you, Longie; I want you to lay me."

"Take it up with Paul," he said and began to laugh. There was nothing bitter, nothing hysterical about this laughter, which followed her down the path to the waiting car. No, it was the laughter of a man much amused by a cosmic joke, and the joke — whatever it was — was not on Longie Zwillman.

The wedding took place on the evening of July 1, 1932, and Jean, in a gesture perhaps intended to show Zwillman that ambition, not love, was being served, chose to make a personal appearance at a local theater in the hours before the ceremony. The house where she lived with Mama and Marino was full of flowers when, tired and fretful, she returned home. She ignored the white roses from Berns, the yellow roses from Howard Hughes, the pink roses from Clark Gable, and searched in vain for the white gardenias that would indicate Longie had stopped laughing.

Jean changed into a full-length white dress and sandals with low heels, but still she towered over her husband. John Gilbert, a fading star of the silent screen, was best man and looked down on both of them. A justice of the peace performed the ceremony, but Louis B. Mayer was there on behalf of the studio and the Republican Party to make it official. The day had not yet come when he would refer to Jean Harlow as "that whore." The cake was cut, the toasts were drunk, the jokes were made, and finally, after midnight, the bride and groom were left alone in the little house. The wedding reception would be held the next day in the afternoon at Paul's house, and when *Red Dust* was finished there would be a honeymoon in Europe.

There in the space of an hour all plans collapsed.

Jean, feeling more curiosity than anticipation, went into the bedroom and put on a white silk nightgown. Paul sat in the living room, drinking steadily. Seeking to encourage him, she called. He crossed the bedroom without looking at her and began undressing in the bathroom. She turned out the night lamp and in total darkness Berns at last approached the nuptial bed. She opened her arms to clasp the small body to her breast — strange, the nipples were sleeping — and realized for the first time just how tiny her husband was without the camouflage of padded clothing. Like a small child, really. She dropped her hand to explore and caress. At first she could not believe the truth.

Paul had the penis and testicles of a boy before puberty.

He was pressing against her, pushing, grunting with effort, but the pitiful organ remained inert beneath her fingers. And suddenly she knew why Longie Zwillman had laughed. The sonofabitch had known the truth.

Her hand fell away, and she pushed backward in bed. Berns sensed rejection and in a flurry of movement changed position and buried his face in Jean's crotch. She could feel his tongue, licking, searching. Hell, it wasn't much longer than his prick.

"Get off," she said, and it was the first time either had spoken. "Cut the comedy."

And then she screamed in pain. Instead of obeying, Berns bit deeply, sinking his teeth into the soft flesh of her pudenda. Suddenly he was an animal, out of control, cursing, crying. Jean rolled away from him and off the other side of the bed. Instantly, he was at the night switch. The lights came on, and they stared across the bed at each other. Jean began to laugh hysterically at the sight of the unformed male organs. The man picked up a thin cane he often carried and struck at her head. She ducked; the blow landed on her back. He hit her again and again before she ran screaming from the room. He made no attempt to follow.

She picked up the phone to call Roselli. Longie had said to call Roselli if ever she needed help in an emergency. Well, this was an emergency. But pride changed her mind. Longie would be expecting a call. She wouldn't give him the satisfaction.

From the bedroom came sounds as if a small boy was crying.

Jean called her agent, Arthur Landau. In secret he came to the house, took her still in her nightgown to his home, where his wife dressed her wounds and helped her regain control. As Landau — who recorded the whole story in intimate detail in his diary, which was later made public — saw it, Jean had no choice. To leave Berns on her wedding night would create a scandal that would ruin her career. Certainly Mayer, who believed in pure love for everyone but himself, would raise hell. In his rage he would break everyone who had anything to do with Jean or Berns. Whatever the explanation, there was sure to be gossip, but truth was more dangerous. To let the public know that Harlow, the sex symbol for millions, had married a man with a child's penis would make the entire movie industry the laughingstock of the country. No, the appearance of marriage had to be maintained. In a year, perhaps, there could be a quiet divorce. But for some months, at least, the newlyweds had to act as if they were made for each other. That meant, first of all, the wedding reception had to go off on schedule.

Landau returned with Jean to the house. Berns lay naked on the floor in a drunken stupor. The evidence to confirm Jean's incredible story was there to see.

Somehow the agent got Berns awake and into his clothes. Berns was shamed and yet strangely defiant. Under questioning he talked of his life of evasion and frustration. In him, the sexual impulse was no more than the knowledge that as a man, as a male animal, he *should* feel passion and desire. He had no tendency toward homosexuality — indeed, that would have been a blessing. He was asexual, a natural eunuch, by ironic jest fated to work in an environment where men were judged by their virility as much as by their wealth. Deliberately he had cultivated a reputation as a swinging bachelor, a sophisticated man about town with no need to boast of his conquests. To maintain the fiction he rented a small cottage in West Hollywood and installed an attractive if untalented actress to play the part of his mistress. Word of his "love nest" spread around town, confirming the general opinion that Berns was discreet as well as virile. That a high executive at MGM should have to go to such lengths to convince his peers that he was a properly immoral person is perhaps a good commentary on the double standard of Hollywood: on the screen, respect for the Hays Office and the Code; off the screen, anything goes.

Why had Berns sought to marry Harlow?

It had all been part of the dream, the hope, the prayer. He had come to Hollywood originally in the belief that sex flowered there. Perhaps in such a climate he could hope to be stimulated. Again and again he set the stage for passion and hoped for a miracle. The marriage with Jean was but another invitation. She was, after all, the nation's sex queen, the woman for whom all men panted. Surely such a glorious animal could help him. If men could have a sexual climax just looking at her image on a screen, surely he could have an erection when her naked body was his to take and use.

He hated her for failing him.

It was mid-August before Longie Zwillman found time to visit Hollywood. Somewhat to Jean's surprise he was neither angry at her nor contemptuous of her husband. When the car deposited her at the usual bungalow, she was ready for anything but kindness, which was what he gave her.

The conversation, this time, took place in bed. Warmed by love and brandy, Jean relaxed for the first time in months as Longie explained how he knew enough about Paul Berns to laugh so heartily. Meyer Lansky had grown up with Paul in New York. Both were small physically, with good minds, and they found much to talk about. One day Meyer rescued Paul from a group of Irish youths who were engaged in the local sport of "cockalizing." They opened Paul's fly to expose his circumcision, but what they found amused them even more. Meyer had felt sorry for his friend and wanted to continue the relationship, but a shamed Berns avoided him thereafter.

"When Meyer heard you were marrying Paul he wondered what the hell was going on. So he asked me. I figured Joe Schenck was involved." "Why?" Jean was puzzled. "Because Joe knows the truth about Paul. It's a small world, you know. Way back yonder when Joe was hustling for a buck, he was working for this drugstore in New York, and Paul — he was just a kid -- asked him if there was any drug that would help him get a hard-on. Knowing Joe, he probably sold him something. Paul complained about it to Meyer when Meyer found out about him."

"And they say women gossip."

"With Meyer it ain't gossip, honey; it's intelligence information. No guesswork for Meyer; he knows what he's doing."

"I don't think I like him."

"That won't bother him none. He's no playboy. But watch out for his partner, Bugsy Siegel. He thinks he's God's gift to women. He'll be coming out this way before long. Says he wants to meet you."

"I've got enough trouble already."

"Harlean, you don't know the half of it."

Then Zwillman broke the news: Paul Berns had another wife. What's more, she was sore. No, it wasn't blackmail. She'd been in love with the guy. Well, maybe not love exactly but sort of a wife and mother. Anyway, she felt she had gotten a raw deal, and she intended to do something about it. What? Well, there were several possiblities.

Jean was dumfounded, less by the fact that Paul had two wives — where he was concerned she had lost the capacity for astonishment — than by the complications that would follow if the news became public. It could ruin her career. Damn the bastard. He was crazy.

"I'll kill him," she said.

"Leave the killing to me." The voice was mild, but it was serious. "First things first. How are you getting along with him?"

"I'm becoming an actress. It's easy enough in public, but sometimes he gets on my nerves at home and I say something and he blows his top. It's sorta interesting. I never know if he'll start crying or start hitting."

"Has he tried to fuck you?"

"No, I haven't given him a chance." She hesitated. "But I think he'd like to try. He keeps hinting."

"Hope springs eternal," said Longie Zwillman. "Well, I

think you'd better take a few days off and go up to Frisco. The other Mrs. Berns wants to meet you. She's really very nice."

The meeting took place at the Plaza Hotel in San Francisco, where Dorothy Milette Berns was staying. She was ten years older than Jean and ten years younger than Paul. Red-headed, she could have been pretty, but there was an old-maidish air about her as she peeped over her glasses at her visitor.

They drank tea and talked of the little man who had done so much to mix up their lives. Dorothy had been a struggling young actress when she met Paul in New York. They had fallen in love, married secretly, and lived as man and wife at the Algonquin. Like Jean, she had not learned the truth about her husband until the wedding night. The shock had been a lasting one, but under pressure she had consented to provide Paul with the appearance of virility. After a year, however, she cracked up under the strain. Conscience-stricken, he had placed her in an expensive sanatorium in Connecticut. She was still there when he went west in quest of sexual stimulation. Discharged at last, she moved back into the Algonquin and lived there for years as Mrs. Paul Berns. Faithfully, he paid the bills. It was only when he asked for a divorce that she followed him to California. Shortly after she arrived in San Francisco, his engagement to Jean was announced. It had not surprised her, and she had wanted to meet Jean to confirm her suspicions that yet another actress had fallen for the "mind and soul" routine he dished out so well. Having met Jean, she liked her, but there was still the question of what to do about Paul. Before deciding, she wanted to talk to him.

"It could be dangerous," said Zwillman.

"I know," she replied. "That's why I agreed to cooperate with Miss Harlow. I've nothing to lose any more, but I realize she could be badly hurt if this thing isn't handled properly."

"We appreciate your concern."

Jean looked quickly at the gangster, but his face told her nothing. Was there a trace of irony in his voice? His expression was that of a friendly lawyer who as a matter of policy refused to believe in evil motives. Yet a shiver ran across her belly.

When Zwillman promised to arrange a meeting within two weeks — the Labor Day weekend might be a good time — Dorothy agreed to wait. As they left the room she touched Jean's hair.

"It's marvelous," she said.

Zwillman was silent during the ride back to the Mark Hopkins Hotel, where Jean was registered, along with Mama and Marino. A block from the hotel he stopped the car and told her to walk the rest of the way.

"No point in somebody remembering later that they saw us together."

"What are you going to do?"

"Well, I gotta see Tony Cornero about some booze. Then I gotta find Doc Statcher if he hasn't left town and straighten out some vending-machine business. And then I've got to go over to Reno and talk to some politicians. They legalized gambling in Nevada last year, you know, but so far they haven't figured out what to do about it. Then, maybe, if I have time, I'll go over to L.A. and see how my favorite movie star is making out."

Jean left laughing, her fears momentarily forgotten.

The scene in the rain barrel was not going well, but only Jean complained at the endless retakes. After the first day she discarded the flesh-colored bathing suit. It was just too much trouble. Clark Gable, who was supposed to be helping her bathe, had trouble remembering his lines. Her feelings were not improved when she learned she would have to work Saturday and Sunday before Labor Day. Louis B.

Mayer would observe a federal holiday, of course, but there was no law saying the studio couldn't make people work on weekends. Greatly daring, Director Victor Fleming pointed out that there was no law saying actors had to do their best on Sunday either, but Mayer pointed out that a *good* director could get the best out of his actors any day of the week.

Upon arriving at the studio Saturday morning, Jean received a call from Zwillman. His voice was casual, but his meaning was clear. Jean was not to go home that evening. She should spend the night with her mother.

"We're already planning to have dinner with Mama Sunday night," said Jean.

"Fine, sweetheart, but I want you out of the house Saturday night too. Understand?"

Paul Berns did not know that Jean would be away from home that night when Dorothy called to demand he meet with her and her "attorney," so he suggested they have dinner at the Ambassador Hotel. He would reserve a bungalow there, and privacy would be assured. Harold Garrison, who served MGM executives as handyman and chauffeur, drove Berns to the Ambassador about seven o'clock. He was told to have dinner, come back and wait. Dorothy, disguised at Zwillman's insistence in a black wig and dark glasses, was waiting when Berns arrived. She introduced the man with her as Abe Long. Berns, more puzzled than alarmed, tried to keep everything civilized. He called for a waiter and insisted that his guests order a meal. When the drinks arrived, he apologized for the quality of the gin. Bootleggers, he noted, were becoming nervous and were apparently dumping all kinds of rotgut on the market in anticipation of Repeal. Zwillman smiled and said nothing.

When the meal was concluded, Dorothy cut short Berns's jabber. How, she asked, could Paul do to another woman, to Jean Harlow, what he had done to her? If he had an explanation, any excuse, she wanted to hear it. Paul began crying, but then by a masterful act of will he got control. He knew all too well what he had done to Jean, but there had been no choice. He had been asked by the studio to marry Jean. The studio wanted to protect her from an Eastern gangster who had been demanding she marry him.

Zwillman spoke softly. "Do you know the name of this alleged gangster?"

"No," admitted Berns, "but I can find out. Joe Schenck knows."

Zwillman remained impassive, but he asked no more questions of the no longer dapper little man. Dorothy took charge. She was frankly skeptical, and her insight into her husband's problems soon had him wiggling. Finally he acknowledged that he "volunteered" for the job of protecting Jean, and since the marriage was in name only he never worried about bigamy. His only motive was to improve his standing at the studio, to make sure he could continue to care for Dorothy in years to come. Miss Harlow's beautiful white body meant nothing to him. He had put that part of his life behind him long before.

Dorothy was about to call him a liar — her wisdom in talking to Jean first was apparent — when Zwillman interrupted and terminated the interview. They would give Berns twenty-four hours to find proof of his story. Tomorrow night they would come to his home for the showdown. If Mrs. Berns — Mrs. Dorothy Berns, that is — remained unsatisfied, legal action would be taken. There were several possibilities. Berns began to cry. From his knees he appealed to the woman. She knew how he had suffered. He begged for pity.

Tight-lipped, dry-eyed, she walked by him, out into the night. Zwillman followed without a word. Berns composed himself, took a drink of straight gin, and went out to the street, where Garrison waited in the studio car. In silence they drove to his empty house. He got little sleep that night.

Jean spent Sunday in the rain barrel, but nothing went

right. Seeing Clark Gable get hot and bothered simply wasn't as much fun as it had been. Clark announced at day's end that he was going fishing in hopes it would relax him. Marino Bello, who had come to the studio to pick up Jean, volunteered to go along to show him how an Italian tied flies. While they were alone, Bello added, he might even tell Mr. Gable about a map to the Lost Dutchman Mine he had obtained from a dying prospector in Death Valley. Gable looked an appeal to Jean, but she was happy enough to have the hyperactive Marino out of town. Besides, it gave her an excuse, if one should be needed, to spend another night with Mama.

Berns spent Sunday alone, eating little and drinking a lot. After receiving two anonymous phone calls — from Zwillman — which suggested the only manly thing to do was kill himself, Berns took the receiver off the hook. When Jean called that evening, allegedly to remind him to come to Mama's house for dinner, she got a busy signal. And Mama could confirm it.

The hours passed. Zwillman deliberately delayed until almost midnight. All was dark along Easton Drive as Zwillman eased the powerful touring car he had borrowed into the driveway of Berns's secluded home. The two Mrs. Berns were in the rear seat. Neither had said much to the other during the ride.

At Zwillman's suggestion, Mrs. Dorothy Berns stayed in the car, out of sight. Zwillman and Jean went to the door, which was not locked. They entered. Paul was in the living room. He was naked. The fragrance of perfume, Mitsouko, Jean's favorite, was heavy in the room. He had drenched his midsection with it. His penis was wet.

At the sight of Jean he rushed forward and fell on his knees. He put his arms around her ankles, almost causing her to fall.

"Darling," he said. "I did it; I did it. I got an erection."

The front door opened and closed. Mrs. Dorothy Berns entered. In her hand was a .38-caliber revolver.

Zwillman reached forward and pulled Jean away from the man on the floor. Still on his knees, he looked up at the woman with the gun. His mouth gaped wide.

"I'm sorry," she said and pulled the trigger. The bullet struck him in the head at a range of not more than three feet.

"Perfect," said Zwillman, but he spoke only to himself.

Dorothy dropped the gun on the floor beside the body, which toppled forward on its face. She walked stiffly from the room, back to the car, got in, and waited.

Jean watched in horror as Zwillman, a professional in every sense, wiped the gun of fingerprints and placed it in Berns's hand. From an inside pocket he produced an envelope and from it he extracted a note.

"Where was it when you found it?" he asked.

"On my dressing table."

"Then that's where it belongs now," he said.

Jean had found the note on the morning after her wedding night. Apparently Paul had intended to kill himself but had lost his nerve or passed out before he could do so. She had said nothing to her agent about it, nor had Paul ever mentioned it. Perhaps he had not wanted to remember. But in that happy reunion with Longie at the Garden of Allah, she had shown it to him. And he had kept it. Although two months old, it would be the clincher in converting murder into suicide. Besides, it sure as hell would puzzle a lot of people. Poor Paul had produced a masterpiece of innuendo and mystery. The note said:

Dearest dear:

Unfortunately this is the only way to make good the frightful wrong I have done you and to wipe out my abject humiliation.
                                                                    Paul

You understand that last night was only a comedy.

"Good enough," said Longie Zwillman, taking one last look. "I think we can leave the rest to Mr. Mayer and his ass-kissers. This is the type of situation they can handle. They're experts."

He took Jean by the arm, shook her violently. "Save your dramatics for later, Harlean; we've got to get out of here."

Obediently she followed. In the back seat of the car the first Mrs. Berns was waiting. When Jean sat down Dorothy patted her hand.

U ilizing the skills developed in guarding liquor convoys from hijackers, Zwillman took the corner to the street on two wheels. So what if the neighbors hcard and remembered? MGM would make it a suicide. Meanwhile, the quicker they got away the better. A careful man could plan against any contingency except bad luck.

Jean was left at her mama's house with orders to take a double dose of sleeping pills and go to bed. As soon as the body was found she could prove she was an actress.

"Goodbye," said the woman in the back seat. Impulsively Jean bent over and kissed her.

It was almost five hundred miles to San Francisco, but Zwillman drove a Pierce-Arrow with a hopped-up motor, extra gas tanks, and special suspension. Traffic was light in the early hours of Sunday morning, and people were just venturing out for eleven-o'clock church services when he stopped the car near the Plaza Hotel.

Dorothy let herself be seen in the lobby of the hotel that Monday afternoon. On Tuesday morning she bought a paper and discussed the headline story with the hotel manager. In the afternoon she boarded the *Delta King*, a paddle-wheel steamer plying the river between Sacramento and San Francisco. She was not seen alive again.

Later, after her body was fished out of the river some thirty miles southwest of Sacramento, Jean asked Longie if the woman really killed herself.

"It's always nice to have some people willing to do your work for you," replied the gangster. "She was a very understanding person, a lady."

Presumably, decided Jean, if Longie had been forced to kill the one witness to Berns's death who could not be relied upon to keep silent, he wouldn't have considered her a lady.

In true movie tradition, Berns's body was found by his butler just before noon. The butler, who knew the ways of Hollywood, called MGM. Louis Mayer was there, brooding over the money being lost by a senseless holiday. He called his executive officer, Irving Thalberg, for whom Berns had worked. Thalberg assigned his wife, Norma Shearer, to spread the alarm.

Mayer was first on the scene and managed to find and pocket the suicide note. After checking out everything and conferring with his aides, he at last consented to notify police. When they arrived he displayed a blend of grief and bewilderment, promised complete cooperation, and departed to comfort his heartbroken child — well, she *seemed* like his child — with the suicide note still in his pocket. Luckily for Zwillman, Mayer met Howard Strickling, his publicity chief, down the road. Strickling, who knew his problems were big enough already, persuaded Mayer to turn his car around and return the note to the house. He had forgotten all about it, he told police, and they, of course, accepted his explanation. The incident, however, later caused some cynics to suggest that perhaps the studio forged the entire note in an effort to protect Mayer's blond "child."

Jean, officially informed of the tragedy, put on one of the best acts of her career, complete with a fake suicide attempt. It was all a mystery to her, she insisted. Paul had been the perfect husband.

In the months to come there were some anxious moments as grand juries probed the case and details about the other

Mrs. Berns became public. But Zwillman had been right: Mayer and his people were experts at whitewashing. Rumor had a field day, but the truth remained hidden until long after it ceased to matter.

It was only a few months later in 1933 that Longie Zwillman put together the final pieces of the Schenck— Harlow—MGM puzzle. He had suspected all along that more than brotherly love was involved in Joe Schenck's switching Jean to MGM, and abruptly it became apparent that he was right. A new producing company was announced by Joe Schenck and Darryl F. Zanuck, former boy wonder at Warner Brothers. It was called Twentieth Century. Three years later when the corporate remains of Fox Films was picked up, it became Twentieth Century-Fox. But how did Zanuck and Joe Schenck swing the deal at the height of the Depression? Simple! Half the initial capital of $750,000 was supplied by Nick Schenck, Joe's brother and the president of Loew's Inc., the parent company of MGM. The other half was supplied by Louis B. Mayer, production head of MGM. Both Nick Schenck and Mayer had gained immensely when they acquired "the Blonde Bombshell" for seven years, and they were grateful to Joe for his services. Mayer, however, got an added bonus: He forced the new company to put his son-in-law, William Goetz, on the payroll as well.

In considering the deal, Zwillman remembered Joe Schenck had hinted at that meeting in Cleveland with Jean that he might need a financial favor soon. Obviously, decided Zwillman, when the time came Joe had looked into his crystal ball and decided it was no time to be dealing with mob financiers with the end of Prohibition so rapidly approaching. Better to turn back to the family, where one hand could scratch the other in comparative safety.

Joe was a smart bastard, all right, but maybe he needed a lesson in humility. If he thought "the Outfit" was dead with Prohibition, he was in for a shock. Things were just getting organized. There was talk of a big meeting next year to put together a national combination. And Abner Zwillman would have an important part in whatever organization emerged. For him there would be no more nonsense about going legit, of dropping out. What was the point?

Zwillman retained an affection for Jean Harlow, but the original magic had been lost. When, on October 15, 1933, she underwent an emergency appendectomy, he arranged to obtain a few golden hairs from her pubic zone. Mounted in little gold lockets, he offered them for sale to a select group of businessmen. At five hundred bucks a hair they were considered an art treasure. Bugsy Siegel bought five of them.

Jean's reaction when she heard the hairy story was somewhat similar to Norma Talmadge's comment when Joe Schenck wanted a divorce: "From now on I'm not even going to trust the ass I sit on."

In this business it's dog eat dog,
and nobody's going to eat me.
— SAMUEL GOLDWYN

Look at that bunch of pants pressers
in Hollywood making themselves
millions.
— JOSEPH P. KENNEDY

4

The Revenge
of Longie Zwillman

On February 1, 1935, United States Treasury agents raided an illegal distillery on the waterfront of Elizabeth, New Jersey. The distillery was second in size only to one at Zanesville, Ohio, which ranked as the largest ever found. Suspecting rightly that the same syndicate operated the two distilleries, the investigators assigned Special Agent C.W. DeWitt to do some undercover snooping. Posing as a distiller looking for a crew, DeWitt contacted some of the men arrested at Elizabeth and released on $100,000 bail. Soon he reported: "Ben Siegel, known as 'the Bug,' had a piece of the Elizabeth plant, as did Charles 'Lucky' Luciano." A few days later, having won the confidence of Rubin Lubitsky, DeWitt was able to elaborate: "Jacob 'Gurrah' Shapiro, Louis Lepke and the Bug put up the money. Siegel looks like Edward G. Robinson, the actor. This Mob wiped out the Waxey Gordon Mob, killed Max Hassell, Max Greenberg, Charles Solomon. . . ."

Later it was learned that the Elizabeth distillery was part of a joint venture of the Eastern and Cleveland syndicates. Begun before Repeal, it continued until 1937 — made profitable because illegal booze was cheaper than liquor on which taxes were paid.

The statement that Bugsy Siegel resembled Robinson, "the actor," is of particular interest.

Robinson achieved fame in the 1931 movie *Little Caesar.* Another variation of the Capone saga, it had "Rico" as Capone and "the Big Boy" as John Torrio. Robinson played Rico, a hood with no redeeming virtue except courage. The plot was so absurd as to be funny, and the much touted "realism" of the production was another joke. Every cliché associated with gangsters was used — but, of course, they weren't clichés at the time. The irony is that instead of the movie resembling underworld conditions and real gangsters, it was the real gangsters who soon imitated the actors in talk, dress, and mannerisms. Thus it was that Siegel looked like Robinson, not vice versa. In real life George Raft was a punk. No one would dream of imitating him. But as a movie gangster he became influential and a buddy of Siegel. While the Hays Office required Rico to die in the end and wouldn't even allow him to call on God in his agony, the movie did more to make gangsters popular than even *Public Enemy.* It taught an entire generation how to talk and act tough Hollywood-style.

Siegel, as tough a hood as ever came out of New York's East Side, enjoyed the good things of life as much as Rico. Just as Zwillman had predicted, Bugsy went to Hollywood and liked what he saw. Unfortunately, the junior member of the Bugs & Meyer Mob was pretty involved back east and couldn't get out as often as he wished. Zwillman introduced him to Jean. Her stepfather, Marino Bello, found Siegel receptive to tales of lost treasure. Soon Bugsy dreamed of ruling this land of easy virtue and make-believe. All he needed was an excuse.

Far from the "let's pretend" of Hollywood, a soup kitchen in Chicago provided some thin nourishment for unemployed members of the Stagehands Union and food for thought in syndicate circles. In those soup kettles was cooked an extortion plot so spicy it would ultimately require the services of Bugsy Siegel on the West Coast and, not incidentally, give Abner Zwillman an opportunity to humiliate Joseph Schenck.

It all began when Willie Bioff ran into George Browne and the two men exchanged hard-luck stories. Bioff was an ex-pimp, put out of business by the Depression. As he told it to Browne: "When things get bad there ain't no place for an honest pimp. The Johns are selling nickel apples and the broads are selling two-dollar cherries and who the hell needs me?"

Bioff, who also dabbled as a union organizer, told of his attempts to organize kosher butchers of Chicago into a union. Economic conditions had spoiled that enterprise too.

"When people get hungry enough, they don't care what they eat so long as it's cheap," he grumbled.

Browne, a big man with a bigger thirst — he averaged one hundred bottles of bear each day he could afford them agreed. He had a union, but half the members were out of work, and the other half had suffered a pay cut of 20 percent. Getting them to cough up enough to take care of their unemployed brothers was impossible. In fact, they could barely take care of George, and he was their business agent.

Out of this and subsequent conversations came the Soup Kitchen. The formula is easily understood. Browne had hungry mouths to feed. Bioff knew some minor politicians needing votes. If the politicians would contribute to the Soup Kitchen, Bioff and Browne could guarantee that the grateful stagehands would vote for their benefactors. And, of course, that would still hold true if only one-fourth of the donation was used to buy soup. There were, after all, certain business expenses.

The joint venture worked, and the fact that one of their ideas actually paid off was of greater importance to Bioff and Browne than the few dollars it put in their pockets. Morale restored, they began looking for bigger opportunities. Bioff knew only a few politicians in need of votes, but Browne knew a lot of theatrical people who had plenty of money and were still making it despite the Depression. Such people should be happy to help feed the unfortunate, especially if by doing so they received a "no-strike" guarantee from the employed members of the union.

Their first target was Balaban and Katz. The company owned a chain of movie theaters in the Chicago area, the product of a partnership between a piano player and a singer. Sam Katz and Barney Balaban began operating nickelodeons while still in their teens and, upon joining forces in 1916, went on to become major figures in the new industry. Significantly, as part of the drive to combine production and distribution units, they found themselves in Hollywood. Balaban would become president of Paramount Pictures, and Katz would become a vice-president of MGM. This link between the theaters in Chicago and other cities with the movie studios was to become a key factor in the developing conspiracy.

Bioff, knowing his partner had consumed too much beer to look tough, made the original approach. John Balaban, brother of Barney, listened to Willie explain that the employed union members could no longer contribute to the support of their unemployed brothers unless the 20 percent pay cut was restored. And if it wasn't restored, well, the employed members would go on strike. It was one for all and all for one in the Stagehands union — even in starvation.

Balaban was impressed, but he suggested that the best way to help the hungry was to do it directly; he would give one hundred and fifty dollars a week to buy soup. Bioff said he'd have to consult with his boss. Browne, after all, was the official representative of the union. Soon a second meeting was set at Gibby Kaplan's restaurant. Browne came along this time, a little awed perhaps and entirely willing to let Willie handle the discussions. Willie had done some serious thinking. It was time, he decided, to move up to the big leagues. He told Balaban he would accept cash in lieu of a pay raise, but the money had to be paid in a lump sum. He thought fifty big ones ought to swing it.

This time it was Balaban who needed to think. The next meeting was in the office of Leo Spitz, a Chicago attorney destined to become head of RKO Corporation. Spitz acted the role of umpire, and a compromise was reached. Bioff, with the astounded Browne watching, accepted $20,000 as a reasonable settlement.

Or, rather, Bioff agreed to accept it. He asked that a check be written to a "starving lawyer friend" instead of to him or to the union. Tax reasons, he said. The "friend" was Benjamin H. Feldman. The check to Feldman was drawn against the First National Bank of Chicago, and it was dated February 14, 1934 — St. Valentine's Day of dreadful memory. The shakedown of the movie industry had begun.

Giving Feldman $4,000 to pay for his trouble and taxes, Bioff and Browne took five dollars of the remaining sixteen grand and bought two cases of canned soup for the kitchen. Legal details and duty accomplished, the boys went out to celebrate.

Inevitably they ended up in one of several joints owned by Nick Circella. Back in their youth, Bioff, Circella, and Frank Rio had been bootleggers together and had purchased their supplies from the Greendale Products Company. Greendale was owned by Frank "the Enforcer" Nitti, a major lieutenant of Al Capone. Of the three, Rio made the best impression and achieved high rank in the organization. Circella tagged along, more or less as a bodyguard for Rio, but Bioff was shut out. It was logical, therefore, that he should be eager to "show off" his new wealth in Circella's place. His pleasure increased when he noted that Rio was sitting at Circella's table and that both men were watching his antics with interest. As Bioff competed with Browne for the unaccustomed role of big spender, Circella wondered out loud where two such punks got all the dough. Rio thought it might be a good idea to find out.

Next morning Browne was taken for a ride around Chicago while Bioff was left to walk the streets in fear. Up today, down tomorrow – the story of both men's lives. Browne, convinced that as in gangster movies his only chance was to "come clean," described how his sudden wealth had been acquired. Not knowing *why* Rio was interested, Browne played safe and credited Bioff with the big idea and the implementation of it. Who knows – maybe Balaban had complained to Greasy Thumb Guzik?

Still confused but glad to have survived the ride, Browne was dropped off and told he'd be hearing from Rio shortly. Two days later the word came: "You and Willie get out to Frank's house."

Waiting in Frank Nitti's drawing room was the elite of the Chicago syndicate: Phil D'Andrea, former Capone bodyguard and official head of the Mafia in Chicago; Paul "the Waiter" Ricca, ally of Meyer Lansky and Lucky Luciano; Charles "Cherry Nose" Gioe, a top Capone lieutenant; and Louis "Little New York" Compagna, another syndicate big shot. Most significant of all, however, was the presence of Lepke from New York, whose fame made even the killers of Capone turn pale. That he had been invited meant that more than a local or regional caper was planned; this was the national syndicate.

Browne was wishing he was back in Jilly's Tavern with a dozen bottles of beer before him, but Bioff's heart was beating triumphantly. This was the big time, where he belonged. At last his luck had turned.

And so it seemed. Nitti, wasting no time on punks, explained the "Outfit" was cutting itself in on their racket. From now on the split would be half and half. Later, when the scope of the operation widened and the amount of loot increased, the syndicate took up to 90 percent of the profits. Browne and Bioff had no real objections; their share exceeded by far the amounts they could have hoped to have collected by themselves.

The presence of Lepke was explained when Nitti ordered Browne to run once more for the presidency of the International Alliance of Theatrical Stage Employees and Moving Picture Operators of the United States and Canada. Browne had tried for the office in 1932 and had failed primarily because of opposition from the big locals in the East. There would be no such opposition in June, Lepke said.

The IATSE convention was held in the Brown Hotel on Broadway in Louisville, Kentucky, and complete privacy was assured when the *Courier-Journal*'s offer to provide some publicity was declined. The newspaper then decided to ignore the affair, so the syndicate was able to take over the union without embarrassment. (Some years later when Longie Zwillman got title to a square block of Louisville through nominees — he provided the newspaper with the kind of constructive news it likes to print. On the site would be built, declared Zwillman's spokesman, a high-class department store, a restaurant of national repute, and a 3,500-seat theater. Needless to say, nothing of the type was built, but Longie's speculation was ultimately hailed by the *Courier-Journal* as "one of the most profitable in Louisville's history.")

Accompanying Bioff and Candidate Browne to Louisville was a collection of muscle men Capone might have envied had he been free to do so. One of them was identified by federal investigators several years later as "Joe Arcadia, alias Joe Batters." In time this man who visited Louisville in the summer of 1934 would be known as Tony Accardo, successor to Torrio, Capone, and Nitti as boss of the Chicago syndicate.

The non-delegates occupied suites in one section of the boxlike hotel, and there any bored delegate could find booze and broads. Louisville was one of the few cities still boasting a well-defined red-light district, where the girls were clean and well disciplined. Those who had ambitions to go to Hollywood were selected to "staff" the Brown Hotel and supplement the "stag" movies shown. So persuasive was the entertainment that it was necessary to beat up only a mere half-dozen stubborn individuals who insisted on believing that as president George Browne would make a helluva beer drinker. Needless, to say the hotel bills of the non-delegates, along with other expenses, were paid in cash — and the money came from IATSE coffers.

Victory was easily achieved, and Browne's first act as president was to appoint Willie Bioff his personal representative with full authority. He was happy to do this out of affection for Willie, but the move was prompted by the syndicate, which controlled Bioff just as Bioff controlled Browne.

Little time was lost by the syndicate in exploiting its victory. Bioff and Browne, with Circella sitting in, invited John Balaban to dinner at Kaplan's Restaurant and informed him that the IATSE had voted to demand the restoration of *two* projectionists in every motion-picture theater. Originally, in the pioneer days, two men had been needed, but as equipment was perfected one man was dropped as an economy move. The union didn't like it, naturally, since it meant a lot of members were out of jobs. To back up the demand, Bioff threatened a strike. As expected, Balaban suggested a compromise. The deal agreed upon provided that theater owners would contribute an additional amount — varying according to the size of the payroll — to the union. Allegedly, it would be used to pay unemployment benefits, but neither side had any illusions as to where the money would go. Similar deals were made in New York City and, the pattern established, in other metropolitan areas around the country. And with the cash coming in, the syndicate decided to go for the jackpot — the movie studios.

Prior to Bioff's and Browne's coming to office, the IATSE in 1933 had conducted an unsuccessful strike against the motion-picture producers in Hollywood. Ironically, the strike had been defeated largely because the producers called on their assorted friends and financiers in the underworld to supply the necessary "muscle." Membership in the union dropped to less than one hundred and fifty, and several "company unions" kept all organization efforts diffused.

Bioff, with all the muscle in the country at his disposal, was just the man to change things. He moved into Hollywood late in 1934 and began recruiting. Progress was spectacular once the realization dawned that Bioff represented organized crime. No one, big or little, dreamed at this stage of a national crime syndicate, and indeed, it had just been organized, but everyone in Hollywood was familiar with "the Capone Mob" as portrayed by Cagney, Robinson, Paul Muni, and others. Thanks to such movies everyone also knew that while the Chicago boys would break your back if you crossed them, they were really good guys at heart who loved their old mothers and wanted to be rich only so they could become respectable. They really differed little from the leaders of the movie industry.

By March 1935 Bioff had signed up enough new and old members to obtain the control he wanted. Impatiently he passed the word that he was ready for action. Chicago was ready too, but Chicago itself did not have ultimate power. That rested with the national syndicate, and its leaders were so busy with other expansion plans that Hollywood had to wait its turn. A long and costly civil war in the Mafia had been ended, but the process of integrating hot-tempered members of the Honored Society into civilized gangland society was taking longer than expected and was never to be completely successful. Mafia members loved the vendetta too well. Then, too, the elimination of "independents" throughout the country brought continuing problems of allocation and diplomacy. But most important was the wide vista of opportunity suddenly open to a unified and all-powerful crime entity: narcotics, gambling, liquor, shylocking, stock manipulation, and, of course, labor racketeering. To organize these and other rackets properly, much time and care were needed. Perhaps most important was the selection of executives. There was simply too much for one man, or even a commission, to handle. Efficiency, as well as political expediency, demanded the delegation of authority — either by racket or by region. Luckily, from the syndicate's viewpoint, there were a number of bright young men available. And of them all, the most eager to travel was Bugsy Siegel. He wanted to go where broads were as easy to make as bread and reality was MGM's Louis B. Mayer opposing the making of *Mutiny on the Bounty* because he was sure the public would never accept a mutineer as a hero. A firm believer in law, order, and pure love was Mayer.

Siegel believed in love too, of one kind or another, and had since his first arrest on a rape charge 1926. A cocksman by instinct and circumstances, he sometimes worried his older partner, Meyer Lansky, who felt Bugs valued balls — with all that implied — above brains. Putting Siegel in charge of the West would be great for Bugsy — who would react as promiscuously as a bull in a herd of heifers — but would it be good for business?

The subject came up one afternoon at a meeting of syndicate leaders at the Waldorf, a meeting prompted by an urgent message from Chicago urging that Bioff be given the go-ahead signal in Hollywood. No one, not even Bioff's original sponsors, thought the ex-pimp could handle the Western project alone, so the necessity of selecting a field commander was apparent.

Zwillman, who had perhaps more experience in Hollywood than anyone else, pointed out that investments beyond the Rockies had been made on an individual basis ever since Owney Madden took George Raft out and got him started.

Mention of Raft — born Ranft — diverted the conversation briefly as several men marveled that a former "stand-in crap shooter" at the Club Durant could have abruptly become such a big star by flipping a coin in *Scarface*. Siegel was impatient, noting that Raft was popular with the movie producers because he talked their language and made them feel comfortable.

Challenged to relate how he would run the West Coast if given the assignment, Siegel, who had given the matter much prior thought, outlined a concise action program that made surprisingly good sense. He would concentrate on providing the big shots in Hollywood with easy gambling and unlimited credit, along with the usual fringe benefits of sex and booze. Bioff, and others, would play the heavy, apply the pressure. Then Siegel would intervene, seemingly force a compromise, and win friendship as well as loot. Soon the syndicate would be accepted as a necessary evil, and, once established, it could expand as opportunity offered.

Noting the proximity of Los Angeles to the Mexican border — a fact originally considered when movie makers first took their cameras west — Bugsy described a courier system he would organize to bring in narcotics from Mexico. Commercial prostitution would be organized for the benefit of the businessman who preferred to deal with a professional rather than taking a chance with law and disease by seducing amateurs. And, finally, the ancient business of shylocking would be developed. In a city where everyone needed "front" money as well as huge sums for unexpected emergencies, the loan-shark industry would thrive.

It all made sense. And even Siegel's demand that he be given some measure of control over syndicate investments in order to avoid conflicts of interest was well received. He noted, however, that individuals could still make personal investments in secret if they wanted to run the risks involved.

Zwillman, with Lansky nodding quiet approval, warned Siegel that he, in turn, would have to remember he represented the syndicate and was answerable to the syndicate. Any attempt at building a personal empire would be punished, as would disobedience to any syndicate command.

Bugsy accepted the restrictions lightly enough, and the conversation turned to another pressing problem: Dutch Schultz. As the last of the independents in the New York area, he had to be dealt with quickly before he could carry out his threat to "hit" Special Prosecutor Thomas E. Dewey. The syndicate did not want the heat such a spectacular assassination would inevitably create.

After the meeting broke up with a decision to knock off Schultz, Siegel paused for a private word with Zwillman. He wanted to know if Jean Harlow was "off limits." Longie made it plain that Jean had a mind of her own and was capable of using it.

But to that denial of ownership Zwillman coupled a warning. He would be very unhappy, he said softly, with anyone who used Harlow badly. He also noted that he had some unfinished business with Joe Schenck, who was a fat pigeon and getting fatter daily. There was no hurry about Joe.

No hurry, but on December 19, 1935, the motion-picture producers bowed to the threat of a strike in the vast theater chains owned by studios and at a meeting in New York City recognized the IATSE as the bargaining agent in Hollywood. For the first time in movie history the union obtained a closed-shop agreement. Men such as Louis B. Mayer, Nick and Joe Schenck, and Harry Cohn blamed Franklin D. Roosevelt, not the syndicate, for their troubles. Roosevelt, they agreed, was opening the doors to socialism with all his talk of the New Deal and collective bargaining. More and more it was becoming apparent that private enterprise had to protect itself in any way it could until the American people wised up and returned a hardheaded businessman to the White House. Such action could be effective. The industry proved that in 1934 when it teamed up to defeat Upton Sinclair for governor of California. Ironically, the mastermind of the campaign was Irving Thalberg, Mayer's deputy at MGM, and the man now credited by liberal critics with being the artistic soul of Hollywood. Sinclair's successful opponents' first act was to secure the passage of the state income-tax law. Solemnly, the studio brass assured themselves that if victory brought such bad news, defeat would have brought nothing less than nationalization of the industry.

Flexing political muscle on the state level contributed in 1935 to the belief that the industry was strong enough to deal with crooked unions on its own terms. So what, went the argument, if we have to agree to a closed shop? If we can make a deal with a few union leaders, the closed shop will work to our advantage. And Willie Bioff is the kind of guy who talks our language. He understands the importance of money. The carrot then was as visible as the stick. Pay up, and maybe you can get sweetheart contracts. Resist, and the supply of cash flowing into thousands of box offices will dry up instantly.

Essential, of course, was to cast the production properly. Experience in a thousand pictures had proved the value of the right man or woman in the right role. Joe Schenck, the friendly playboy-gambler with a hundred underworld friends, was obviously the man to represent the studios in any formal discussions. But supporting characters were needed, and two came quickly to mind: Marino Bello and Johnny Roselli.

The stepfather of Jean Harlow, Bello was a vain little man with a libido as large as his ego. For years he had attempted to impress people with boasts of his Sicilian ancestors and dark hints about his friendships with Torrio and Capone. Jean's rising star gave him new and more credulous audiences and an illusion of importance. Unfortunately, his tendency to propose an investment in a lost gold mine or South American oil field shortly after meeting a gilt-edge executive caused a lot of people to question his intelligence.

Suddenly, however, it dawned on studio executives that the mysterious Mr. Bello might come in handy if, in fact, he really knew the big boys in Chicago as he claimed. Questioned about it, Marino was able to prove that such people as Willie Bioff, Nick Cirella, and Frank Nitti came often to his home for dinner. That they came to meet Harlow and to talk to Bugsy Siegel he did not mention. Siegel, not being from Chicago, was not known as a gangster, and he wasn't seeking publicity. Jean, as a courtesy to Longie Zwillman, was happy to introduce "Mr. Benjamin Siegel" to Hollywood. He was, after all, a rather romantic figure.

Curiously, Siegel and Bello became good friends and, even stranger, remained buddies. Both shared a perhaps innocent belief in fortune — a conviction that if you play for big stakes often enough sooner or later you win. And one big win would be enough. Meanwhile, Bello, who had managed to get on a first-name basis with a lot of Hollywood celebrities, was proud to introduce his old friend from "back east" to them all. And drop provocative hints about his "connections."

Mayer and Schenck actually took Bello to one meeting with Bioff but became discouraged when he attempted to interest them in investing in a company to manufacture synthetic mink coats. The parent company of MGM, Loew's, Inc., had been founded by a furrier, and Mayer had no desire to be reminded of it. Besides, if you manufactured mink cheap, what would you use to seduce proud maidens?

Johnny Roselli was another story.

Like Meyer Lansky and Mayer, Roselli was arbitrarily assigned July 4 as an easy-to-remember birth date, though in later years he moved it back to June as part of his bid for a more inconspicuous image. There was even confusion as to the year he was born, with Roselli listing it as 1905, making himself a year younger than some police records indicated.

Whether Johnny was born in Sicily or Chicago is also in question, but there is no doubt that at a young age — "fifteen or thereabouts" — he moved to California, where he worked as "an extra in pictures and at various jobs, odds and ends." He first came to the attention of the Los Angeles Police Department in 1925 when he was arrested for carrying a concealed weapon and for grand larceny. Prohibition offered better opportunities, and he hooked up with Antonio Cornero Stralla, known to the underworld as "Tony Cornero, King of the Western Rumrunners." Tony came temporarily to grief in 1926 while attempting to unload four thousand cases of booze off a mother ship. The Coast Guard interrupted the party and arrested Tony, who escaped to Canada. While there he made contact with the Reinfeld Syndicate and its superintendent of transportation, Abner Zwillman. Roselli, who had managed to get a couple of thousand cases of liquor ashore while the Coast Guard chased Tony, was instructed to deliver the booty to Longie. The two men liked each other, and Johnny was appointed Zwillman's personal representative in the West. The association carried sufficient prestige that on a visit to Chicago in 1928 to see the Dempsey—Tunney heavyweight championship fight, Roselli met Al Capone at a party for Al Jolson at the Metropole Hotel. Capone invited him over to the Lexington Hotel, his headquarters, for a talk. Two years later when Capone spent two days in Los Angeles, one day was devoted to Roselli. All of which did much to help Roselli's prestige among show-business personalities, who depended on the goodwill of gangsters for their nightclub bookings.

Shortly after the strange death of Paul Berns — and the

unrelated passing of Prohibition a few months later — Roselli
was in the market for a new job. By no coincidence he was
living in the Garden of Allah, that swinging bungalow complex favored by Zwillman. The 1933 drive by legitimate
unions for better salaries and working conditions was under
way. It would end in disaster and prepare the way in 1935
for Bioff and the syndicate. One of the reasons it failed was
Johnny Roselli. He was hired by the Hays Office — that
organization devoted to keeping the movies pure — as a
"labor conciliator." Nearly two decades later in testimony
before the Kefauver Committee, Roselli explained it this
way:

> At that time, to go back, I didn't have much money.
> They had a strike in the industry and the unions — that
> is, the studios — were in difficulty. The unions were try-
> ing to get on to this — I don't know whether it was a
> demand for higher wages or recognition or what it was. I
> have forgotten just what it was at the time. There was a
> little rough play around and the studios naturally didn't
> want it. They didn't want their workers hurt. They
> needed some cameramen to go back to work, and they
> had been threatened through some people. They had
> asked if I could help. I said: "The only way to help is to
> fight fire with fire. You don't have to knock anybody on
> the head doing it, but you can just get them enough
> protection for these fellows so no one will approach them
> with any rough play."
>
> So I think at that time they asked me how much I
> would charge for this performance of duties. I said: "I
> don't want anything but I would like to get a job. You
> just pay the men that I will get out and hire to protect
> these people going to work in the studios, and later on
> you can give me a job as a negotiator or assistant or
> something."

He gave me some expenses. Within one week it was all over.

Actually, it was just beginning. But Roselli had his job.

Now a respectable executive instead of a bootlegger, the slender, gray-eyed Roselli married a promising young actress, June Lang, and became a buddy of studio bosses. Born June Valasek, twelve years younger than her husband, June was an accomplished dancer. Her first screen role was in *Chandu the Magician* in 1932. When after a few years it became apparent that Roselli would never become a producer, she divorced him. The producers, however, found him useful, and their regard for him increased immensely when Bugsy Siegel reorganized the betting business and Roselli was given a piece of the local wire service. Controlled by Moses Annenberg, the national wire service supplied essential information on racing odds and results to bookies in 223 cities in the United States and Canada. Fourteen corporations were necessary to handle the business. While nominally independent, Annenberg, who also published newspapers and magazines, was a member of the board of directors of the crime syndicate and played a vital role in its expansion. For Roselli to be given a piece of the Los Angeles "action" was added proof he was well established in syndicate circles. But there was more than personal prestige involved. Siegel was doing what he promised to do — make gambling a weapon with which to win control of key individuals in the movie business. Roselli was expected to exploit every advantage that gambling gave him.

The employment of Roselli by the Hays Office is perhaps the best measure of the hypocrisy of the movie industry of the period. That this bootlegger, strong-arm goon, and illegal gambler should hold a responsible position in the agency created to protect the morals of the American people gives point to an often quoted remark by Harry Cohn of Columbia

Pictures. Speaking of the industry one day, Cohn told Ezra Goodman: "It's not a business; it's a racket."

Unwittingly, Roselli gave added insight into the relationships when questioned by the Kefauver Committee's chief counsel, Rudolph Halley, about Bugsy Siegel.

Q: Did you know Bugsy Siegel?

A: Yes, sir.

Q: How long did you know him?

A: Oh, I don't remember, but I know it was a number of years. He used to come out to California all the time.

Q: You would see him when he came?

A: Yes, sir. I think he has lived there since maybe '34, '35, '36; somewhere along there.

Q: What business was he in?

A: To tell you the truth, I never did know what his business was at that time. He seemed to get along all right. He had plenty of money. He went around with the best people.

Q: Who are the best people?

A: In that circle, the motion-picture industry, you would always see him with very nice people.

Q: Who, for instance?

A: Oh, Countess DeGracio.

Q: I can just see the wheels working in there, Mr. Roselli, trying to think, "Who can I mention that I won't hurt?"

A: Not at all.

That Roselli classed Harry Cohn among the "best people" goes without saying. Since Roselli had arranged with Zwillman for the half million Cohn needed to get control of Columbia from his brother, the two had become great friends. Gambling was just one of the things they enjoyed doing, and until July 22, 1935, the place they went to gamble was Agua Caliente, near Tijuana, Mexico.

"Paradise in the midst of Hell," Ovid Demaris has called it, and for a time it served Hollywood and Southern California as the ultimate retreat. Modeled after a Mexican's idea of what a Spanish estate *should* be, Agua Caliente provided green lawns and formal gardens in which were hidden Continental restaurants, a plush hotel, swimming pools, health spas, stables, golf courses, etc. Central to all was the glittering casino, which made available every gambling game known to man. For the elite there was the Gold Room, where the stakes and the steaks were high. The service was of solid gold, and dinner prices began at fifty dollars. Only highrollers were admitted. Occasionally Joe Schenck would rent the Gold Room for a private party, but Joe was a privileged character, having invested $403,000 in the Compania Mexicana del Agua Caliente — the company that owned the oasis. Jean Harlow was a frequent visitor, and almost all the stars from Clark Gable to Mary Pickford came often. It was, basically, a place to let down your hair.

Mexican President Lazaro Cardenas suffered an attack of virtue in 1935 and banned gambling throughout Mexico. The casino and race track at Agua Caliente were padlocked, and Schenck was lucky to receive $50,000 for his share of the property. Gambling interests attempted a revolt against the government, but it failed. Two years later, however, the race track was reopened by the crime syndicate. Johnny Roselli was one of the investors, with money supplied by Harry Cohn.

This beautiful friendship between the gangster and the movie magnate was symbolized when Roselli bought two identical star rubies and had them set in hardsome rings. He gave one to Cohn and kept the other for himself. It was, he explained to Jack Dragna, the closest he could come to reproducing the blood-brother ceremony of the Mafia with a non-Italian. Cohn was very impressed and continued to wear the ring long after June Lang had disposed of the one Roselli gave her.

That friendship, and all it represented, came in handy when

Bioff began shaking down individual studios or, as he might have explained it, allowing himself to be purchased. Columbia, as one of the smaller studios, was near the bottom of the list, so it was 1937 before Cohn was told the price was $25,000 a year. This seemed reasonable, since some of the larger studios were shelling out a hundred grand each. But Cohn had just given Roselli $25,000 to invest in Agua Caliente, and he saw no reason to pay twice.

There was some confusion. Bioff apparently failed to understand that Cohn was a member of the same team. When he didn't pay, Bioff ordered a strike at Columbia, and the disciplined union members obeyed. Shocked and angry, Cohn, who had boasted to his peers that he had "someone taking care of me," called Roselli and pleaded for help. Johnny has described in rather melodramatic terms how he went to Bioff's office for a showdown. Willie had a gun on his desk, said Roselli, and was, of course, chewing on a cigar in the best gangster tradition.

The boys talked it out. At one point, said Roselli, Bioff said, "Well, you know Frank Nitti is my friend."

"To hell with you and Nitti," Roselli said he replied.

"Well, I'm going to have to tell him," blustered Bioff.

"I said, 'Don't care who the hell you tell.' "

While the dialogue sounds like a Warner Brothers picture of the period, it is revealing for what it doesn't say. Roselli had to protect his real bosses — Zwillman, Siegel, and the syndicate. Bioff, for all his ineptness, was not stupid. While he may have believed, and rightly, that Nitti and the Chicago syndicate were in charge at the beginning, he had surely gained better perspective in three years of syndicate operations. The point is, however, that few in Hollywood and fewer outside had learned the truth. They haven't learned it yet. Most books today make only a passing reference to the "Bioff-Browne Case" and give the impression that the entire movie shakedown was the work of a couple of unlikely independents.

Disregarding Roselli's version of his private conversation with Bioff, he apparently straightened him out in a hurry. The pickets were called off, the strike ended, and "King Cohn" was once again boasting of his influence with the mob.

Some others weren't so lucky. As previously indicated, Joe Schenck was designated by the motion-picture producers to come to an understanding with Bioff and the forces behind him. Prodded by Siegel, who, in turn, was being personally directed by Longie Zwillman, Schenck was pulled in deeper and deeper. He contributed greatly to his own misfortunes by assuming the whole affair was just another business deal which men of goodwill and sophistication could work out to the satisfaction of all. That there was a more sinister purpose — the revenge of Zwillman — he could not credit. To do so would have been to acknowledge the reality of a crime syndicate that could plan deviously over a period of years and utilize fantastic resources of men and money. Like many another business executive, before and since, Schenck didn't want to acknowledge even to himself that he was in bed with gangsters. Better to be considered a naive shnook than an exposed crook.

The first installment was delivered in cash to Bioff in his private room at the Garden of Allah by Joe Schenck and Sidney R. Kent, the top executives of Twentieth Century-Fox. The money was in two parcels, each wrapped in brown paper, a total of $100,000. At subsequent meetings, Louis B. Mayer, who had conspired with Schenck to form Twentieth Century and to sign up Jean Harlow for MGM, paid tribute in person. Not even his friendship with syndicate gangster Lou Wertheim, with whom he once traveled to Europe, could get him a reduction. Nick Schenck, head of Loew's, Inc., and with Mayer the financial backer of Twentieth Century, was forced to pay and pay again. Nick later admitted he got the money by having his New York executives list large but false items on their expense accounts. And so the guilt was spread downward from the top.

As it turned out, the payment of large sums — be they considered bribes or tribute — was not enough to satisfy Zwillman. Schenck could afford them, and so long as they were kept secret his pride was not hurt. Something more was needed. That something more was set in motion by Robert Montgomery, president of the Screen Actors Guild. Fearing the reason that Bioff might try to move in on that organization once he finished with the studios, Montgomery took the offensive. The Guild, an honest union, displayed more integrity and more courage than all the producers combined. An investigation was begun into Willie Bioff, and it easily produced the information that Willie was a convicted pimp. What's more, it discovered that Willie had neglected to serve the six months in jail he was sentenced to in Chicago in 1922. Not that anyone in Chicago cared very much.

Montgomery, greatly encouraged, soon uncovered evidence that seemed to indicate Joe Schenck had given Bioff a personal check for a hundred grand. This puzzled the dickens out of the Treasury Department's Intelligence Unit, which had taught gangsters the value of cash transactions, so the men who had convicted Capone and Waxey Gordon launched a major investigation. It was the first IRS movie probe since Marion Davies was nicked for $750,000 in back taxes and penalties.

Had Longie Zwillman been inclined to forget and forgive Mayer and Schenck, the events of the summer of 1937 would have changed his mind. Jean Harlow, the girl Zwillman had made into a star and dreamed of marrying, was ill. Nevertheless, she was being pushed into finishing *Saratoga* with Clark Gable. As the picture fell behind schedule, Mayer decided to take personal charge of his blond bombshell. He invited her to come alone to a beach house at Malibu. After a cozy chat, he offered her a fabulous mink coat and made it plain he wanted a roll in the hay as payment. According to Jean's version of the incident — for obvious reasons Mayer's side of the story has not been heard — she told him the only thing she would like to give him was a dose of clap. The horrified Mayer ordered her out into the night in true Victorian tradition. Next day he removed Jean's picture from his office and ordered the movie she was making completed by June 5 — or else.

Under Mayer's pressure, production continued at a frantic pace. And on Saturday, May 29, Jean's body went limp in Gable's arms as a love scene was filmed. She was taken home to rest over the weekend. Mama, who had recently broken with her Latin lover, Marino Bello, and become a devout Christian Scientist in compensation, welcomed the chance to treat her beautiful daughter. Studio officials — not eager to seem overly concerned in the face of Mayer's rage — left Jean to her mother's care. Despite prayers and meditation, Jean became steadily worse. On Monday she was too ill to report to work. Mama, however, told all callers that her daughter was recovering nicely, and no one in the outside world had any inkling as to her real condition. Gable tried to visit her on Tuesday but was not admitted. Alarmed, he reported his fears, and a delegation of movie stars and production people descended on the house. After much argument they got inside. Although it was obvious that Jean was dangerously ill, Mama at first refused to allow a doctor to be called. When at last one was able to examine the stricken star, he reported she was suffering from inflammation of the gall bladder. Immediate hospitalization and surgery were recommended, but Mama stood on her interpretation of Christian Science doctrine and refused. The public was told that Jean was the victim of a bad cold.

Conditions got worse as Jean's kidneys failed and uremic poisoning developed. Finally, on June 4, Mama permitted her daughter to be hospitalized, but by then it was too late. Jean Harlow died early next day.

The funeral was on June 9, 1937, and the flowers that

filled the chapel were valued at $15,000. In her bronze coffin she wore a pink gown, one that she had worn in the movie *Libeled Lady*. And in her hand she clutched a single flower, a white gardenia. Attached to it was an unsigned note: "Good night, my dearest darling."

Longie Zwillman, who flew west for the funeral, became so ill that he required medical treatment from Dr. Benjamin Blank, a friend of Bugsy Siegel.

Shortly thereafter, Mayer and Joe Schenck sailed for Europe on a combination junket and talent hunt. Apparently shaken by Jean's death, both men decided to consult a famous blood specialist, Dr. Isidore Snapper, in Amsterdam. Dr. Snapper happened to be vacationing in Norway, but Mayer, who had been unable to get Jean to a hospital in time, pulled strings and brought him back to his office. Dr. Snapper told both men they needed more relaxation. On the same trip Mayer "discovered" Greer Garson in England.

Two years after Jean's death, Longie Zwillman married for the first time. His bride was a widow and former socialite, Mary de Groot Mendels Steinbach, of Asbury Park and Allenhurst, New Jersey. She had a son by her first marriage, and, in time, gave Longie a daughter. She also gave him respectability, a sense of roots, which at age thirty-five he had begun to want. But revenge remained inevitable as the wheels set in motion kept turning. There was the matter of the personal check Schenck had given Bioff.

Investigation revealed that Wee Willie wanted to buy a ranch. All his movie friends had ranches. He owed it to his union members not to be placed in an inferior social position. But all he had was cash — cash he couldn't justify having. Sure, Willie knew that in secret deals cash was best, but he wanted to buy and own the ranch in his own name. Otherwise, why bother? So there had to be a gimmick. And, of course, good old Joe Schenck had been eager to please. According to the official explanation, Willie gave Joe a hundred grand in cash, and Joe promptly gave it back to him via that famous personal check. Willie planned to call it a loan if asked, but Montgomery assumed it was a payoff and precipitated the probe. The gimmick, if that's what it was, killed the payoff theory, but by then the IRS had plenty of evidence. Eventually, the great Joe Schenck was indicated on income-tax charges.

As far as Schenck was concerned, the code of the underworld was something you heard about in gangster movies. Cagney or Raft could die (in the movies) without squealing on their fellow rats, but Schenck had no intention of giving up the gay life of Agua Caliente, Santa Anita, and the boulevards of Paris if he could help it. And he could. All he had to do was talk. And he did.

As a result, Bioff and Browne were indicted on extortion charges and sent to prison. To reward Schenck for talking, a deal was made. The tax charges were dropped, and he was permitted to plead guilty to one count of perjury. He was also forced to pay a lot of back taxes, but it was the year in prison that really bothered him. Joe Schenck had become a felon. His parole after serving only four months did not change that terrible fact.

The chain reaction continued. Bioff and Browne sat in prison awhile before also deciding to talk. (Life in Hollywood had corrupted their hoodlum principles.) As a result, the top leaders of the Chicago syndicate — Bioff's evidence didn't extend beyond — were indicted along with Johnny Roselli. Frank "the Enforcer" Nitti, who had already served one term in prison for tax evasion, killed himself rather than serve another. The others were convicted and sentenced to ten years in prison.

Unlike Schenck, Bioff, and Browne, who talked, Roselli and the Chicago hoods did not squeal. And the syndicate rewarded them. Strings were pulled, and after only three years — the absolute minimum — all were paroled and sent home to resume their careers. At the same time Joe Schenck received a full pardon, which restored his civil rights. Nevertheless, he had been publicly humiliated, and he never recovered from his days in jail.

As far as Longie Zwillman was concerned, he had gained his revenge. To paraphrase Samuel Goldwyn, he had passed a lot of water since that day in Philadelphia when he first touched Jean Harlow's hair. He would remember her as men always remember their first love, but the pain was gone.

There is irony in the fact, however, that many years later when, due to pressure from IRS and other factors, Zwillman became a liability, his murder was officially declared a suicide. Someone high in syndicate circles obviously arranged things so police could declare that Longie hanged himself in the basement of his New Jersey mansion. There is also irony in the fact that in 1952, a year after Louis B. Mayer resigned from MGM, the American Academy of Motion Picture Arts and Sciences presented Joe Schenck with a special award. The accompanying citation praised his "long and distinguished service" to the industry.

In the land of make-believe, the pot was calling the kettle white.

Only the naive identify social status with probity.
—LEO ROSTEN

5

Why Bugsy Blew His Cool

In his non-violent conquest of Hollywood, Benjamin "Bugsy" Siegel owed much to such people as Jean Harlow, George Raft, Mark Hellinger, Wendy Barrie, and Johnny Roselli, but his greatest debt was to the dark-haired daughter of a Watertown, N.Y., leather-goods manufacturer.

Dorothy Taylor, blue-eyed and buxom, was suddenly much in demand when her father died and left millions to be divided between her and her brother, a member of the Board of Governors of the New York Stock Exchange. Her first marriage was to a British pilot who apparently didn't want his wings clipped. Finding Dorothy a bit possessive, he made a secret landing in the bedroom of her best friend. The friend, who understood the situation, had the bedroom ceiling repainted to resemble a blue sky out of which a plane swooped toward the bed. When Dorothy heard about it she got a divorce and married a penniless Roman with a title. As the Countess DiFrasso, she went to Rome and bought her husband a suitable palace. Leaving him there to bask in the ancient grandeur of his station, she moved to Hollywood in search of true love. One day while sitting in a box at the Santa Anita race track — the creation of Producer Hal Roach — with a cousin of Anthony Eden, she was introduced to Bugsy Siegel.

Immediately bells clanged, sirens sounded, whistles blew, and sparks flew. Or at least Dorothy was convinced these traditional symptoms were activated. Mr. Benjamin Siegel was handsome, romantic, and seemingly entranced. That somewhere in the background he had a wife made no difference. Back in Italy Dorothy had her count, and she liked his title. This was Hollywood, where people were sophisticated, where Marion Davies' birthday parties for William Randolph Hearst were the social event of the season. Perhaps movie stars had to maintain a facade of respectability, but wealth and good old Carlo's title were enough for her and Benny. Within a week, Siegel was standing beside her in a receiving line at a formal affair in the Mary Pickford—Douglas Fairbanks home, which Dorothy had leased until she could buy a suitable mansion of her own. The junior partner of the Bugs and Meyer Mob looked distinguished in evening clothes.

Siegel decided he needed a suitable house as well. Upon arriving in Hollywood he rented the home of opera star Lawrence Tibbett. Plush enough by everyday standards, it was not sufficient for the companion of Countess DiFrasso. But there was a vacant lot on Delfern Avenue in Holmby Hills that had possibilities. In the neighborhood were such residents as Bing Crosby, Sonja Henie, Humphrey Bogart, Anita Louise, Judy Garland, Vincent Price, and Alan Ladd. The house Siegel built cost $150,000 and included everything from an Olympic-sized swimming pool to a row of slot machines, from six "vanity rooms" for women guests to sliding panels and secret trap doors, from a well-stocked wine cellar to a hidden arsenal. For a man who had never worked at a legitimate job in his life, Siegel was throwing it around for the world to see.

The world wasn't watching. The national crime syndicate was expanding all over the country, but attention, such as it was, centered on New York, where "the fighting D.A.," Thomas E. Dewey, was building himself a political platform. But there was no national organization to keep tabs on the syndicate, to put together the scattered pieces of the jigsaw puzzle and inform local police and local newspapers that syndicate gangsters were in town. Bugsy Siegel might be recognized as the partner of Meyer Lansky in New York, where Police Commissioner Valentine might describe Lansky as "the brightest boy" in crime, but in Los Angeles Siegel was a "wealthy sportsman" and Lansky was unknown. Tony Cornero might operate a fleet of gambling ships three miles off the California coast, but no one knew that Siegel was an investor personally as well as 'on behalf of the syndicate he represented. For that matter, no one would have cared.

It was a ship of sorts, the schooner *Metha Nelson*, that led to newspaper publicity in Los Angeles for Siegel. Exactly how the Countess DiFrasso obtained the crude map is not clear, but the inclusion of Marino Bello, ex-stepfather of the late Jean Harlow, in the expedition is presumably the answer. Marino had been attempting to interest the wealthy in treasure maps for years, and he got his chance through the good offices of his delightful friend, Bugsy. As might be expected, the treasure at the end of the rainbow was large enough to stir the imagination — ninety million smackers. It was supposed to be hidden on remote Cocos Island, a dot of land three hundred miles off the Pacific shores of Costa Rica.

The treasure, if a blend of history and legend is believed, was actually hidden on the island in three installments over a period of one hundred and fifty years. Pirate Captain Edward Davis allegedly looted the city of Guayaquil in Ecuador in or around 1685 and stashed his rather bulky spoils – thousands of pounds of bar silver and gold plus seven casks of gold coins – on Cocos, which was a favorite watering place of pirates. Thereupon he sailed out of history, the victim of a sudden squall or mutiny or disease. The next chapter opened in 1818 when a Captain Grahame of H.M.S. *Devonshire* turned pirate and amassed a great fortune by raiding the western coasts of Central America. He also captured Eliza, a good-looking lady of Spanish descent. Eventually the turncoat captain ran into a fleet sent out by the Admiralty to punish rebellion and was captured and hanged. Eliza and the crew were "transported" to Tasmania. After twenty years she escaped, got somehow to the United States and told a tale that interested a lot of people. It seems, she said, that Captain Grahame stored his loot – estimated by Eliza at sixty million dollars – on Cocos Island. Eliza actually led an expedition to the island and found the hidden cave she had described, but it was empty.

Three years after Captain Grahame met disaster, the greatest treasure of them all was hidden on Cocos. Rebels inspired by Simon Bolivar threatened Lima, the capital of Peru. Some residents fled, but church officials and their supporters who believed their wealth was given by God waited too long. When at last they recognized the revolution was for real, only one ship, the *Mary Deare*, remained in the harbor, and its captain, Richard Thompson, was little better than a pirate. But there was no choice. All the wealth remaining in the city was piled aboard the ship – gold, silver, and jewels in casks and caskets. Seven high churchmen also boarded to keep an eye on it. Once at sea, Captain Thompson tossed the churchmen overboard and sailed to Cocos Island, where eleven trips by the ship's boat was needed to get the booty ashore. It was stored in a cave, a cave that had to be enlarged to hold the treasure. Once filled, the cave was sealed with a door that opens only if a secret pivot stone is pushed. Thompson sailed away and soon came to a pirate's end. One man survived, however, and went to Nova Scotia. Keating was his name, and it was he who drew the map which purported to show where the treasure was buried. It was passed on from hand to hand over the years until, in 1938, an alleged copy of it, drawn on a table-cloth, came into the possession of the Countess DiFrasso.

The countess was determined to take an active part in the treasure hunt even if the shortage of space reduced her personal attendants to one maid. No sacrifice was too great if it made Benny happy. Siegel brought along his personal physician, Dr. Benjamin Blank, who had treated Longie Zwillman after Jean Harlow's funeral. Dr. Blank also happened to be the official physician for the Los Angeles County Jail. Marino Bello, who claimed a bad heart, brought along a personal nurse, but after four days at sea he persuaded Captain Bob Hoffman to marry them. Others in the party included Richard Gully, the cousin of Anthony Eden and social secretary to producer Jack Warner.

Landfall was made, and for ten days the gangsters dug and blasted the uninhabited island without finding a peso, a shilling, or a brass ring. A typhoon was approaching, the rains fell, heat and the insects took their toll. Finally, Bugsy gave up and ordered the captain to sail for Panama, where he, ungallantly, abandoned the ship and his lady for urgent business in Los Angeles. He flew home while the *Metha Nelson* battled a storm until she was helpless. An SOS brought aid, and the schooner was towed into Acapulco, where Dorothy followed the example of Siegel and flew home. When the vessel finally got back a month later, the crew of gangsters had threatened to mutiny. Charges and countercharges gave reporters a field day. It was some time before Siegel's role in the affair became known – his wisdom in quitting the ship at Panama paid off – but the affair ultimately brought him publicity. And when that happened, someone – perhaps a disgruntled member of the treasure hunt – tipped off Jim Richardson, city editor of the Los Angeles *Examiner,* and his newspaper proceeded to shock Hollywood by disclosing that Bugsy was a gangster.

Richardson, like other allegedly hard-boiled editors of his day, has been romanticized as a crusading fighter for truth and justice, but the *Examiner* was a Hearst paper, and William Randolph Hearst had a vested interest in motion pictures and California politics. He might ruffle the waters now and then but always on a limited basis. Perhaps Siegel, with his capacity for making friends of the famous, irked Richardson personally, but his main task was to promote Los Angeles and Hollywood, not clean it up. In fact to suggest it was even slightly soiled was to risk dismissal.

Nevertheless, the newspaper exposé, such as it was, shook up Siegel to the point where he sent his old friend, Mark Hellinger, in to have a one-newspaperman-to-another chat with Richardson. A former New York gossip columnist of the Runyon — Winchell school of journalese, Hellinger had just come out to Hollywood "to write and produce crime pictures" for Warner Brothers. Richardson, who apparently suffered the usual illusions common to newspapermen outside "Big Town," was allegedly shocked when Hellinger asked him to "lay off" Bugsy. Perhaps the experience so disenchanted him that later he tried to make a pal, and informer, out of a certain Mickey Cohen. Billy Graham later made the same mistake.

It is hard to believe that the Hellinger — Siegel friendship shocked Richardson very much. Certainly there was no secret about it in New York. Jim Bishop, the biographer of Hellinger, surely wasn't shocked when he wrote that Hellinger "cultivated the gangsters, racketeers and hoods of his time. He liked them. And they liked him." In fact, if Bishop is right, the gangsters "agreed to stop killing each other and named Mark Hellinger as personal arbiter of the underworld." Jack Warner, the most colorful of the three Warner Brothers, has acknowledged that Hellinger "knew all the Eastern racketeers." Crime pictures became the staple product of Warner Brothers in the 1930s following the success of *Public Enemy* starring Cagney and Harlow. Even after the public recovered sufficient faith in its economic future to turn to other subjects, a special unit headed by Bryan Foy kept turning out "B" pictures to be used as the second half of double features. It was to this unit that Hellinger was assigned. When Johnny Roselli was paroled, he too became a producer under Foy. The public wanted realism, didn't it? According to Jim Bishop, Hellinger believed that "practically all bad men were really good men who were forced by circumstances to work outside the law." That would explain Roselli, George Raft, and Bugsy Siegel as well.

Warner, who came from Youngstown, Ohio, a steel city which had its share of gangsters and gang wars over the years until the Cleveland syndicate put the Mafia families there on short rations, loved to gamble and took every opportunity to do so. Once he mentioned to Hellinger that he planned to visit Hot Springs, Arkansas, for a turn at the baths on one side of Central Avenue and the tables on the other.

"Better not," said Hellinger, assuming the air of a well-read thug. "You might get in the way of a bullet."

Warner, always ready to believe anything about gangsters, asked for details. Hellinger obliged. Hot Springs, he pointed out, was run by Owney "the Killer" Madden, the former New York gang boss who had retired to Arkansas to escape a contract on his life. It had been six years, but sooner or later the syndicate would go after Owney and there would be a battle royal. Madden wasn't the type to be taken easily.

"I didn't want to be around there even with wide-open gambling as a special attraction," Warner said later.

For the record, it should be noted that Madden lived on undisturbed for another quarter century and died peacefully of old age.

Thanks to Countess DiFrasso, Siegel — a member of the

syndicate that allegedly was threatening Madden — was a frequent visitor at the Warner home. And, thanks in part to Bugsy, Warner didn't have to go to Hot Springs to gamble; he could visit one of several gambling ships the syndicate was operating off the coast of California. As usual, there was insulation. Most people assumed that the ships were the private property of Tony Cornero, the former "King of California Bootleggers." When on occasion Siegel went out to the *Rex*, the flagship of the gambling fleet, on business, he used a private boat. When, however, he accompanied the countess and her guests on a social expedition, he used the water taxis provided by Cornero for the suckers.

The taxi was an old launch which had been jazzed up with a glass roof covering three-fourths of the boat. Although there were only two couples in the party, the big boatman shoved off immediately. Dorothy snuggled up to Siegel, assuming this was standard VIP treatment for her man. But Bugsy had a frown on his handsome face as he stared at the boatman's back.

On the other side of the breakwater there was enough swell to bounce the boat about. Three miles, more or less, out to sea were the neon lights of the *Rex*. A searchlight mounted on the ship served both as an advertisement and a security measure as it sent its beam revolving slowly over the black water. Cornero felt he was outside the jurisdiction of Los Angeles and California, but he knew renegade hijackers observed no limitations of law or custom. The casino's bank, plus the jewels, furs, and pocket money of the guests, was a tempting target. Thinking about it, Siegel felt a pang of regret for the pre-syndicate days when the Bugs and Meyer Mob operated as it pleased. As his mind roamed backward, his eyes centered again on the big boatman who was attending strictly to business. And suddenly he recognized him — Big Greenie.

Harry "Big Greenie" Greenberg had been a member of the Bugs and Meyer Mob but had been attached much of the time to Lepke and his garment-industry rackets. As a strong-arm goon, Big Greenie knew a mistake could cause him to be deported. A refugee from Poland, he had jumped ship to enter the United States.

Ironically, it was a police roust that caused Greenberg's downfall. Siegel had called Lepke and Joseph "Doc" Stacher into conference, and each had come with his contingent of bodyguards and gunman. The meeting was at the Hotel Franconia, and for some reason the cops raided the joint. All nine present were hauled off to headquarters, where their picture was taken. Greenberg was standing to the left of Lepke in the photo. Nothing came of the affair as far as Siegel was concerned, but someone checked up and found that Big Greenie was in the country illegally. After some delay he was put on a freighter under guard for return to his native Poland. But Big Greenie was no dope, as Lepke had discovered, and he somehow managed to jump ship in Germany. Eventually, he got back to Montreal, working as a seaman.

What happened next? Bugsy flipped the file cards of his mind. Oh yes, the letter. Big Greenie's return to the American continent coincided with the "Big Heat" resulting from the search for Lepke. It had begun in 1937 and was still continuing in 1939. From his hiding place Lepke had ordered all potential witnesses killed, and the troops of Murder, Inc., the enforcement arm of the syndicate, had obeyed. The hunt for Lepke waxed hotter as the FBI put its prestige on the line in a race with state authorities. And in this moment of tension came a semi-illiterate letter from Big Greenie in Canada. Exactly what he was trying to say no one could comprehend — there is nothing to indicate they tried very hard — but it was clear Greenberg was all steamed up about something and wanted money badly. It was easy to assume the guy was threatening to talk if he didn't get the dough, but, in any case, he knew too much and was obviously unreliable. Another contract was let.

Allie Tannenbaum got the assignment, but by the time he

reached Montreal, Greenberg had disappeared. There were plenty of mobsters in New York who disapproved of Lepke's war of extermination, and their counsels would soon be heeded. Meanwhile, one of them apparently told Big Greenie to get lost. Greenberg surfaced in Detroit but vanished again before Tannenbaum could get there. And this time he stayed lost. Months passed and no trace of the fugitive was found. Siegel, who had only secondhand knowledge of the affair, had been told to put out an alarm for Greenberg on the West Coast but had neglected to do so. Privy to Lansky's plans, Siegel was ready to write off Lepke as an effective force in the syndicate. Thanks to the publicity he had received, "Lep" had become a liability, and it was to eliminate liabilities, not protect them, that Murder, Inc., had been formed.

To decline to look for Big Greenie was one thing; to ignore him in the flesh was something else. Personally capturing, or executing, someone the syndicate had been seeking for months would be a feather in his cap, and Bugsy liked feathers in his fedora. But the matter had to be handled carefully. A scandal on the *Rex* wouldn't be appreciated by either Cornero, Zwillman, or Lansky.

Siegel decided to wait. While taking a few precautions to keep Big Greenie available, he would give the impression he hadn't recognized his old companion. Turning to Dorothy, who was beginning to sulk, he began talking loudly about the time Mark Hellinger intervened with "Legs" Diamond to save Al Jolson from a beating. Newly married Jolson was so grateful that he invited Hellinger to go to Europe with him on his honeymoon. Hellinger, never one to pass up a freebee, accepted — and felt hurt when Jolson neglected him for his bride.

"The bum actually complained he was bored," said Siegel.

The landing stage of the *Rex* was lit up like a theater marquee, and Big Greenie displayed the skill of a practiced seaman in bringing the water taxi up against the hemp fenders.

Music floated down from the deck, and a searchlight cut the water fifty yards out. A hard-eyed gunman in evening clothes helped the countess and her guests mount the stage. As Siegel stopped to tip the boatman, Big Greenie whispered, "I gotta talk to you, Ben."

Siegel realized there was no way of delaying a decision. Well, so be it. Tony would have plenty of muscle on board and a spare anchor or two to weigh down the body.

"C'mon up," said Siegel and stepped onto the *Rex*.

Greenberg threw a line to a sailor and clambered aboard. Telling Dorothy he would join her shortly in the casino, Siegel led the way up some slippery steps to the boat deck. The only light there was reflected from the water. It made Big Greenie's face look like newly butchered beef.

"Long time no see," said Greenberg, holding out a hamlike hand. Siegel ignored it.

"You're hot, Greenie, and you know it. If you've got anything to say, let's hear it."

The big man chuckled deep down in his chest. "Still the big shot, huh, Benny?" he said. "Well, I guessed right. Figured you'd come along sooner or later."

Siegel looked at Greenberg for a second, took his hand off the belly gun he carried, and put the action section of his brain into neutral.

"Talk," he said.

Big Greenie wasn't the most articulate hood in the world, but he could talk better than he could write. As he explained it, a threat to Lepke was the last thing he was thinking about when he wrote from Montreal for money. Hell, he was trying to do Lep and the boys a favor. On his travels he had lucked into something big, and, naturally, he had looked to New York for the dough to develop it.

It all happened on that slow boat to Europe the feds put him on. There was another passenger, a lousy little Kraut. They got to talking as men do, and the Kraut turned out to be a spy for Krupp, the big German arms manufacturing family. Seems he had scored big and was just busting to brag about it. From an eccentric old scientist up in New Haven he had stolen a formula that would revolutionize warfare. Had to kill the old man to keep it exclusive, of course, but since nobody knew what the guy had been working on there wasn't any problem. The Kraut was sure that Krupp would make him rich once he tested the formula, and Hitler would give him the Iron Cross with diamonds.

Well, naturally, Big Greenie took all this with several grains of salt, but it was the only game in town, so to speak, and he played along. The Kraut knew that his fellow passenger wasn't exactly returning to Poland for pleasure, and he just took it for granted that Greenberg had no loyalty to anyone. Greenie encouraged him, told him a lot of stories about Prohibition and won his confidence. Turned out that the Kraut wasn't as sure of being rewarded as he pretended. He figured Krupp might just take the formula and cash in on it as his divine right. In other words, the thief wanted to do a little bargaining and he wasn't sure he knew how to do it. He needed a little help from a man versed in free-enterprise procedures, and the only such man available was Big Greenie. With that kind of edge, it didn't take Greenberg long to get a look at the mysterious formula the Kraut carried in a watertight money belt around his waist. The symbols on the paper meant nothing to him, but the Kraut in an awed whisper told him they added up to nothing less than the atomic bomb.

Siegel, who had been listening with growing interest, broke into laughter at this point. He had read enough Sunday supplements to know the A-bomb was something people had been dreaming about for years. As far as he was concerned, it belonged in the same category as rocket ships to the moon and heart transplants. Urgently Big Greenie kept talking.

On the night before the ship made port, he managed to

knock the Kraut in the head and roll him overboard — after removing his money belt, of course. He wasn't missed until next day, and by then there wasn't much anyone could do about it. The excitement, however, gave Greenberg a chance to jump ship, and he took it.

Over the next few years Greenie bummed about as best he could, always holding onto the stolen formula but not really worrying much about it. Not until he got back to Canada did he think seriously of it and only then because he ran into an old friend from New York who had specialized in making bombs for the late Dutch Schultz. In the course of professional chitchat Big Greenie mentioned the formula for the atomic bomb he had been carrying around so long. Stinky Pete — so called because he smelled of cordite in the old days — was interested but skeptical. Through his contacts he was able to get the required ingredients, and in a deserted farm house far from town he mixed up a small batch. From behind a stone fence some one hundred yards away, he detonated the explosive. Big Greenie, who didn't trust things he didn't comprehend, watched from his car a half mile away. The blast shook the car, blew down the stone fence and Stinky Pete and obliterated the farm house.

"It scared the bejesus out of me," said Big Greenie. "There wasn't enough left of Pete to bury."

No longer doubting he had the secret of the atomic bomb, Big Greenie sensed that the potential was too great for one man. This was a job for the Outfit with its money and connections. But he remembered the Kraut and his fears. The problem was to make connections with somebody who would listen and deal fairly. He wrote to New York, but the difficulty of expressing himself on paper while remaining deliberately obscure had been too much for him. The boys, concerned with fears of their own, had misunderstood, and Big Greenie had been on the lam ever since.

"When I got to L.A.," he said, "I heard you were running things out here, and I figured you would listen to me if I could get to you without being gunned down first. Some guy told me you had a piece of the *Rex*, so I took this job on the chance you'd show up some night and, by God, it worked out the way I hoped."

The story was fantastic, but that was the best evidence of its veracity. Big Greenie could never have dreamed up such a tale, and, what's more, why should he bother? Quickly making up his mind, Siegel pulled out his roll and peeled off ten C-notes — a thousand dollars. He gave the money to a grinning Greenberg and told him the address of a "safe" house. He was to check in there at once and wait. Siegel would see him later.

Countess DiFrasso was plainly peeved when Siegel joined her in the casino. It was early, and there weren't enough people present for Dorothy's neglected state to go unnoticed. To cheer her up, Bugsy told her he was working on a big deal — the atomic bomb. No fool in money matters, the countess instantly understood the commercial possibilities.

With an elbow on the glass bar and a foot cocked on the brass rail, she puffed a Turkish cigarette and suggested, "If it really works we'll let my husband sell it to Mussolini. It'll make him a big shot in Italy."

Dorothy knew someone who knew a professor at Cal Tech who could recommend a couple of experts to test the magic formula. No mention of the atomic bomb was made — why start rumors? It was all kept low-key and unofficial. The experts whipped up about five pounds of the stuff and detonated half of it out in the desert. It blew the hair off jack-rabbits a mile away and persuaded Siegel he had stumbled into something valuable.

Count DiFrasso talked Mussolini into advancing $40,000 American dollars, and the countess, Siegel, and, of course, that distinguished son of Sicily, Marino Bello, sailed for Italy.

They took along their hired experts, but Siegel soon became convinced they were Russian agents out to steal the prize for Stalin. Somewhat nervous at being involved in international intrigue, Bugsy became heavy-handed and succeeded only in getting the experts angry. By the time the party reached Rome they were ready to go home. Siegel had no intention of letting them out of his sight until a deal had been worked out with Mussolini.

Countess DiFrasso was also a little nervous at the prospect of meeting Italian society in the company of an untitled gangster. Carlo, being a man of the world, couldn't object to her having a lover, but he had every right to demand she show good taste in her selection. Fortunately, a solution worthy of Hollywood suggested itself. She proceeded to introduce her dear friend as Bart Siegel. If everyone assumed that Bart was an abbreviation for baronet and that Siegel was a titled Englishman, well so much the better. Elsa Maxwell has since insisted that one of those so assuming was King Umberto.

The day of the big test, the convincer, came. The top commanders of the New Roman Legion gathered, eager to see the weapon that might restore a lost empire. Siegel and Bello were just as anxious, but their concern was whether to demand a flat sum or accept a royalty arrangement. The Count and Countess DiFrasso were arguing about a new villa; the old one, obviously, would not befit their new dignity.

The experts pressed the button. Nothing happened. Siegel pressed the button. There was a thin trickle of smoke. Bello pressed the button. The smoke stopped. Sabotage, said Siegel. Those Red agents had double-crossed him. He would kill them all. Not so, said the Italians. Investigate first, kill later. Someone has fooled someone, but who? Italian experts took over. Several days later they reported that "Atomite," as Siegel had named the plasticlike substance, did not contain enough power to stun a gnat. It was a hoax. Then what had blown up back in the Imperial Valley of California? What had blasted Stinky Pete into nothingness? The Italians shrugged. Whatever happened there, this stuff didn't cause it. This was worthless, they told the furious Siegel.

Bugsy was still raging when Count DiFrasso got bad news. To punish him for attempting to defaud the state, Villa Madama, the huge palace Dorothy had purchased for her husband, was confiscated. The count and his guests could, if they desired, move out to the stables. The villa was needed immediately to house Field Marshal Hermann Goering and German Propaganda Minister Paul Goebbels, who were in Italy to accept an award for a German film which had won first place in the Venice Film Festival.

The stables were quite comfortable, but Siegel was crazy with rage at the insult. He called Lansky by transatlantic telephone to ask for the names of local Mafia leaders he could contact to arrange the assassination of Mussolini. Lansky warned him that the Mafia in Italy had quit fighting Il Duce in 1927 and wasn't about to try again. If Mussolini was to be bumped off, Bugsy would have to do it himself. He was mad enough to try. And when he saw Goering and Goebbels drive up to the main house in the glory of medals, glittering uniforms, and Nazi salutes, he added those two characters to his death list.

Jack Warner, who had come to Italy to enter his film *The Life of Emile Zola* in the festival, takes credit for persuading Bugsy to change his mind. "I talked him out of it," said Warner, "on the grounds we couldn't fix the local harness bulls if we got caught."

And so the maker of gangster movies restrained Bugsy Siegel — killer, English lord, and lover of a countess — from bumping off leaders of two nations and perhaps, incidentally, breaking up the Rome–Berlin axis. Having done so, Jack Warner went back to Hollywood to continue his standing feud with his writers at Columbia, whom he accused of lacking originality in plot development. Siegel and Dorothy headed north to the French Riviera, where George Raft was consoling Norma Shearer, the widow of the late lamented genius, Irving Thalberg. Raft took time out to tell Bugsy about the Battle of Long Beach.

Somehow or other a do-gooder, Earl Warren, had been elected Attorney General of California, and in July he declared war on Tony Cornero's gambling fleet. Tony ignored him, because the best attorneys available had assured him the ships were outside the jurisdiction of the states. But legal niceties did not stop Warren, who, obviously, had ambitions to be Governor and maybe President. What's more, he was pretty smart about it. Without any warning or explanation he rounded up a small army of deputies and locked them up so no word could get out. When time came for the raid, he put the deputies into sealed buses and took them to the attack boats he had assembled. The deputies had absolutely no chance to tip off anybody.

The surprise was complete at three of the gambling ships, and no resistance was encountered. But Tony was aboard the *Rex*, and he wasn't the kind of guy who got surprised. Heavy steel doors prevented the deputies from getting inside, and water hoses drove them back to their own craft. Warren ordered a blockade. If he couldn't get on board he wouldn't let anyone get off. He figured there was plenty of guests on board who needed to get home before their wives, or their employers, discovered they'd been out gambling. Sure enough, pressure from the angry suckers soon forced Tony to compromise. If Warren would let the customers go home, he would permit an armed guard over his anchor – thus making sure he wouldn't sail away. Warren agreed, and the stalemate continued for ten days while the lawyers fought it out on shore. It turned out Warren's legal gimmick was the fact that Tony had been operating those water taxis without getting a license for them as a public conveyance. With his clout with local officials he just hadn't thought it necessary, never dreaming the state would stoop to such technicalities. A deal was worked out. Tony agreed to pay fines, taxes, and expenses totaling $13,200 and to the destruction of all gambling equipment on the *Rex*. A raiding party busted up twenty crap tables, twenty roulette wheels, one hundred and twenty slot machines, and a lot of other stuff. Tony proceeded to forget his troubles in a high-stake crap game and lost the ship itself on a throw of the dice.

This sad tale helped Siegel put his own troubles into perspective. He had lost nothing in Italy except face, whereas he had money invested in the *Rex*. Accordingly, his anger settled on that unlucky slob, Big Greenie. It was irrational, but Siegel had to have a scapegoat, and Greenberg had been directly connected with the *Rex* and with the mysterious, non-explosive "Atomite." Upon reaching Los Angeles, Siegel checked with Mickey Cohen, a young lieutenant sent out from Cleveland and the personal protégé of Moe Dalitz's partner, "Uncle Lou" Rothkopf. Mickey had been ordered to keep an eye on Greenberg, and the precaution had been well taken. Big Greenie had slipped away one night from the "safe" house where Bugsy had left him and was hiding out in a roominghouse on Vista Del Mar. Fine! Bugsy scratched himself in pleasure. It was an unconscious gesture, one the countess deplored. Largely at her urgings, he trained himself to conceal his hand in his pocket before reaching for his scrotum.

But there was one hitch. On August 14 Lepke had surrendered to Walter Winchell and John Edgar Hoover. Lansky had arranged it and tricked Lepke into thinking that he was bypassing Dewey and would escape with a rap on the knuckles. Unknown to Lepke, the Federal Narcotics Bureau had built a solid case against him, and over in Brooklyn an assistant district attorney was on the verge of blowing the veil off Murder, Inc. Under the circumstances there seemed little point in executing the contract against Big Greenie. Siegel flew to New York to argue that the hit should still be made. Greenberg, he said, was a danger to Lansky as well as Lepke, and if he ever decided to talk he could put others in the soup. Why take a chance?

No one bought the argument. Lansky was in Cuba, amusing himself until the Big Heat ended by laying the foundation of a gambling empire in Havana. Siegel was told that Greenberg was no longer a danger to the syndicate. If, for his own reasons, he wanted to knock the guy off, the boys would cooperate, but the hit would be Siegel's responsibility. Only Lansky offered cautious encouragement, and it never occurred to Siegel that his old partner might be setting him up the way he so smoothly had Lepke.

More determined than ever, Siegel went ahead. He had been pushed around too much. His pride demanded that he kill someone, and Big Greenie was handy. Writers who have since wondered in print why a high-ranking official of the syndicate would turn back the clock and kill as he had while still a punk do not understand how Siegel reacted to frustration.

Tannenbaum, the original hit man assigned the contract, didn't want anyone to boast about succeeding where he had failed, so he volunteered to help finish the job. Longie Zwillman, who owed Siegel a favor, arranged to have a couple of "clean" guns stolen off the New York docks. Frankie Carbo, a fight promoter for the syndicate, happened to be in town, so Siegel recruited him too. Siegel had discovered that Big Greenie left his hideout every night to drive to a drugstore to get the next morning's newspaper. It was a perfect setup, and on the night of November 11, 1939, Greenberg was blasted by two guns as he sat at the wheel of his ancient Ford. According to Tannenbaum, the guns were fired by Siegel and Carbo, while he, Tannenbaum, waited nearby in the "crash" car — the vehicle assigned to block possible pursuers. Others have whispered that Allie's testimony was self-serving — that it was he, the assigned killer, and Siegel who shot Big Greenie while Carbo waited in the other car. In any case, Bugsy called Lansky in Havana and told him to start celebrating Thanksgiving Day.

But Big Greenie was not so easily forgotten. Over in Kings County (Brooklyn) New York, William O'Dwyer was district attorney and no real problem except he was too busy being a good-time politician to keep an eye on his assistants. One of those assistants was Burton B. Turkus, who had the quaint notion that he was supposed to make good cases against killers and send them to the electric chair, regardless of whom they might know. It is rare indeed when chance gives such a man the power and also the opportunity to use it, but such was Turkus' good fortune. More good luck came when Abe (Kid Twist) Reles, an active member of the enforcement arm of the syndicate, decided, for reasons Turkus never did understand, to "sing." Reles had taken part in a dozen contract murders and knew intimate details of hundreds of others. Moreover, he was gifted with the faculty of total recall, and his tales of violence wore out a team of stenographers and filled twenty-five notebooks with shorthand code. And one of many Reles fingered was Allie Tannenbaum.

Picked up on a murder charge and held without bail, Allie brooded awhile and then decided to "cut myself a piece of cake." He talked. Since New York and California law required the testimony of an accomplice to a crime be corroborated by other witnesses or evidence, Tannenbaum's cooperation magnified many times the value of Reles' confessions. And, as it turned out, vice versa. Reles could corroborate some murders in which Tannenbaum was the accomplice.

Such as Big Greenie, for instance.

On August 16, 1940, Siegel was indicted for murder and an arrest warrant issued. He was found hiding in the attic of his mansion, having reached that secluded spot through a trap door in the closet of his bedroom. No bail was set. Countess DiFrasso had hysterics when she saw the headlines. Calming down, she tried to think. Who was the most powerful, most influential person she knew? William Randolph Hearst, of course. If anyone could spring Ben, clear him of this outrageous charge, WR was the one. Stopping only to collect her $50,000 diamond and ruby necklace, she chartered a private plane and flew to San Simeon. But neither her tears nor her necklace moved the old man to intervene. There was nothing he could do, he said.

If Dorothy could not get Siegel out of jail, Dr. Benjamin Blank, a jail physician, could at least make him comfortable. Bugsy's former shipmate on the voyage to Cocos Island arranged special food, drink, and visitors hours. One of the visitors brought in by George Raft was cute young British starlet Wendy Barrie. Apparently she and Bugsy made a date. Dr. Blank not only gave permission for Bugsy to have dental work done — a continuous process requiring a visit every day or two — but he supplied the civilian clothes Siegel wore while out on the town. Someone tipped Jim Richardson at the *Examiner*, and reporter Howard Hertel was assigned to get the story. He succeeded and followed Siegel to a tryst with Wendy. The picture made as Siegel emerged caused a sensation when published, and an official probe not only documented Dr. Blank's favors but disclosed a box of canceled checks signed by Siegel and cashed by Blank. The doctor explained that the $32,000 represented the repayment of a loan he had made to the gangster. But, under newspaper pressure, Dr. Blank was fired. The public was assured that Siegel henceforth would be treated like any other prisoner.

That being the situation, it was perhaps lucky for Bugsy that a new district attorney took office and promptly secured the dismissal of the murder charge on grounds of insufficient evidence. The fact that Siegel had contributed thirty grand to his election campaign had nothing to do with his decision. Or so he said.

John Dockweiler defeated incumbent Buron Fitts — the man who had "investigated" the Paul Berns mystery — despite the fact that the movie industry supported Fitts financially and otherwise. Heavy contributors to his campaigns included Jack Warner and Louis B. Mayer. In a front-page editorial following Dockweiler's victory, the *Hollywood Reporter* noted that "many here in the studios are a bit nervous because ALL the financial support handed out by the industry for the campaign went to Fitts and nothing to Dockweiler."

Under such circumstances the $30,000 of syndicate money Siegel gave to Dockweiler speaks for itself and eloquently demonstrates Bugsy's political acumen that was soon to be exercised again and again in Nevada. Of course, in giving the money Siegel didn't expect to need a personal favor so soon, but the value of having friends in high places to protect you against the unexpected was never better illustrated.

True, the publicity about the Siegel gift forced Dockweiler to announce he was returning the money — it had helped him get elected, of course — and some ten months later he bowed to continuing pressure and secured a new indictment against Siegel and Carbo for Big Greenie's murder. Within a few days, however, Reles won lasting fame in New York as "the canary who could sing but couldn't fly." He was tossed to his death from the heavily guarded hotel where he had been kept under the tightest security Turkus could devise. The murder remains an unofficial mystery today, but there's no mystery about its consequence. Reles represented the necessary corroboration of Tannenbaum testimony, and the case against Siegel went out the window with Reles. Once again Dockweiler secured the dismissal of the charges, and Bugsy was more of a celebrity than ever.

Countess DiFrasso was prey to mixed emotions. She was

glad Ben was free, but her joy was tempered by the knowledge that he could now see Wendy Barrie, or Marie "the body" MacDonald, or Virginia Hill, or any number of nubile young starlets any time he desired. She sensed that, despite her best efforts, she had failed Siegel. She had tried to work behind the scenes, use influence that Ben really didn't want or need. It was Wendy Barrie who gave him what he wanted, going boldly to the jail to see him in spite of public opinion and meeting him openly outside the jail.

Ben was established now. And confident. Soon he would dream dreams that would influence show business for decades to come.

The Strip outside Las Vegas!

And he would pay the price.

PART II

Syndicate City

It was legitimate business. Like the Andrews Sisters, Durante, Cugat, or Henry King. I felt there was no valid reason to turn it down.

—HANK GREENSPUN

Senator Tobey: *Before you got into bed with crooks, to finish this proposition, didn't you look into these birds at all?*
Wilbur Clark: *Not too much; no sir.*

Kefauver Committee,
November 15, 1950

Frank Sinatra, I consider him a good friend.

—MICKEY COHEN

6

The Flamingo

It was 1947.

Jean Harlow had been dead for ten years. The Second World War had been fought and won. A year had elapsed since Winston Churchill proclaimed that an "Iron Curtain" had fallen across Eastern Europe. Joe McCarthy had taken his seat in the United States Senate.

For show business a new era was beginning. Television was officially born, and in Las Vegas a report was prepared by IRS Special Agent Howard J. Werner. Dated February 27, the report was filed "for the purpose of placing on record the names of some of the individuals involved in the gambling industry in Las Vegas." Excerpts follow:

> Perhaps the investigation which will prove most interesting, and profitable, concerns the latest addition to amusement centers of Las Vegas which opened on De-

135

cember 26, 1946, under the name of "The Flamingo." This monstrous establishment covers acres of ground and consists of a hotel, restaurant, cocktail lounge, gambling casino, shopping center, swimming pool, outdoor cafe, and a nightclub and dining room that seats in excess of 700 persons.

The Flamingo is owned and operated by a syndicate using the name "Nevada Projects Corporation" and is incorporated in the State of Nevada. The central figure behind the corporation is the notorious Benjamin "Bugsy," or "Benny," Siegel who is having a private penthouse erected on top of the hotel building. The Flamingo . . . is advertised and broadcast as having cost $5,000,000. Actually, information was received from one of the contractors that the cost was in excess of $6,000,000, most of which was derived from black market operations during the war.

The theory that the funds originated in the black market is fostered by the fact that the backers wanted the structure erected in the desert in approximately eight months, despite the scarcity of various materials, fixtures and labor. To achieve this, plasterers and electricians were paid $40.00 per day; common laborers often received in excess of $100.00 per week; fabulous prices were paid in the Los Angeles market for commodities that could not be purchased elsewhere because of the national shortage of certain building materials; and no expense was spared to provide the finest quality obtainable in every phase of construction.

Opening night at The Flamingo, which cost $15.00 per person admission, including dinner, featured Xavier Cugat and his orchestra and Jimmy Durante. George Jessel was master of ceremonies. The show is reputed to have cost $35,000.00 per week, and a reliable informant told me that Benny Siegel paid Cugat an additional $4,000.00 per week "under the table," which money was taken "off the top" of the winnings in the gambling casino. Cugat's engagement lasted approximately five weeks.

In September, 1946, Siegel made a trip to New York to obtain additional funds for the construction of the resort. . . . When Siegel returned he is said to have carried $1,100,000.00 with him to Las Vegas. He has a safe built into the floor of his inner office at the Flamingo.

Benny Siegel's partners in New York are said to be: Frank Costello, leader of the Union Sicilio (spelling uncertain) and notorious gangster of the east coast; Joseph A. Doto, Alias Joe Adonis, who is rumored never to have reported more than $16,000.00 gross receipts for taxation in any year although that amount is only a small fraction of his total annual income; and Meyer Lansky, well-known gambler in New York, Florida and Chicago.

Siegel, Costello, Adonis and Lansky are said to own the Colonial Inn and the Greenacres in Hollywood, Broward County, Florida, and control all gambling activities in most of the State of Florida. The foursome allegedly had an income in excess of $10,000,000.00 in Broward County during 1946.

Siegel's wife's name was Esther, but she obtained a divorce from him in Reno, Nevada, in July 1946, and obtained custody of two minor daughters. A property settlement was drawn up in June, 1946, voluntarily by Siegel, under which he is to pay to her $32,000.00 per year.

Pending completion of the hotel section of the Flamingo, which is advertised as ready for occupancy March 1, 1947, Siegel is registered in room 412 of the Last Frontier Hotel, Las Vegas. His reputed mistress is one Virginia Hill, who also lives in room 412 at the same hotel. . . .

One of the most active characters in the gambling business in Las Vegas is Morris Sidwirtz, alias Moe Sedway. He and one Gus Greenbaum purchased the El Cortez Hotel from Mr. Marion Hicks and a Mr. Grayson early in 1945. Sedway was formerly a part owner of the Copacabana nitery in New York and is contemplating opening a replica locally. He is financially interested with Benny Siegel in The Flamingo, and is affiliated in one way or another with several gambling ventures in town. In 1942, he reported a net income of $3,272.76. No other returns are available at this time.

Mr. Marion Hicks, mentioned hereinabove, from whom Moe Sedway and Gus Greenbaum purchased the El Cortez Hotel, Las Vegas, also owns the El Cortez Hotel in Reno, Nevada, as well as several gambling ventures in that city. He also owns the Savoy cocktail lounge and casino in Las Vegas, which place operates one of Siegel's race books. Plans now are being negotiated by Hicks and Clifford Jones, the latter of whom is a local attorney, for the construction of a hotel in Las Vegas to be known as the Nevada Ambassador. . . . Other partners associated with Sedway and Siegel include David Berman, who came here from Minneapolis after a vice cleanup in that city where his brother, Charles "Chickie" Morton Berman, was convicted and sentenced to five years for being involved in negotiating the ransom in what was known as the Bremer kidnapping case; Israel Alderman, alias "Izzy" Alderman, also a refugee from the reform movement in Minneapolis; and August Bertrand Greenbaum.

In the midst of all this scheming and tax evasion are the local city and county commissioners who hold the authority as to whom shall be issued liquor, cafe and gambling licenses, as well as issuing permits for construction and remodeling. Graft and bribery are rampant in Las Vegas. . . .

Special Agent Werner's report is a remarkable document for its day, outlining as it does both the nature of the syndicate investment in Las Vegas and the techniques it would employ. The expressions "under the table" and "off the top" became part of the language of show business as non-taxed salaries were paid to "name" entertainment from non-taxed gambling profits. While such financial techniques were not new, they had never before been used on such a lavish scale. Together with the mushrooming media of television, this so-called "black money" revolutionized the entertainment industry. As in the 1920s when only those with access to ample boot-leg booze could successfully operate nightclubs, so it was that the stars of mid-century America were dependent upon gambling — legal or illegal. Las Vegas was but one of several gambling centers developed in various sections of the country: Saratoga, New York; Revere, Massachusetts; Miami Beach and Broward County, Florida; Gretna, Louisiana; Hot Springs, Arkansas; Galveston, Texas; Cicero, Illinois; and, of course, Newport, Kentucky.

While there were some exceptions, the entertainment industry as a whole prostituted itself to serve as shills for a gambling racket controlled by gangsters and kept in business by continuing public corruption on every level of government.

Some entertainment figures such as Sinatra went into business openly with mobsters, accepting them as partners in the operation of club-casinos. Others attempted to compromise, and one such was the durable Jimmy Durante.

Back in the 1920s Jimmy was performing at the Dover Club, one of several joints owned by Waxey Gordon. On one occasion the spotlight was on Jimmy's nose when a battle royal developed between the occupants of two tables. Champagne bottles flew through the air, and four innocent by-standers were knocked cold. Unmoved by the violence, Durante finished his routine. Greatly impressed by Jimmy's performance, Waxey — a former professional pickpocket — opened a new club and called it the Club Durant.

More than thirty years later Durante was starring at the plush Beverly Hills Club outside Newport. The plush Beverly called itself "The Show Place of the Nation," and it had the right. The food and liquor were the very best, and it was reasonable. The Beverly featured the biggest stars of Hollywood, and it offered "honest" if illegal casino gambling. For decades the club served as a lightning rod. In the area around Newport—Covington—Cincinnati there were literally scores of dishonest casinos, handbooks, brothels and bust-out-joints. Yet whenever demands arose that anti-vice laws be enforced, corrupt officials could point to the Beverly Hills and wax pious: Simple justice demanded that if one dump was closed, all places violating the law should close; if the Beverly was allowed to operate, then so could the meanest bust-out joint. So long as the joint paid off, of course. The argument worked for years until, in 1961, local citizens rejected it and began pressing for a complete cleanup. Word reached the *Courier-Journal* in Louisville that the Beverly had closed voluntarily, apparently in the hope of blunting the reform drive by disappointing all the good citizens who had planned to take their wives or girlfriends out for dinner and a look at the Durante show. No one would comment for publication, but the author got through to Durante at his Cincinnati hotel. He confirmed the story. The entertainer talked willingly enough of his canceled show, of the good food and fine people who ran the club, but as far as the casino was concerned — the illegal heart of the entire operation — Durante said he was not involved. "I don't go near the tables," he said, ignoring the fact that his high fee for appearing was paid solely to draw others to those same tables. Like other big "names" who appeared over the years at the Beverly and helped charm local citizenry into tolerating hoodlum government and open vice, Durante was nothing but a shill.

Unlike the other regional gambling centers, Las Vegas had the advantage of legality. Originally Siegel saw "the Strip" as drawing most of its suckers from the Los Angeles area in the tradition of Agua Caliente in Mexico. For once, however, the reality outstripped the vision. Thanks to its legality and the jet plane, the town became a national center and caused Siegel's partner, Meyer Lansky, to seek its eastern counterpart in Havana and, later, in the Bahamas. Over the decades, to an entertainer an engagement at one of the glittering hotel-casinos on the sands of Nevada became the symbol of success — because everyone knew the "under the table" payoff, drawn as it was from the "off the top" skim, was almost limitless. Besides, since the payoff did not have to be reported for taxes, it meant more money in hand for the high-bracket stars. No longer was the big money in Hollywood, and, inevitably, the old star system began dying. New names flashed across home television screens like meteors, and the reward for a successful show was a contract at the Sands or the Stardust. Only the new market for old movies kept the reputations of many veteran stars alive.

In 1947, however, all this was little more than a dream in the minds of a few gangsters. And Bugsy Siegel, who had risked the most to make the dream a reality, would pay the price often paid by pioneers and trail blazers. He had become too independent to suit his colleagues in the national crime syndicate. The personality traits he had displayed in the murder of Big Greenie — a murder that had caused far more trouble than it was worth — were threatening to dominate the handsome gangster. Time and again he ignored the advice of his old friend Lansky and pushed ahead as he pleased. Rumors that he was stealing syndicate funds instead of just wasting them began circulating. Ironically, a quarter century later the discovery of a locked safe in the floor of the Flamingo created great excitement — excitement based on the theory that the safe might contain millions squirreled away by Bugsy. It proved to be empty, of course. But Lansky and his trusted associates were less concerned about rumors of theft than with reports that Siegel had lost his head over a woman and was ready to quit the rackets. He was reaching the dangerous age. His love affairs, especially the latest one with the mysterious Virginia Hill, brough him notoriety instead of respectability. There was good information that Siegel intended to break with the syndicate and take off with its liquid assets just as soon as the Flamingo produced enough of them.

Lansky restrained the others until the Flamingo was finished and in the black. He knew very well that his old partner would do a better job than anyone else in making the dream a reality. But Bugsy's usefulness ended with his success. Moreover, a Los Angeles city councilman had charged that local Communists were in league with "an eastern gambling syndicate," and Lansky — a man who believed in the freest enterprise possible — was alarmed. Much of the syndicate's power depended upon its alliance with right-wing elements in the United States, elements that wanted the status quo maintained above all else. If this working relationship was put into jeopardy by extremists, great damage could be done. In Los Angeles, Bugsy Siegel symbolized the "syndicate"; eliminate him and maybe the Redhunters would look elsewhere for victims. Hollywood offered plenty of targets.

On June 20, 1947, Siegel flew to Los Angeles. He conferred with his lieutenant, Mickey Cohen, talked to his attorney and visited George Raft's home in Coldwater Canyon. Raft disclosed that he was trying to start a motion-picture production company of his own. That night Siegel went to Virginia Hill's home on North Linden Drive. Virginia was in Europe — and some people believed she was waiting for Bugsy to join her with the Flamingo's bankroll. Allen Smiley, a veteran of the old Bugs and Meyer Mob, dropped in for a chat. Smiley was alone with Siegel when the shots came through the window and knocked out one of Siegel's "baby blue eyes."

Bugsy died instantly.

Six months later to the day, Smiley dropped in on Siegel's old friend, the ex-columnist turned movie producer Mark Hellinger. The visit came on the heels of an announcement that Hellinger would soon set up his own motion-picture production company. Apparently, in the interval since Bugsy's execution, Raft's plans to do the same thing had come to naught. Smiley was closeted with Hellinger for an hour, and, as with Siegel, he was the last visitor Hellinger ever received. Two hours after Smiley completed his mysterious business and departed, Hellinger suffered a heart attack.

He died.

A coincidence perhaps. Who knows? More secrets remain with the syndicate than ever get exposed in books. One thing is sure, however. The national crime syndicate was alive and well, and not even Senator Joseph McCarthy linked it with communism again.

And on "the Strip" outside Las Vegas, new hotel-casinos sprouted like the flowering cactus.

I didn't inherit any money.
— MOE DALITZ

7

The Desert Inn

Moe Dalitz, ex-bootlegger and co-founder of the far-flung Cleveland syndicate, approached the dangerous age cautiously. He had been married for many years, but there had been little time for home life. Unlike some of his colleagues, he had never learned to play.

World War II provided him with the excuse and the opportunity. Upon being commissioned a lieutenant, Dalitz had been assigned to operate a laundry on Governors Island, New York — an assignment that was logical enough in that Dalitz had owned a few laundries along with nightclubs, gambling joints, steel companies, and assorted other business ventures.

Not a man to complain, Dalitz settled down to his billet in the swank Savoy-Plaza and did his part to keep the army's linen clean. The job left him a lot of free time, however, and permitted him to sample the pleasures of New York nightlife. Even with a war on, a man with Dalitz's wealth and connections could find just about anything he desired.

As the war neared its end, Dalitz found himself restless. He took leave, went back to Cleveland, and ran into an old friend on the street. Their conversation ended a few hours later with the Cleveland syndicate owning a big hunk of Detroit Steel stock. But the deal, while quick, painless, and profitable, didn't satisfy Dalitz as it might have in the old days. His feeling grew that something was missing – or someone – or something *and* someone. Then Sam Stein, an old friend and something of a loser – he was just out of federal prison after serving a stretch for gold smuggling – came to town to celebrate his new marriage. Moe met the bride and liked her. But he liked her friend, a cute little model named Toni, even more.

The inevitable happened. Toni read her man well and acted on the reading. She was tired of the bright lights, she said, tired of moving about from place to place. More than anything, she wanted to settle down in a nice ivy-covered townhouse on some quiet but fashionable street in some small – well, Cleveland would do – town, with some solid, mature, and wealthy husband. They would put down roots, raise a family, and grow old together, secure in the love of their grandchildren and the respect of the community. Dalitz was approaching his forty-sixth birthday, and the picture Toni painted was, he suddenly realized, exactly what he had been craving. Something and someone suddenly added up, so Dalitz got a divorce from his wife and married Toni. They moved not to Cleveland – his reputation had gone to pot there – but to Detroit, where folks had forgotten, if they ever knew, that he had begun as a member of the Purple Gang.

After some discussion the happy couple decided it was more sensible to adopt a child than start from scratch. This they did. Moe also bought a boat and named it *Toni Kid,* but he didn't use it much. It was too difficult to cruise Lake Erie or the Detroit River without recalling the days when the Cleveland syndicate operated a rumrunning fleet that brought millions of gallons over from Canada.

To take one's mind off the past, a man needs a new project for the future, and, as usual, Dalitz's old friend and partner, Meyer Lansky, was ready with one: Consolidated Television, Inc. The venture was the syndicate's bid to get control of the new industry, which they saw as a logical outgrowth of movie-making. For once, the syndicate's business executives vastly underestimated the potential.

"I think we went in at the wrong end of it," Lansky explained a few years later to the Kefauver Committee. "We thought that the commercial end was the best part. We should have gone into the home-set end, and maybe I would have been a very rich man today."

In other words, the syndicate shared the view of Hollywood executives who felt about the home screen as they had about the "talkies." One movie-maker, to show his contempt, had furrier Al Teitelbaum — long accustomed to providing mink-covered toilet seats — drape a TV set in skunk. (Later, when the movie mogul sold a few old movies for the late, late shows, he changed the fur to mink.)

Lansky and Joe Adonis and Frank Costello and Joe "Bananas" Bonanno and Longie Zwillman and Moe Dalitz, and a lot of others, decided that people would never stay at home to watch pictures. They thought the men, at least, would go to the neighborhood bar and look at the screen while getting loaded. The future of television was, therefore, in supplying bars, taverns, and casino lounge areas with king-sized television sets and perhaps making some "soundies" — short subjects featuring French dancers — for presentation on those sets.

In addition to relying on the judgment of the movie-makers, the syndicate boys were reasoning on the basis of their experience with jukeboxes. Lansky had been a major distributor of Wurlitzer, and syndicate figures all around the country controlled most of the competition. Routes were set up much like the beer routes of Prohibition days, and woe betide the tavern owner who tried to operate with a non-syndicate machine. Moreover, control over the boxes gave the syndicate a measure of authority over the records offered the customers, and that, in turn, had much to do with deciding which tunes made the "Hit Parade" each week. Just as Willie Bioff could make Hollywood tremble by threatening a strike at local theaters, so Lansky could determine which singing stars would shine by controlling jukeboxes. More than one personality had to sell, literally, much of himself before he was able to cash in on his natural talent. It was natural, then, for the syndicate to assume that the new gadget, television, would work the same way.

Moe Dalitz, who had a piece of Consolidated Television, was especially anxious to get a corner on the production of special "soundies." Luckily, his tour of duty at the Savoy-Plaza had given him a wealth of contacts. One of the men he met there was Robert Goldstein, a navy man during the war but in peaceful times a big shot at Universal International pictures. To discuss the production of the "soundies," Dalitz sent Sam Stein to Goldstein.

It was, in retrospect, Toni's fault. Once they were happily settled in Detroit, she had begun worrying about her girl-friend who had married Sam. The girl deserved a break, and Sam, who had been in and out of jail since serving a rap for grand larceny in 1920, was hardly the man to give her the life she deserved. Couldn't Moe with all his friends and con-nections do something for Stein? After all, Sam *was* his friend.

If Dalitz had not been so much in love he would have explained that where business was concerned friendship was unimportant. Sometimes one became friends with a business associate who had proved himself, but seldom if ever did a friend become a business associate. The explanation was simple. Suppose in the course of business it became necessary to knock off or frame an associate? If he happened to be a friend as well, it could be a little awkward. Lansky certainly had not enjoyed having Bugsy Siegel hit.

But Toni was insistent, so on a visit to Cleveland Dalitz met at the Theatrical Grill, that delightful joint on short Vincent Street behind old Hollenden Hotel, with a Consolidated Television executive and recommended Sam Stein for a job. No one knew the bars and taverns of the Midwest better than Sammy, said Dalitz, and he would be the perfect contact man to place those commercial TV sets.

Stein went to work for Consolidated TV, and Dalitz went back to Detroit and the respectable life of a laundry owner. And what happened? The next thing he knew Sammy dropped out of Consolidated, along with the executive Dalitz had met, and the two had formed a new corporation. Masthead Export Corporation was the name of Sam's new outfit, and Dalitz was not surprised to find that Stein was listed as a vice-president. Goldstein was president, and that wasn't unexpected either. The real shocker, or so Dalitz always maintained, was to discover that he, Dalitz, was a vice-president too, and in a deal to sell planes to Egypt.

Well, a deal was a deal, and upon careful study it did look as though there was money to be made in selling surplus planes. So Dalitz invested a little cash, and the project went ahead. At the last minute the planes were seized, and then, sure enough, Dalitz, Stein, and the rest all found themselves under indictment on conspiracy charges. It was all very embarrassing, the more so since in the interim Dalitz had become associated with the Desert Inn in Las Vegas and the Desert Inn had a publicity chief, Hank Greenspun, who had been indicted for shipping arms to Israel to use against Egypt.

Dalitz managed to keep the publicity at a pretty low-key, and eventually the indictment against him was dismissed.

Somehow the experience soured him on being a family man and helping out his wife's friends. He put the *Toni Kid* into dry dock and gave his attention to the big project in Vegas. The concept of legal gambling on a big scale had a strange fascination for him, and Toni, who was beginning to enjoy being a society matron, didn't mind too much when her husband flew to Las Vegas for a week at a time. She could assume if she wanted to that Moe's talk of a new plant which would take people to the cleaners was some sort of mechanized laundry.

Wilbur Ivern Clark was the front man at the Desert Inn, the name in lights. The Cleveland syndicate shared Meyer Lansky's distaste for publicity and was happy enough to push Clark forward. Wilbur was made into a miracle man, a promoter par excellence, by publicity director Hank Greenspun, who had worked earlier for Bugsy Siegel at the Flamingo. In reality, Clark was just another professional gambler. He had worked as a crap dealer in Reno in the early 1930s, moved up to the gambling ship *Monte Carlo* off Long Beach, and had a tour of the syndicate casinos at Newport, Kentucky, and Saratoga, New York. In 1947, impressed with Siegel's achievement in the desert outside Las Vegas, Clark bought the Players, a small bar and casino on the road to Los Angeles, and formed Desert Inn, Inc. Dalitz and his associates took over there, pouring in the money to build a huge resort similar in scope to the Flamingo. Wilbur was happy enough to take the credit and let Dalitz and his friends have the cash. Unfortunately, one man with great expectations was not so pleased.

Allen Smiley, the man who sat beside Bugsy Siegel when a rifle spoke through the window, had been waiting since 1947 for a reward. He had been told that he could not be given a "piece" of the Flamingo for obvious reasons but to hold on until the Desert Inn was ready. Three years had passed, and as the opening date of April 24 approached he was becoming uneasy. To get the "skinny," he called Jack Dragna from New Orleans, where he was working for "Dandy Phil" Kastel at the Beverly Club. Dragna, head of the Mafia in California, was playing second fiddle to Mickey Cohen, Siegel's successor. Fortunately, Los Angeles police had thoroughly bugged Dragna's apartment, so Jack's side of the conversation with Smiley was recorded for posterity.

When Smiley apparently mentioned rumors that the Cleveland boys were not going to cut him in on the new resort, Dragna replied: "I don't know what in hell they've got to do with it. After all, you got in here. . . ."

"It's for you to say and them to. . ."

"All you've got to say is that whatever you've got there is no special name and that is enough. . . ."

"Them dirty bastards. . . ."

"There is plenty that goes out with the dish water in there. . ."

"No, I was told they were supposed to give you five and now they're going to give you money instead. . ."

"That's what I was told. . ."

"He didn't specify what he was going to give you. . . I mean Lou himself. . ."

The "Lou" referred to was Louis Rothkopf, a charter member of the Cleveland syndicate but because of his unique criminal record not officially an owner of the Desert Inn. At one time a boxing promoter, Rothkopf had managed Mickey Cohen during the latter's efforts to earn a living with his fists. In fact, it was Rothkopf who sent Cohen to California and persuaded Bugsy Siegel to use him. But whatever Rothkopf had promised Dragna on behalf of Siegel, he lacked either the desire or the power to deliver. In a subsequent recorded conversation, Dragna could only sputter to Al, "I'd show them people whether you could face it or if I could face it. We're as clean as them anytime."

The Desert Inn opened on schedule. Politicians, movie

stars, and gangsters rubbed elbows at the dice tables and drank champagne in this most lavish of all "rug joints." Among the stars on hand were Van Heflin, Gail Storm, Bud Abbott and Lou Costello. There were rumors that another star, one of the most beautiful in Hollywood, was present but found the entertainment in the penthouse more interesting than the floor show or the casino. When she decided to jump out the window and fly around the building, a visiting physician gave her a hypodermic. She was allowed to sleep it off in privacy.

Also a guest was Chet Lauck, the "Lum" of the long-running radio program "Lum and Abner." But Chet hardly counted as a visitor since he owned a huge ranch near Las Vegas. Eventually he would sell the ranch to Vera Krupp, divorced wife of the German munitions-maker. Vera got her start in Hollywood, so it was only natural (when her marriage failed) that she could seek solace in the new capital of the entertainment industry. After buying the ranch, she got a license to operate a casino in downtown Las Vegas but neglected to get an "okay" from the real boss, Meyer Lansky. Eventually she sold both the casino and the ranch to Howard Hughes. When Howard set up his headquarters in the penthouse of the Desert Inn, he installed his wife, actress Jean Peters, on the ranch. The marriage ended in divorce shortly thereafter.

But we are anticipating. Shortly after the Desert Inn opened on April 24, 1950, Moe Dalitz divorced Toni and moved permanently to Las Vegas. Two years later, having learned how easy it is to shed wives, Dalitz married a still younger model who just happened to be employed at the Desert Inn. Easy come, easy go, and still plenty of time to create an empire and be remembered as a pioneer.

8

The Strip

With the Flamingo and the Desert Inn showing the way, everyone wanted to get into the act and own a "piece of the action" in Las Vegas. The combination of legal gambling, high-class male and female prostitutes, and show-business celebrities was enough to make any staid businessman drool. Syndicate executives, too. Usually, however, they sought participation in an "approved" project. No one tried to build a hotel-casino all for himself.

Benny Cohen, the friendly little political boss of Miami Beach, was an exception. In excuse of his folly it can be said he assumed he was part of the "in" group and didn't need an "okay" from anyone. He had longed for a return to big-time gambling since the Kefauver "heat" closed illegal casinos along the Florida Gold Coast and broke up the S & G Syndicate. The S & G — for Stop and Go — had operated large handbooks in the beach hotels. Ben had been counsel to the

S & G and had also received a third of his brother Sam's share as full-time partner.

Despite doleful predictions that the tourist industry would die without gambling, Miami Beach had enjoyed a tremendous boom as many veterans, remembering the warm sands and blue skies from service days, brought their young families back on vacation. This fact of life blunted the drive for legalized gambling and caused Benny to look enviously at Nevada, where the economy was, in fact, largely based on the sucker trade.

Meyer Lansky's approval could have been obtained, but Cohen remembered the free-and-easy days of the S & G — before the Chicago syndicate muscled in — and saw no need to pay tribute to the Chairman of the Board if he could avoid it. Convincing his brother and assorted friends such as Morry Mason was not difficult, since in his own circles Benny was considered a genius. Mason controlled the Taylor Construction Company, which had just built the pride of Miami Beach, the Fontainebleau Hotel, so it was logical to assume he could construct a hotel-casino on the Strip outside Las Vegas.

The financial wheeling and dealing was complicated enough to confuse the Internal Revenue Service, and the presence around the new hotel — named the Riviera after the famous casino in New Jersey — of Charles "the Blade" Tourine apparently caused Nevada officials to assume the project had syndicate approval. Exactly what Tourine, an illiterate Mafia figure of some reputation, was doing at the Riviera was never officially established, but he soon moved to Havana, where Lansky was building "the Las Vegas of the East." Busy as he was, however, Lansky still had time to teach his good friend Benny a lesson when the Las Vegas Riviera opened in March 1955 with the usual gaggle of Hollywood free-loaders. Business, to put it politely, was lousy. Despite the odds that always favor the house, the casino lost money fast, lots and lots of it. It turned out that Benny Cohen was no idealist, determined to hang on to realize a dream. Perhaps he remembered the fate of Bugsy Siegel. So, after a decent interval and the loss of more than $1,500,000, he was ready to quit. Lansky, as always, was generous. He allowed Cohen and his associates to keep the building and the land it sat on. It was the heart of the operation, the casino, that interested him, and it was the casino he got. Drafted somewhat reluctantly to operate it was good old Gus Greenbaum.

Moe Sedway and Gus were the ones who marched into the Flamingo some twenty minutes after Siegel died in Beverly Hills and took command for the syndicate. Greenbaum was a tough old bird and a good businessman. He had put the Flamingo into the black very quickly and kept it there. But the strain had taken its toll. After seven years he retired to Phoenix, Arizona, where he had lived off and on since 1928. Among his many friends there was a former Phoenix city councilman turned United States Senator, Barry Goldwater. Barry was a frequent visitor to Las Vegas, flying there in his private plane. Perhaps as an excuse for his trips he opened a branch of his clothing-store business there. Goldwater's of Las Vegas was located at the Desert Inn. Later, after Barry achieved national prominence, the name was changed to "D.I. Distinctive Apparel," and Moe Dalitz was proud to claim it as a tenant.

Perhaps Greenbaum wasn't anxious to go back to Las Vegas, but all the troubles that had beset the Riviera vanished upon his arrival. Soon it was paying off officially as well as under the table and off the top. Still Gus was getting old, or careless. That became obvious when he appointed as his Director of Talent a figure out of the past. On paper, perhaps, Willie Bioff seemed a logical candidate, for Willie had been a boss of the IATSE, the union that controlled the motion-picture industry. Yet Gus had to know that it was Bioff who had violated the gangland code and "squealed," sending several top Chicago hoods to prison briefly and causing Frank "the Enforcer" Nitti to kill himself. Bioff served time too and, upon release, settled in Arizona under the name of William Nelson. It was by that name that Goldwater knew him — he said. Anyway, they became friends, and Bioff — protected by a Lansky lieutenant on the one hand and a United States Senator on the other — felt safe enough to show himself in the neon jungle of Las Vegas. Occasionally he would even fly up and back with Senator Goldwater.

Lansky has owed his successful survival — survival when most of the gang leaders who began with him have been killed or imprisoned — to his reputation for honesty and fairness. His handshake has sealed many multimillion-dollar deals, and he has never let friendship interfere with what some might call justice but what he would be content to call the best interests of the syndicate. Certainly, under any standards, Willie Bioff deserved anything he received, and the fact he had developed important friends meant nothing. As far as Lansky was concerned, if the Chicago gang or anyone else wanted to make an example of Willie, it was okay. As a matter of fact it didn't look good for such a man to be connected with the Riviera; someone might recognize him from the past and give the joint, and Vegas, bad publicity.

So on November 4, 1955, Willie turned on the ignition of his pick-up truck back in Phoenix and was blown to bits when a bomb went off. Back in Hollywood a lot of people felt confirmed in their fears. They had *known* all along that Chicago gangsters played rough, and this proved it. So who in his right mind could blame good old Joe Schenck for playing ball and maybe saving himself and others from getting blown up like Bioff? By God, Joe really deserved that special Academy Award they gave him five years earlier. Greenbaum and Goldwater bore up bravely under their loss.

Arizona has been a syndicate target since 1936 when Moe

Dalitz developed sinus trouble in Cleveland and went to the Tucson area for his health. He liked what he saw, and he passed the word to the boys back east to come out and take a look. Frank Costello couldn't come, but he sent his personal aide, Joe Zucker, who called himself Joe Baker. Trigger Mike Coppola, needing a vacation, also came from New York, and "Big Al" Polizzi, — who had been promised some big-game hunting, — came down from Cleveland. The boys bought a lot of land in the area, which they did not develop until the population contained more people and fewer lizards. That happened right after the war. Peter Licavoli, who began his career as a hired gun for the Purple Gang, bought the Grace Ranch near Tucson and developed it into a desert showplace and hangout for mobsters everywhere. While Licavoli made a fortune in land deals, other syndicate figures such as Sam "Gameboy" Miller and Edwin "Butts" Lowe — the only gangster with a ring in his nose — set up gambling operations. An "underground pipeline" for smuggling in narcotics and illegal aliens was also perfected. It stretched across the Mexican border to Vera Cruz, where Frank Milano, an original leader of the old Mayfield Road Mob in Cleveland, owned a huge ranch and coffee plantation. As tourism developed in the postwar period, Tucson and Phoenix boomed, and fueling much of that boom was syndicate cash. The state was classed with Florida and California as not only a good place to visit but a fine place to live and invest.

How cozy things became was illustrated in 1963 when Alvin Malnik of Miami Beach sent a telegram to Sam Ford Fishbein in Los Angeles. Malnik was a young attorney involved in multimillion-dollar syndicate deals that ranged from Paris to Honolulu. In 1962 Malnik made a number of calls to Fishbein in Phoenix, and his telegram contained an obscure reference to that town:

The Fish was to duke me with a fin,
Came through the back door with only a min,

Am sending you an ink pen so you won't be so lax,
For this quill will only let you write a max.
There's a big difference between a max and a min,
So in the future don't treat them as next of kin.
I take leave now and say goodby until,
Our next song fest at the *house on the hill.*

Investigators noted in their reports that Senator Goldwater's home near Phoenix has an Indian name which, when
translated, means "house on the hill."

Gus Greenbaum wasn't around to attend a song fest. The
syndicate retired him permanently in 1958 when Moe Dalitz
and his friends at the Desert Inn decided to add another
casino to their string in Las Vegas after pulling out of the
Nacional in Havana.

Reading the political signs better than some United States
diplomats, the Cleveland syndicate decided Fidel Castro was
about to take over Cuba. How, then, to dump the Nacional
on someone and get out? The Nevada Tax Commission came
to the rescue by "discovering" that the joint ownership of
casinos in Las Vegas and Havana could have "serious reper-
cussions." It suggested a choice between the two locations be
made. The official action was the perfect cover for the Desert
Inn crowd, and they sold the Nacional to Mike McLaney. The
deal was completed on September 30, 1958, three months
before Castro became dictator of Cuba and put McLaney in
prison.

So there was capital available for a new investment, and
where better to put it than the Riviera, which Greenbaum
had turned into a gold mine? But Gus had developed illusions
of grandeur and of independence. Some writers insist he had
become a heroin addict. In any case, he was having such a
good time chasing broads and shooting dice that he didn't
want to step down. Gus just didn't want to go home.

But he went to Phoenix for Thanksgiving, and there on

December 3, 1958, he was found dead in bed. It wasn't exactly a natural death. Someone had cut his throat so completely that his head was almost severed from his body. They had been neat about it. Pillows had been placed on each side of Gus's neck to soak up the blood.

Down the hall in another bedroom was Mrs. Greenbaum. Her throat had been cut as well, but apparently only after she had been knocked unconscious with a heavy bottle. Newspapers and towels had been used to soak up the blood and keep it from staining the carpet. As some syndicate wives have learned, blood is almost impossible to get out of rugs, coverlets, and the like. The Greenbaum killer had been most considerate.

The murder remains a mystery, in the same class with the shooting of Bugsy Siegel. But the sequel is not. The Cleveland syndicate took over the Riviera and operated it pending official approval by Nevada officials. Eventually, when arrangements had been made with certain nominees, the Cleveland boys officially withdrew and their application was formally denied. But their aim had been achieved.

The Riviera was not the only new jewel in the Cleveland syndicate's crown. Moe Dalitz, comforted by a new and younger wife, was wheeling and dealing all over the place while his co-equals — Sam Tucker, Morris Kleinman, and Lou Rothkopf — settled in Cleveland and Miami Beach. And Moe couldn't help but be interested when that old rumrunner and gambling-ship operator, Tony Cornero, began building the huge Stardust just across the street.

The new hotel-casino was only 70 percent complete, at a cost of some six million, when Tony fell dead while shooting craps at the — where else? — Desert Inn. It was all a little mysterious. No autopsy, and the body was shipped to a mortuary in Beverly Hills for burial. They gave Tony a good funeral, and someone sang his favorite song, "The Wabash Cannon Ball," presumably on the theory that Tony could hear it. And only then was it disclosed that Cornero had agreed to lease the Stardust to Dalitz, since he couldn't get a license for himself. The terms Tony wanted were pretty steep, however, a cool half million a month. John Factor, better known as "Jake the Barber," took over and finished the hotel. He couldn't get a license either, much to the disgust of the Chicago branch of the syndicate. He twisted and turned to no avail, but finally bowed to reality and announced he would lease to the Desert Inn group.

That was fine, although there were still a few details to work out. Dalitz didn't intend to pay out six million a year in rent — not when he held all the trump cards, thanks to his "in" with Nevada authorities and his old partnership with Lansky. It took a western Apalachin to solve the matter. Meeting in Beverly Hills were Lansky, Zwillman, and "Doc" Stacher, representing the syndicate; Dalitz and his partner, Morris Kleinman, representing the boys from the Desert Inn; and, representing Chicago and Jake the Barber, Marshall Caifano and John "Bats" Battaglia. It was decided that the lease would cost only $100,000 a month, a rather low figure when it is remembered that the Stardust quickly became the second largest money-maker in Las Vegas. With everything settled, the group boarded a Western Airlines plane and flew to Las Vegas to implement the decision. Had that plane crashed, organized crime would have suffered a blow far more serious than anything achieved by federal and local lawmen in fifty years of accumulated effort.

John Drew, a tough little character who convinced the press he was an Irishman from Chicago, was given 5 percent of the new casino and put in charge. Actually Drew had once been Jacob Stein, a partner of Dalitz and Lansky in the liquor business at the end of Prohibition. He legally changed his name and, for good measure, secured on July 30, 1952, a birth certificate showing he was born John F. Drew on November 21, 1901, in the village of LaFarge, Wisconsin. The certificate was based on what is called a "Declaration of Self" — in other words, on Drew's word. The gimmick worked, however, and a lot of writers have insisted Drew was given his job at the Stardust to represent the hidden interests of the Chicago syndicate — still the bogeymen of crime. When the author asked Drew about it, the foul-mouthed gambler tossed off several anti-Semitic statements and then insisted, "My life is an open book." But he refused to discuss its specific contents.

Over at the Tropicana Club, Philip "Dandy Phil" Kastel had no such identification problem. He had been a bucket-shop operator for Arnold "the Brain" Rothstein back in the innocent days when bankers were heroes and Lillian Gish was starring in *A Romance of Happy Valley,* and Dandy Phil was proud of it. When Rothstein pioneered in rumrunning, Kastel had become acquainted with Frank Costello and then Meyer Lansky, and his subsequent career as their representative was something to boast about in Las Vegas circles.

The crime syndicate, in one of its first acts after its formation, sent Kastel to New Orleans to develop that territory. After the murder of political boss Huey Long, Kastel experienced some rough times before things stabilized. At one point he was reduced to operating a strip joint in the French Quarter at a salary of $100 a week. Eventually, however, Lansky opened the Beverly Club and put Kastel in charge. Second in splendor only to the Beverly Hills Club in Kentucky, the Beverly soon became nationally known, a fixture in the nightclub circuit for top show-business personalities. Like its counterpart at Newport, it became the excuse to allow the meanest bust-out joints to operate as once again law-enforcement officials proved how difficult it is to be half corrupt. But then in 1951 the Kefauver Committee came to town, and the Beverly was forced to close. The bust-out joints moved off Jefferson Highway to Gretna, across the Mississippi River, and that little town became as vice-ridden and as corrupt as Newport or Cicero. For the masses there was still plenty of action, but the more respectable middle class deplored the loss of the Beverly and its big-name shills.

Kastel, with time on his hands, wandered down Bourbon Street, where an old friend, Blanche Monte, introduced him to a charming brunette named Margaret. She had class, Dandy Phil decided. Not only did she want marriage, but she wanted dignity and respect. Of course, that meant solvency. Soon Kastel found himself trying to impress her with tales of his important friends who might, if he asked, assign him to run one of those wonderfully legal hotel-casinos they were building all over the place out in Nevada. Soon they were planning a dream castle of their own, and Margaret promised to marry Phil on the day he got the go-ahead to build it. She even supplied the name — the Tropicana. Las Vegas wasn't the tropics exactly, but it was hot — Death Valley being near — and there were some imported palm trees.

Inspired by his late-blooming love, Kastel bestirred himself, found financing and got an okay from his old friend Lansky. By the time he was ready to build, Morry Mason had just completed the Riviera and had the men and equipment available for a new job. With a boom on in syndicate construction, Mason was almost too busy in Las Vegas and Havana to gamble with his new friend, Charles "the Blade" Tourine. But he found the time to lose back the money paid him, and before too long his construction company was bankrupt.

Reassured, Margaret became Mrs. Kastel. The happy couple moved to Las Vegas, where Margaret spent many of her daylight hours climbing over the construction to savor the wonder of it all. Since she usually wore mink over an ankle-length gown and flourished a long cigarette holder, the workmen found her conspicuous. She explained her interest in detail by comparing the Tropicana to the Taj Mahal — a monument to true love. It just had to be perfect.

It was indeed a lavish place, and its first twenty-four days of operation netted a neat if not gaudy "handle" of $651,284. Everyone was quite pleased, and Margaret was in heaven as she was introduced to such distinguished personalities as George Raft, Icepick Willie, Swifty Morgan, and Frank Sinatra. But then in New York someone bounced a slug off Frank Costello's skull, and in his pocket police found a slip of paper bearing the words "Gross casino wins as of 4/25/57, $651,284."

Even the New York cops were able to figure that one out, and Nevada authorities professed dismay to think that Kastel and Costello were associated. Their connections had all been brought out by the Kefauver Committee six years earlier, but no one expected investigators to check that far back. Whitewash was needed, and quickly, before someone remembered that Kastel had also been associated with Lansky as well.

Inevitably, policy considerations took precedence over friendship, and Kastel was forced to end his relations – officially, at least – with the Tropicana. And that was very important to Margaret. Being the wife of a *secret* owner wasn't any fun. She became so unhappy, Dandy Phil finally had to tell her to go to hell. Their marriage ended in the divorce court. Easy come, easy go, in Nevada. The Tropicana endured, of course, but few who gambled there remembered the girl from Bourbon Street who inspired its construction.

Margaret may have retained only her memories of Las Vegas, but Benny Cohen came away with something more substantial. True, he lost his Riviera and his chance at a piece of the action, but he came up with something equally profitable – a friendship with Jimmy Hoffa of the Teamsters Union. Money from the union's pension fund built many syndicate projects in Las Vegas and the Caribbean: hotels, high-rise apartment buildings, hospitals, shopping centers, etc. Benny soon became one of "the men to see" if one wanted a Teamster loan. His commissions from such deals were so large that he finally had to serve a few months in prison for failing to pay taxes on all of them. But, after all, Hoffa went to prison too and stayed there — until President Nixon released him.

And in 1972 Benny and Jimmy were seen lunching together at the Jockey Club in Miami Beach. Whether they were looking back or looking ahead only time would tell. Both had helped make Syndicate City — Las Vegas — the show-business capital of the world, but it seemed a safe bet that so long as there was money to be made they would not rest on their laurels. As Henry Grunewald, another famous "money man," once put it: "You never get enough."

9

Of Love and Crime Wars

At age sixty-nine, Joe Schenck was fat, bald, and squint-eyed. He looked like Kubla Khan after too many years in Xanadu. But still he had an eye for a shapely body and an inviting smile. This broad swinging along a company street had both. Joe told his chauffeur to stop, and he called the girl to his limousine. When she disclosed she was under contract to Twentieth Century-Fox at $74 a week, he gave her his telephone number and told her to call him sometime soon for dinner.

Listed as Norma Jean Mortensen on her birth certificate and baptized Norma Jean Baker, the twenty-year-old starlet didn't know the name of her father, but she did know that her mother had named her after Norma Talmadge, the first wife of this same Joe Schenck who wanted to take her to dinner.

Only a few weeks before, in July 1946, Ben Lyon, the man

who allegedly "discovered" Jean Harlow for Howard Hughes, had signed her to a six-month "option" contract. Just as he rejected Harlęan Carpentier as a suitable name for Harlow, he sought a new name for his latest find. And abruptly Marilyn Monroe was born.

Like Harlow, Marilyn had married early — at age sixteen — in a desperate effort to find stability. Since she had no father and a mother she saw only occasionally, her early years lacked both security and affection. Her beauty and shyness that invited protection while concealing a sharp intelligence were her chief assets. Blond and blue-eyed, with a body that would grace a million calendars, Marilyn was something extra, something unique — sex with the promise of fun. Jean Harlow, forced to play the gangster moll in an era when the gangster had to die at the end to please the Hays Office, had been heavy with sex. Implicit in her performances was dark passion and tragedy. But Marilyn, with her uncertain smile and wiggly walk, radiated a gaiety that warmed the heart while heating the libido.

Despite such qualities, Schenck made no move to push his new friend. Perhaps he recognized that he could keep her only so long as she was hungry. He permitted her option to run out and made no move to renew it. Eventually, in his own good time, he spoke to his old friend of Bioff—Browne days, Harry "King" Cohn, and Cohn gave Marilyn a similar six-month contract at Columbia.

In Hollywood it is difficult to separate truth from ballyhoo. People sometimes lie when there is no need to conceal the truth because to lie is to conform. Thus there are several versions of the Schenck—Cohn transaction that passed Marilyn from one aging satyr to another. In his excellent book *The Moguls,* Norman Zierold credits Schenck with arranging the shift with Jonie Taps, one of Cohn's favorite producers. Taps gave her a small part in a film called *Ladies of the Chorus.* When Cohn saw the first-day rushes he allegedly asked, "Why'd you put that fat cow in the picture? You fucking her?"

When Taps denied it, Cohn bet him a buck she would never get anywhere.

In any case, the rushes got King Cohn to thinking about Marilyn. Perhaps his question to Taps was simply designed to make sure the coast was clear. A strong believer in the principle "He who eats my bread sings my song," Cohn was nicknamed "White Fang" by writer Ben Hecht. All starlets at Columbia traditionally had to endure "Hell Week," and Cohn decided to make Marilyn his personal target.

Marilyn, however, was no naive maiden who could be convinced that the rocket to fame began with a blast-off on a casting couch. She knew Cohn's reputation, and her experience with Joe Schenck had been educational. She was ready to hitch her wagon to a star if necessary, and at that moment she believed she had found one in Frank Sinatra.

Albert Francis Sinatra, a high-school dropout with a skinny frame and a voice bobby-soxers screamed to hear, was having his troubles in 1947 too. In February he had visited Havana, where he met with Charles "Lucky" Luciano, the exiled head of the Mafia. Luciano had been paroled from prison at the end of the war, allegedly for help given Naval Intelligence. Under terms of his parole he was supposed to go to Italy. He went, but soon he was back in Cuba, where his friend Meyer Lansky had been operating for more than a decade. Many top gangsters hastened to Havana to pay their respects and supply their old colleague with cash. Sinatra came with his old buddies, the Fischetti brothers, cousins of Al Capone. Columnist Robert Ruark, who broke the story, noted: "The curious desire to cavort among the scum is possibly permissable among citizens who are not peddling sermons to the nation's youth, and may even be allowed to a mealy-mouthed celebrity if he is smart enough to confine his social tolerance to a hotel room." But Sinatra, he added, "seems to be setting a

most peculiar example for his hordes of pimply, shrieking
slaves. . . ."

Sinatra's friendship with gangsters before and since has
been frequently reported, so much so that apparently it has
become accepted by a public grown hardened and indifferent
to the connections between crime and the entertainment
business. But in 1947 Sinatra's visit to Lucky created quite
an uproar. On top of that, Sinatra was accused of being pro-
Communist. The House Un-American Activities Committee
reportedly planned to probe his associations with left-wing
groups.

So "King" Cohn was doubly insulted when Marilyn told
him she couldn't accept his friendly proposition because she
was in love with Sinatra. To be jilted in favor of "a skinny
little Red" was a bad blow to Cohn's ego, but he had to
restrain himself. He could make sure Marilyn's contract was
not renewed, but Sinatra required more careful handling.
Cohn had enough contacts in the syndicate to know that
Sinatra too had friends and that these men of power considered him a valuable commodity.

Marilyn, of course, was exaggerating when she spoke of
being "in love" with Sinatra. There is little doubt that she
welcomed his friendship and sponsorship, but she soon
realized that his own career was in a state of transition and
that he had no time to spare for hers. Moreover, Sinatra was
attracted to power and success. An unknown Marilyn Monroe
might be fun to play around with, but an Ava Gardner —
successful as well as beautiful — was his passion.

As Sinatra sought to halt his downward slide — his records
as well as his movies were failing — Marilyn struggled to begin
her climb. A brief walk-on scene with Groucho Marx in *Love
Happy* gave her a chance to display the twitchy gait that
seemed at once so natural and yet so deliberately sexy.
Shortly after that she posed nude for a calendar shot,
"Golden Dreams." It paid her only fifty dollars in cash, but it

was worth a million in publicity. It also brought her to the attention of Johnny Hyde, executive vice-president of the old and powerful William Morris Agency. Hyde fell in love with Marilyn and divorced his wife in an effort to win her. When that failed, he asked old Joe Schenck to put in a good word for him. That failed too. Marilyn, accustomed by now to being used, saw a chance to turn the tables. She kept Hyde's hopes alive while he advanced her career by getting her parts in such movies as *The Asphalt Jungle* and *All about Eve*. Suddenly Marilyn had arrived, and by the end of 1950 all Hollywood knew it.

Sinatra, meanwhile, was pursuing Ava Gardner with a passion worthy of a teenager's first love. The affair created something of a scandal since Frankie was still married to Nancy. After a time Ava fled to England to get away from the stink. Sinatra's voice gave out completely, but he followed his lady love to Europe and allegedly fought with a bullfighter over the doll from Smithfield, North Carolina. It was all great copy, but it did nothing for Sinatra's career or his romance.

Months passed, and by April 1951 Ava told Frank she wouldn't see him again until he was divorced. It took some doing, but by November 1 he was free. Within twenty-four hours he was applying for a marriage license in Philadelphia. All seemed settled until Ava got mad and hurled her six-carat emerald engagement ring out a window of the Hampshire House in New York. It was never found. Sinatra got another one, and at last the wedding took place. The bride and groom flew to Miami Beach and hid in a syndicate-owned hotel in Sunny Isles, near a syndicate-owned casino. Then, after two days, they flew to Havana to stay at the Nacional — a hotel-casino long operated by United States gangsters. Whether the bills were "comped" is not a matter of record.

Having made it legal, the Sinatras simply started fighting more regularly. Frank was intensely jealous — the Italian concept of manliness, requiring that his woman be completely, exclusively his property. (Marilyn Monroe was to have somewhat similar problems on a lesser scale when she married Joe DiMaggio.) Ava, whatever her feelings for her husband, was not so much in love that she was ready to play the role of old-country wife. Moreover, her own career was ascending as Frank's declined.

In his darkest hour — his career in ruins, his marriage a joke, his unpaid back taxes due — Sinatra grasped at a straw. James Jones had written a huge book, *From Here to Eternity*, and Sinatra was convinced that the role of Private Maggio was made for him. Perhaps he could start again and build a new career as an actor. There was just one problem. Columbia Pictures had the rights to the book, and King Cohn had a grudge against Sinatra.

So what happened? Sinatra got the part. For two decades Harry Cohn had eaten the bread of the syndicate and, on demand, sang its song. Sinatra had friends in a position to demand, and he got the part of Maggio and an Academy Award.

A new career opened for Sinatra. Eventually he even recovered his voice, and most critics agreed it came back better than ever. Now he was both a singer and an actor, and though he carried a torch for Ava he had recaptured his dignity. Strangely, when he should have been on top of the world, columnists reported that George Wood of the William Morris Agency was assigned to stay close to Sinatra to "try to keep him from slashing his wrists." Perhaps. But George Wood was a syndicate-owned man, a friend of Jimmy Blue Eyes Alo (who owned part of the Morris Agency), and his assignment to Sinatra may have been nothing more than a desire to keep a valuable property under close supervision.

Meanwhile, Marilyn Monroe, having achieved fame and fortune, was still seeking personal happiness. Johnny Hyde had signed her to a seven-year contract with Twentieth

Century Fox — with a little help from Schenck — just before his fatal heart attack. His family disregarded Hyde's whispered last instructions to treat Marilyn "as one of the family" and ordered her to move out of his home. She had not loved Hyde enough to marry him, but she had depended upon his faith and advice. Now, abruptly, she was alone again.

In an effort to get her back into circulation, a girlfriend made a blind date for Marilyn — with a ball player, "Jolting Joe" DiMaggio, the "Yankee Clipper," now retired and living in San Francisco. She liked the handsome, well-dressed celebrity, and he responded immediately to the gay beauty of Hollywood's new sex queen. The courtship lasted more than a year, and in January 1954 they were married in San Francisco. The romance interfered with Sinatra's schedule, since he was supposed to co-star with Marilyn in *Pink Tights*. The film had to be shelved when his co-star decided she would rather get married. Sinatra didn't mind — he had his choice of films these days, and, besides, he liked his fellow Italian-American almost as much as he did Marilyn. But not in the same way, of course.

If Sinatra had a hero, it was Humphrey Bogart, a member of "Murderer's Row" at Warner Brothers for many years. Bogart wound up "dead" in many movies before switching from a well-cut overcoat to the trench coat of the private eye. But unlike George Raft and Sinatra, Bogart felt no need to play the tough guy in private life. He had a great sense of humor, enjoyed mocking the pompous and shocking the self-righteous, but he never took himself seriously. Around him assembled the original "Rat Pack," a group of characters who shared his outlook on life, which, basically, was one of compassion.

Bogart, after two failures, was lucky to marry a woman who complemented him in every way. Lauren Bacall was, as Ezra Goodman put it, "a sort of Humphrey Bogart in skirts." Their marriage was happy. Marilyn Monroe, who starred with

Lauren in *How to Marry a Millionaire,* could envy the long-legged blonde.

When Bogart died of cancer in 1957, Sinatra undertook to console the widow even as he attempted to take over "Bogie's" image as the leader of Hollywood's middle-aged delinquents. Bogart had done what came naturally, but Sinatra seemed to be playing a part — a part dictated by a need to cultivate an ego that would conceal a basic insecurity. To fight with reporters, consort with gangsters, curry favor with the politically powerful, and throw money around as if it was meaningless — all was part of the pattern. Bogart was an admirer of Franklin Roosevelt, a cynic about Douglas MacArthur, in both cases as a matter of principle. Sinatra supported men in power; their politics were immaterial. His passion was aroused only when his vanity was hurt, and the price of his friendship was "respect." Perhaps that is why Lauren Bacall, "a real Joe," as Bogart put it, when asked to comment in 1958 on published reports of an impending marriage to Sinatra, said bluntly, "Marry that bum? I ought to clobber you."

As Bogie always claimed, Lauren had "class."

Ava Gardner, on the other hand, felt it necessary to explain the quiet life she was leading in the post-Sinatra era by telling a British writer, "Don't get me wrong, honey. I think fucking is a great sport. It's all the fucking talk you have to listen to from the man before."

As much as anything, these comments by women close to Sinatra testify as to his failure as a human being and explain his compulsion to be bigger than life, the friend of Presidents, a law unto himself.

But in 1954 Sinatra was still courting the powerful, willing to forget his friendship with Marilyn Monroe to help her new husband try to surprise his wife in a compromising situation.

The Monroe—DiMaggio marriage had built-in problems from the start. An ability to hit a home run is much admired but it can scarcely compete with sex. DiMaggio enjoyed his fame and was hardly pleased on occasion to be ignored by fans who mobbed his wife. Then, too, there was perhaps a touch of old-country tradition in his background that said a woman's place was in the home — if not in the kitchen, at least in the bedroom. He did not enjoy being forced to share Marilyn's beauty with millions of men. Indeed, the incident that finally broke up the marriage is supposed to be the scene in *The Seven Year Itch* when air blowing through a subway grating sent Marilyn's skirt up to expose her skintight white panties. DiMaggio watched the shot being made, as did a thousand New Yorkers. Only he failed to enjoy it.

More basic, perhaps, was the conflict on the intellectual level. DiMaggio was a man's man, an outdoor type who liked hunting and fishing. Marilyn went along on many of the trips and even learned to fry his fish. In return, however, she sought to include him in the adventures of her mind. Although she lacked a formal education, she flirted with ideas and with men of ideas. Long before meeting DiMaggio she had come close to an affair with playwright Arthur Miller. Only the fact that he was married had prevented it from becoming serious. DiMaggio had to know of this and, unable or unwilling to compete in such a field, was inclined to dismiss his wife's interests as an affectation. Marilyn, of course, resented his attitude. On November 5, 1954, one day after Marilyn completed shooting *The Seven Year Itch,* Sinatra teamed with DiMaggio to "raid" an apartment on Waring Avenue. Marilyn's car was parked in front of the building where it was supposed that she was celebrating the completion of the picture with a male friend.

The professional in charge of the attack force was Barney Ruditsky, a former New York cop and alleged expert on syndicate personalities. He had come to Hollywood to open a detective agency which did little more than collect gambling debts owed in Las Vegas. Among his clients were such notables as Bugsy Siegel and Al Smiley.

Ruditsky brought along his own man, Philip Irwin, a former Los Angeles policeman. Sinatra brought along Hank Sanicola, his manager and later his partner in the Cal-Neva Lodge in Nevada where Chicago gangster Sam "Mooney" Giancana liked to cavort with singer Phyllis McGuire. But Sanicola may have come along for reasons other than friendship; he was a financial backer of Jimmie Tarantino, publisher of *Hollywood Night Life,* described by Earl Wilson as "one of the most scandalous of all the Hollywood scandal sheets." Had the raiders been successful and caught Marilyn *flagrante delicto* with a lover, the photographer in the party would have had some very valuable pictures and *Hollywood Night Life* its most smelly scoop.

Unhappily for the raiders, Ruditsky was a better bill collector than detective. The invaders blundered into the wrong apartment, scaring a strange woman into "acute hysteria." Marilyn, it developed, was having dinner with a girlfriend in the apartment above.

Why DiMaggio, whose latter actions proved he still loved Marilyn, allowed himself to be involved in this shabby adventure has never been explained. One can only surmise that he surrendered momentarily to jealousy and the impulse to humiliate his wife. Ordinarily, where hoods were concerned, DiMaggio had 20/20 vision. Three years later, as one particular group of Mafia members schemed to win control of the brand-new Habana Hilton and its glittering casino from Meyer Lansky, an attempt was made to use DiMaggio as a front. A delegation of Cubans allied with Albert Anastasia went to New York to talk to "Jolting Joe." The discussion was "strained," according to one of the Cubans, and it ended the moment Anastasia entered the room. DiMaggio simply walked out. A few days later Anastasia was "executed" and the threat to Lansky's power ended.

Two years passed before the story of the bungled "raid"

leaked out. There were grand-jury investigations, which, as might be expected, produced nothing for the public record. And there was a civil suit by the woman whose door had been mistakenly knocked down which ended in an out-of-court settlement. All of which prevented the affair from becoming widely known. In and of itself, as far as DiMaggio is concerned, such secrecy is probably justified. For Marilyn, however, it may have had a terrible significance for the future. Did the episode inspire a tragic sequel eight years later?

Meanwhile, it could be forgotten. Marilyn went to New York in 1955 to pursue Arthur Miller. In a few months the couple obtained divorces from their respective spouses. And Marilyn worked her way into the intellectual circles frequented by Miller, circles much different from the sporting world of DiMaggio. Despite resentment at her beauty and fame, and some amusement at her occasional mistakes in pronunciation, she was more or less accepted, and today — in the second decade since her death — it is those with pretensions to culture who have made of her a goddess of love and art. There is an undertone of guilt in this posthumous recognition, an almost naive hope that bright legend will live while dark memory fades. Few have said it better than Edward Wagenknecht, author and professor, who wrote: "I am as sure as I can ever be of anything that her soul inhabits that world of light where the excellent becomes the permanent. . . ."

The marriage took place on June 29, 1956, a civil service followed immediately by a Jewish ceremony. Marilyn had no fixed religious convictions and was happy enough to accept her new husband's faith. But while eager to please, Marilyn was not humble. DiMaggio had combined their honeymoon with a long-planned business trip to Japan. He had been annoyed when Marilyn upstaged him by flying on to Korea to entertain — incite to riot is more accurate — American troops there. The Millers honeymooned in England, and this time Marilyn combined pleasure with business. She had agreed to make a movie with, and directed by, Laurence Olivier. Miller, whose own writing career was in a slump, sided with Sir Laurence when Olivier and Marilyn argued about Olivier's direction. Marilyn found herself frustrated on the set and at home, and her feelings weren't improved when Miller left a notebook containing some unflattering observations where she was sure to find it. Anyhow the marriage of two proud and sensitive people fell apart over the next four years.

In 1962 reporter Alan Levy embarked on a career as a free-lance writer. His first assignment was to interview Marilyn Monroe — an interesting challenge at any time and, given the circumstances, a unique one. But Levy was always lucky on assignments; he just happened to be vacationing in Cuba on the day President Batista went on the lam. When Levy asked Marilyn about her marriage to Miller, she gave him two statements of importance to this history: "At the beginning of our marriage there was a pupil-teacher relationship. I learned a great deal from it, but there was more to the marriage than that. . . ."

And, still speaking of Miller: "He introduced me to the importance of political freedom in our society."

The marriage also gave her two miscarriages, an addiction to Nembutal, and a commitment to co-star with Clark Gable in *The Misfits,* a screenplay based on a short story by Miller and tailored by Miller for his wife. It proved to be a great movie. The strains caused by Marilyn's physical and emotional condition were blamed by some for the heart attack Gable suffered one day after the picture was completed. His death followed on November 16, 1960. The man who, while holding Jean Harlow in his arms, had realized she was seriously ill and sought in vain to get her the help she needed had been patient and kind with Harlow's successor. Gable sensed that she too had troubles.

A week before Gable's death Marilyn finally broke with Arthur Miller and in her loneliness began to reach out to former friends for the emotional support she needed to supplement her sleeping pills. Among those she began to see again were Joe DiMaggio and, somewhat ominously, Frank Sinatra.

In those years when Marilyn had sought with Miller a marriage of mind and body and had refused to settle for less, Sinatra had come to terms with himself. Ruthlessly he had made himself the man who used others. No longer would he beg for a starring role or pursue a woman. He could make a movie, *The Joker Is Wild,* about the life of Joe E. Lewis, and then walk out of the post-premiere party in Las Vegas when asked by Lewis to sing. Such bad manners won admiration from an industry which believes above all else in the virtue of being on top. And Sinatra was on top. "Not since the late thirties when Louis B. Mayer ruled from his Metro throne has anyone had such power," wrote John C. Bowes in the *American Weekly.*

A king must have his court, a tyrant his sycophants, and a Sinatra his clan. "To his friends," wrote Ezra Goodman, "Sinatra dispenses flashy and expensive gifts like a gang overlord. There were years when he averaged $50,000 in gifts." And around him he gathered a successor rat pack of his own, a curious crew, a combination of talent and servility, a blend of arrogance and humility that approached sheer hypocrisy.

Most conspicuous was Sammy Davis, Jr., who sought to be the Jackie Robinson of show business. For much of his success he credited Sinatra. Some of Sinatra's friends also backed Davis. Yet these men had their prejudices and didn't hesitate to enforce them. Once Davis appeared on the verge of marrying Kim Novak, a star developed by Harry Cohn to replace Rita Hayworth. Cohn, as we have already seen, was vulnerable to syndicate pressure, and conveyed threats to Sammy. Everything from broken legs to castration. Hurriedly Davis married a black girl. As soon as the storm passed, he divorced her and eventually married Mai Britt, a Scandinavian blonde. Defiantly he announced he didn't care if their babies were polka dot in color. The cynical noted that no one cared who he married so long as he didn't hurt a valuable property like Kim Novak.

Dean Martin had no need to break color barriers, but early in his career he changed his name and his nose. Born Dino Paul Crocetti in Steubenville, Ohio, Martin grew up in a gangster town. Steubenville for many years was notorious as the home of more bust-out gamblers than any city in the country. They learned the basics in the back rooms of that dirty town and attended graduate school downriver in the plusher dives of Newport, Kentucky. Those with skill and luck eventually made it to Las Vegas. In 1961 an official investigator noted that more than three hundred former residents of Steubenville were employed as dealers, stickmen, pit bosses, and bouncers in Las Vegas. Dino might easily have been one of them, but he could sing as well as shoot dice, and he had friends who made sure he came to the attention of people of influence. Even so it was necessary for him to get a new nose. It cost five hundred bucks for a down payment to a plastic surgeon, and the bookies of Steubenville put up the money. The operation was a great success. With a streamlined schnozzle Dino was on his way to wealth, fame, and the right to be present when "Il Padrone," as Sinatra was known to fellow Italian-Americans, removed his hair piece. Still another "Knight of the Toupee" was Peter Lawford, whose brother-in-law became President of the United States.

While the idea that Sinatra helped Robert Kennedy in his war on crime is absurd, he did do everything in his power to elect John Kennedy in the campaign of 1960. Not only did he take part in vote-getting, fund-raising rallies, but he forced the Clan and all others who sought his favor to follow suit. That Sinatra did have political influence with Italian-Americans as with millions of others who admired him soon became apparent. But it was also apparent that Sinatra supported Kennedy for practical reasons unrelated to the principles and issues with which the candidate was identified. Gambling that the handsome young Irish-American, with the beautiful wife, would be a winner, Sinatra utilized the edge his friendship with Lawford gave him and hoped to incorporate the Clan into the so-called "Irish Mafia" which surrounded the Kennedys.

So eager was he to be accepted, he issued a statement in August denying the very existence of the Clan. Some observers saw this move as an attempt to convince John Kennedy that he was, indeed, a serious citizen. A similar sacrifice was forced on Sammy Davis. To avoid the possibility that his planned marriage with Mai Britt would be used by Republicans as a racial smear to hurt Sinatra and thus Kennedy, Davis postponed the wedding until the Sunday after the election. It was only after Kennedy's victory that Sammy became bold enough to talk of polka-dot children.

On election night as millions waited for the outcome, Sinatra became furious because Richard M. Nixon wouldn't concede. According to *Time* Sinatra tried unsuccessfully to reach the Republican candidate on the telephone to tell him to give up and get it over with.

The reward for all Sinatra's efforts came on January 19, 1961, when he and Lawford, assisted by the Clan, produced the Inaugural Gala in Washington. It was the social high spot of the season. The following day Sinatra breakfasted with Robert Kennedy and attended his swearing in as Attorney General. Of all the public events of Sinatra's political life, it is perhaps his presence when organized crime's most effective foe took the oath of office that is most ironic.

Marilyn Monroe was not in Washington to welcome the opening of the "New Frontier," although she had supported John Kennedy since the moment it became apparent that Adlai Stevenson was out of contention. She watched the inaugural ceremonies on television at the Dallas airport during a stop-over on a flight to Juarez, Mexico, to divorce Arthur Miller. The trip was timed in the expectation that the new President would dominate the next day's newspapers. Perhaps the break-up of the marriage would be little noticed. Reporters were on hand, however, and their questions did nothing to soothe a lonely, confused woman who desperately needed something or someone in which to believe. Instead, there were only sleeping pills. Reluctantly she agreed to treatment in a New York mental hospital, then called Joe DiMaggio and asked him to rescue her. DiMaggio flew to New York and took her from the hospital to another institution where she felt more comfortable. Marilyn was able to obtain three weeks of rest and privacy. But New York, with its memories of Miller, proved unbearable. She told friends that she almost jumped from a window one day but held back at the last second when she thought she recognized a woman on the street below. Since her principal motive for suicide was to escape a world too full of the casually curious, she wanted anonymity in the act of death. Better the land of make-believe than the reality of New York. She returned to Los Angeles and, significantly, spent the first weeks there at the home of Sinatra. He was away most of the time, but they dated often enough for the columnists to begin speculating.

At this time Sinatra began to be puzzled by an increasing coolness from the White House. Again the columnists had an answer — both John and Robert Kennedy had engaged in too many Clan "summit meetings" to please their wives. Certainly, the Republicans made much of the alleged disgrace Sinatra and his pals were bringing to the Kennedy Administration. No one, not even William Buckley, Jr., dared suppose that eleven years later Sinatra would be seated as an honored guest in the box of a Republican Vice President as the Grand Old Party renominated Richard M. Nixon for a second term.

In an effort to make himself more respectable, Sinatra "cooled" the Clan and dashed about the world doing good deeds. Nevertheless the freeze deepened. In anticipation of a visit by President Kennedy, Sinatra added five rooms to his Palm Springs home. But when Kennedy did go west he stayed instead with Bing Crosby. Sinatra, unable to bear the humiliation, left town.

Sinatra also broke with Peter Lawford, Kennedy's brother-in-law. Sinatra and Lawford had been more than friends; they had been partners in a restaurant. This association was dissolved, and soon the two weren't speaking to each other. Once again the "insiders" blamed the rift on the lovely Jackie. As usual, they were wrong. Robert Kennedy, not Jackie, was responsible.

As Attorney General of the United States, Robert Kennedy had two assets unique in the history of that office. He had personal insight into the problems of organized crime, insight gained through his work as counsel of the McClellan Committee in its long investigation of James Hoffa and the Teamsters Union. Hoffa, as has been noted earlier, was deeply involved with the real leaders of the syndicate and through the pension funds he controlled had financed countless syndicate projects. In probing these deals Kennedy learned much about crime and its relation to business and politics. Moreover, as brother of the President of the United States, Robert Kennedy had the political muscle to get things done. Other Attorney Generals had been forced to rely on J. Edgar Hoover for their understanding of crime – and Hoover was neither well informed nor objective. Worse, he was whimsical about investigative action. Robert Kennedy knew more about organized crime than Hoover, who had for decades denied its existence, and he had no political need to *ask* when he could *order*.

Immediately after his brother's inauguration, Kennedy

launched a "coordinated war on crime," forcing the several federal investigative agencies to cooperate with each other. Coordinating their activities was a special "Organized Crime Section" in the Justice Department. Shortly after it began to function a conversation between Salvatore "Mooney" Giancana — currently considered Al Capone's successor in Chicago — and a friend was intercepted. Giancana indicated to the friend he was trying to use Sinatra as a link to Kennedy.

A probe of Sinatra was begun. Unlike most of the others getting under way, it wasn't designed to bring about the subject's indictment and conviction. Basically the effort was to put Sinatra into better perspective. There were two principal questions:

1. Is Sinatra "owned" and controlled by organized crime?

2. If he is so controlled, is his courtship of the Kennedy family a matter of personal pride or is it the type of thing Giancana was talking about — a syndicate attempt to win influence?

It was easy to see how a Sinatra, or any other entertainer with vast popularity and status as an international celebrity, could be used by the syndicate in the normal course of business: as a front for mob investments, as a means of promoting casino gambling, and as a way of attracting business to syndicate hotels, restaurants, nightclubs.

On the other hand, it was also easy to see why Sinatra, a man who loved power and the spotlight, would be attracted to the most powerful man in the world and would seek his favor. Nothing unusual or sinister about that. But Robert Kennedy, through his pursuit of Jimmy Hoffa, had learned much about corruption, and Giancana's remarks about Sinatra made it imperative that the matter be probed. Assume Sinatra was being used, consciously or unconsciously, by organized crime. Assume the President and his Attorney General had no inkling of that fact. The possibilities for the mob would be endless. Those possibilities could range from securing confidential information about criminal investigations to influencing pending legislation, from recommending appointments of corrupt judges to setting up the President or a member of his family for blackmail.

No conclusions were possible in the months remaining of 1961, and no effort was made to embarrass Sinatra by a public break. Some citizens, unaware of the behind-the-scenes investigation, were distressed. Nevertheless, evidence of Sinatra's involvement with mob figures poured in. Typical was a call received in the office of the Chicago Crime Commission on December 6, 1961. The call came from a deputy sheriff in Clark County, Nevada (Las Vegas), who, according to a memo of the conversation, said that "a few days ago he was in a Greek restaurant in Las Vegas. In this restaurant for a meal and in intimate conversation were Frank Sinatra, Joseph Fischetti, Rocco Fischetti, and the crime boss of Joliet, Illinois." The deputy added "the belief that in view of Frank Sinatra's close associations with President John Kennedy, the associations with gangsters he constantly maintains are bad for the President."

At least three formal reports on Albert Francis Sinatra were made to Henry Peterson, deputy chief, Organized Crime Section: on May 15, July 2, and August 3, 1962. The last one was nineteen single-spaced pages long and contained many cross references to reports on many other gangsters of note such as Joseph Stacher and John Roselli. It traced in considerable detail the intricate threads of mob ownership, and it was spiced with occasional episodes of action. For example:

The Cal-Neva Lodge at Lake Tahoe has just completed extensive remodeling and reopened on June 29, 1962. Frank Sinatra, a 50 percent owner of this establishment, was the headline entertainer and was scheduled to appear for the first week. However, according to the Washoe Sheriff's office, Sinatra made improper advances to a beautiful cocktail waitress who is married to a deputy sheriff. Sinatra reportedly failed to heed the deputy's warning to stay away from his wife and continued his advances. On or about June 30, 1962, this resulted in Sinatra receiving a punch on the nose from the deputy which knocked Sinatra to the casino floor and apparently made it necessary to call on replacement entertainment.

There was much information about Sinatra and the Sands Hotel in Las Vegas, a sample of which went like this:

On March 28, 1962, Lionel R. Brooks of Miami Beach advised that he originally obtained five shares of the Sands Hotel in Las Vegas through attorney Bryant Burton and gave Burton power-of-attorney to handle the voting of his shares in any directors' or stockholders' meeting.

According to Brooks, approximately two years ago he was notified by Burton that inasmuch as he did not take an active part in the affairs of the Sands Hotel, two of the five shares he owned had been selected by the management to be sold to Frank Sinatra. Burton pointed out to Brooks [that] in order for the Sands Hotel to have leading entertainers, it was necessary to sell shares of stock not only to Frank Sinatra but to Dean Martin and Sammy Davis.

The long report made no attempt to answer the second question which puzzled Kennedy — Sinatra's motives in seeking friendship with the President — but it left no doubt about his relations to the mob. It concluded:

Sinatra has had a long and wide association with hoodlums and racketeers which seems to be continuing. The nature of Sinatra's work may, on occasion, bring him into contact with underworld figures *but this cannot account* for his friendship and/or financial involvement with people such as Joe and Rocco Fischetti, cousins of Al Capone, Paul Emilio D'Amato, John Formorsa and Sam Giancana, all of whom are on our list of racketeers. No other entertainer appears to be mentioned nearly so frequently with racketeers.

Available information not only indicates that Sinatra is associated with each of the above-named racketeers but that they apparently maintain contact with one another. This indicates a possible community of interest involving Sinatra and racketeers in Illinois, Indiana, New Jersey, Florida and Nevada.

It appears that IRS and FBI investigations of Frank Sinatra may reveal not only Federal income tax violations on the part of Sinatra and various racketeers, but also new insight into the activities and operations of Sinatra's racketeering associates. Such insights would be particularly helpful to our program in the Las Vegas and Miami areas.

Sinatra, the good-time guy and eager friend when Robert Kennedy was a private citizen campaigning for his brother, looked different to the Attorney General of the United States who had declared war on crime. He looked Dangerous. The Kennedys were through with Sinatra, and Robert, not Jackie, was responsible. There was, of course, still no public break, no effort to embarrass Sinatra or harm his image. Most citizens, in fact, still didn't know what was going on. Sinatra no more than the Kennedys wanted to advertise the situation. Reluctant at first to believe he had been rejected, Sinatra began to sulk as the truth penetrated his ego. Self-pity soon turned to rage — rage directed primarily at the Attorney General.

In hating Robert Kennedy, Sinatra was, of course, not alone. No law-enforcement official in history — and that would include Thomas E. Dewey and J. Edgar Hoover — has ever been so thoroughly hated. While all kinds of excuses were given, the truth wasn't complicated: Kennedy was hated because he was effective. For the first time since crime became organized, there was organized opposition. Kennedy knew the score. He was fond of quoting a paragraph from Raymond Chandler's famous essay "The Simple Art of Murder," wherein Chandler speaks

> of a world in which gangsters can rule nations and almost rule cities, in which hotels and apartment houses and celebrated restaurants are owned by men who made their money out of brothels, in which a screen star can be the finger man for a mob, and the nice man down the hall is a boss of the numbers racket . . . where no man can walk down a dark street in safety because law and order are things we talk about but refrain from practicing.

Armed with his insight and the power that falls to a President's trusted brother, Robert Kennedy threatened to topple the complex organization constructed so carefully by syndicate leaders over three decades. Aware of the danger, organized crime's rage was increased by the knowledge that the Attorney General could neither be bought with money nor promises of political help. He had enough money of his own, and so long as his brother was President he needed no other sponsor. Only one possibility existed — blackmail. An old weapon, it could still be effective if properly used. Recently it had been attempted in Newport, Kentucky, in an effort to discredit and destroy a citizen's revolt against the syndicate. George Ratterman, a retired professional football player, had been drafted by the reformers to run for sheriff. The gamblers tricked Ratterman into having drinks in a Cincinnati hotel with Tito Carinci, a former Steubenville grid star turned gambler. Carinci put chloral hydrate into Ratterman's Scotch mist, rendering him dazed but conscious. He was then taken to a bust-out joint in Newport and put to bed with a stripper.

Unfortunately for the conspirators, the photographer scheduled to take the incriminating pictures didn't show. An alternate plan was used. Cooperative cops came in, pulled the trousers from Ratterman's unconscious form — he had been knocked out upon reaching Kentucky — and arrested him. The case became a national sensation, and it backfired. Ratterman proved he was framed. Moreover, the incident gave Robert Kennedy, who had followed the case closely, the legal justification he needed to close down the syndicate casinos which had operated undisturbed for more than twenty years. Just another reason to fear Kennedy — and to frame him too if possible. The stakes were high enough to justify fantastic risks.

While Sinatra and his pals were ostracized, Marilyn Monroe was moving into that inner circle from which Frank had just been ousted. Thanks to Peter Lawford, she was invited to sing "Happy Birthday" to President Kennedy at a giant celebration in Madison Square Garden in New York. She accepted. It was May 18, 1962.

New York had bad memories for Marilyn, and she was half drunk much of the time she was there. Yet her performance for the President was a triumph. Dressed in a long, shimmering, clinging gown that outlined every curve, she sang the familiar song in a breathless, sultry style that made it sound like "That Old Black Magic." The crowd went wild, and President Kennedy, a wide grin on his youthful face, drew laughter by remarking, "Now I can retire from politics after having had 'Happy Birthday' sung to me by such a sweet, wholesome girl as Marilyn Monroe."

What Sinatra thought of Marilyn stealing his thunder, so to speak, isn't on record, but ominously he continued to be one of her few friends in Hollywood. Earlier he had given her a small poodle which Marilyn, aware of Frank's friendships with hoods, had promptly "initiated" into the Mafia. Naturally such an animal could only be called "Maf," and that became his name. She grew very fond of the dog, and Maf came to symbolize her friendship with Sinatra. As a symbol, Maf is rather revealing.

To sing at the President's party Marilyn had taken "French leave" from the set of the movie *Something's Got to Give* in which she was co-starring with Dean Martin. The studio was thoroughly annoyed. An effort was made to patch things up, and the shooting of the movie continued long enough for Marilyn to do a nude swimming scene. Direction called for her to wear a tight-fitting flesh-colored suit, but once in the water she stripped if off while delighted photographers made the most of their opportunity. *Life* paid $10,000 for the U.S. rights to the pictures, and foreign magazines competed eagerly for the right to publish in a dozen countries.

Marilyn's delight in the pictures was perhaps partly due to her realization that at age thirty-six she still had the figure of a "cover girl." There was a reverse side to the coin, however: the knowledge that she was approaching middle age. Just something else to worry about. Her thirty-sixth birthday was her last appearance on the set of *Something's Got to Give*. When she failed to return, the studio suspended her, not caring that she was too ill to work. A studio spokesman was quoted as saying, "We can't afford to risk millions on unreliable stars."

Depressed, deserted, desperate, Marilyn was ready for a new love.

Enter Robert Kennedy.

He had met and admired Marilyn at his brother's birthday party in Madison Square Garden. Now, in the summer of 1962, he combined personal business and a vacation to fly west to Hollywood. The business concerned his book *The Enemy Within*. The story of his experiences with the McClellan Committee, it expressed his belief that organized crime and corruption, not a Communist conspiracy, represented the real danger to America. First published in 1960,

Kennedy's book had been an immediate best seller, with all the author's profits assigned to help retarded children. The book was dedicated to his wife.

Eager to get his message about crime to as many citizens as possible, Kennedy commissioned Budd Schulberg to do a screenplay. Schulberg, the distinguished son of a Hollywood producer, had written of crime and waterfront corruption before and was eager to take on the more difficult assignment. Producer Jerry Wald was interested in making the movie. Kennedy wanted to make sure that Schulberg's screenplay would be followed; he wanted an accurate picture that would inform as well as entertain. And he knew the subject was dynamite for an industry built in part by mob money. Wald was famous for his energy and his willingness to talk about anything, uninhibited by lack of knowledge. Schulberg had, in fact, used him as a model for the principal character in his novel of Hollywood, *What Makes Sammy Run.* Wald certainly knew the value of talking business with the Attorney General of the United States, the brother of the President. And, of course, nothing was too good for such a celebrity.

In the course of their several conversations Wald mentioned to Kennedy that he had produced two of Marilyn's movies, *Clash by Night* and *Let's Make Love.* When Kennedy expressed his admiration for Marilyn, Wald offered to arrange a meeting. Kennedy refused. He was too discreet to allow a Hollywood producer to do him a favor involving a beautiful woman. Besides, he didn't need Wald's help. Despite Peter Lawford's withdrawal from Sinatra's Clan, the Attorney General's brother-in-law had remained friends with Marilyn, who, in fact, had been to the Lawford home many times and enjoyed playing with the Lawford children.

A meeting with Marilyn was easily arranged. A healthy, virile man, Kennedy could not help but be fascinated by Marilyn's beauty. A compassionate man, he realized she was emotionally distraught and needed help badly. While he loved his wife and was a faithful Catholic, he was also a sophisticated man of the world. Where women were concerned he was like Raymond Chandler's hero who would willingly "seduce a duchess but never spoil a virgin." Marilyn was no virgin. What's more, Kennedy was the type of man she had been seeking. He combined, or so it seemed to her, the best qualities of her last two husbands. A man of action, a lover of adventure, he resembled DiMaggio. An author, an educated man of ideas, he resembled Miller, who had first introduced Marilyn to the ideals of intellectual and political freedom. And, in addition, he had the confidence that wealth and power gives, plus the ability to laugh at himself and others. He was also a celebrity.

The first meeting was quickly followed by another and another. Within a week a routine developed. They saw each other every day. When urgent business required, he would fly back to Washington for a couple of days and then return. He was, of course, in touch with his aides every day by telephone as the war on crime gathered momentum. The official excuse for his trips to Los Angeles remained the talks with Wald about a movie version of *The Enemy Within.*

It's doubtful if such an affair could have been kept secret in Hollywood for long despite the elaborate precautions Kennedy insisted be taken. In any event, Marilyn confided in friends, among them Sinatra, whom she still saw during Kennedy's absences. The hopelessness of the affair was obvious to Marilyn — it had no place to go. By personality and by training, Kennedy was not the kind of man to damage his brother's career, break his wife's heart, and destroy his own political future for love. Marilyn knew this, accepted it at first without tears, and even respected her lover for his toughness of spirit. To be his mistress on a permanent basis seemed the most she could hope to attain; yet even that possibility was fraught with dangers to his career, and the arrangement presented practical problems of great complexity.

The old adage that a politician, especially a politician fighting crime and corruption, should be as pure as Caesar's wife was peculiarly appropriate in Kennedy's case. Every time he saw Marilyn he left himself open to blackmail. And certainly he could not continue to come to California on anything approaching a regular basis. To think of keeping Marilyn in a comfortable brownstone house in the Georgetown section of Washington was attractive, but Marilyn would have had to abandon her career and become a recluse. The sacrifice was too much to ask.

Since the affair apparently had no future, the limited opportunities of the present became more precious. While one can wonder if Kennedy knew that Marilyn and Sinatra were still friends, there can be no doubt that he was completely unaware that she had told Sinatra about their affair. For Kennedy knew in the early summer of 1962 that Sinatra hated his very guts. And he knew also that Sinatra's gangster associates would do anything to destroy him. The Kennedy-ordered investigation even then under way into the true ownership of Las Vegas casinos and the distribution of the "off the top" skim threatened to undermine the entire structure of organized crime. And the Las Vegas probe was but one of many. Equally important was the attack on Teamsters boss James R. Hoffa. A special squad under the leadership of Walter Sheridan was aggressively examining union-syndicate deals in every major city, and scores of Hoffa's underlings were being indicted in the hope that some would "squeal" on the boss. In other words the "heat" was on, and the man responsible was the man who was seeing Marilyn Monroe at every opportunity. Kennedy must have known it was a reckless thing to do, but he enjoyed adventure and was fascinated by Marilyn.

The summer dragged on. Marilyn told DiMaggio of her new

friend and he became angry. His disapproval shook Marilyn and made her more vulnerable to those less sincere who might want to use her. When Kennedy had to return to Washington in the latter part of July, she sought relief from anxiety by visiting the Cal-Neva Lodge at Lake Tahoe, the casino in which Sinatra had an interest. To her usual fears was now added the suspicion that Kennedy would not return to see her. He had promised to come back, but Marilyn had little faith in men's promises. Already emotionally upset, her despondency increased, and she took an overdose of sleeping pills. Somehow, before passing out, she knocked off the telephone by the bed. An alert operator sounded the alarm, and Marilyn was found nude and unconscious on the floor. Sinatra, who had been at the lodge not long before, must have heard about the entire incident.

In attempting to reconstruct the events of early August 1962, certain persons — of whom the author is one — have concluded that Marilyn's suicide attempt at Lake Tahoe provided the final inspiration for a plot to blackmail the Attorney General of the United States into calling off his war on organized crime. The plan conceived by organized crime and its allies was modeled on the frame-up of George Ratterman at Newport in 1961. There the reform candidate had been drugged in order to get him someplace, anyplace, where the conspirators could control the action. The cautious Kennedy would give no one such an opportunity. How, then, to lure him into a situation he could not control? By using a woman. Surely Robert Kennedy could not let a beautiful woman who loved him die of an overdose of sleeping pills. The conspirators familiarized themselves with Marilyn's household, the people in her entourage, her lawyers and her doctors. They quickly realized that their first problem would be to obtain Marilyn's cooperation. Obviously, she would not join a conspiracy against the man she loved, but her love could be skillfully manipulated to obtain the desired result.

More than anything, Marilyn wanted some assurance that her romance with Kennedy could continue indefinitely. She knew the risks he was taking and couldn't help wondering how soon reason and practical difficulties would prevail. She would be more than glad to cooperate with anyone who suggested a way that would be sure to get Kennedy to agree to continue the affair. Maybe she should go east, perhaps to New York, an hour from Washington by shuttle plane, where she might make a movie. There would be plenty of opportunity in the huge city for privacy. By setting the right scene, Marilyn, and the people she regarded as her friends, could not fail to convince Kennedy that the plan which had been suggested to her made sense. And once the pattern was established there could be similar arrangements further in the future. Marilyn was so important a star that she could, if necessary, refuse to work in Hollywood. Thus we can assume that when Marilyn was approached by one of the conspirators, she, believing her own happiness was at stake, agreed for her own purposes to try to get Kennedy to her own home, which was at the end of a dead-end street behind a ten-foot-high brick wall, built to assure privacy.

"Can assume." Those words are necessary today, for Marilyn Monroe is dead. Many believe she was mentally unstable and took her own life. Many believe that she, like other unfortunates, simply miscalculated the dosage of the medicine she took. But the possibility also exists that Marilyn's death was an accident resulting when someone underestimated Robert Kennedy. Obviously, at this late date, no one is likely to prove Marilyn's death was not suicide, but those who understand — as Robert Kennedy understood — something of the power and ambition of organized crime and its allies will not accept that conclusion precipitously. The very same facts support each conclusion or combinations thereof.

Marilyn came home from Lake Tahoe excited about a plan

to make a movie in Brooklyn of Betty Smith's best-selling book *A Tree Grows in Brooklyn.* In confirmation, on August 3, 1962, producer-composer Jule Styne telephoned Marilyn from New York to discuss the movie. Dean Martin, Shirley MacLaine, Sinatra, and Marilyn would star in it. Styne wanted to use the score from *Pink Tights,* the picture Marilyn had been scheduled to make with Sinatra when she married DiMaggio. Expecting the call, Marilyn was quick to agree and too happy to conceal her interest. Styne assured her he wanted Sinatra in the picture as well. Months later Styne said she told him, "I'm dying to work with Sinatra." After agreeing to meet with Styne the following week in New York, Marilyn hung up.

And as if to confirm that her luck had turned, another call came. Kennedy would be back in town next day. Would she join him for the evening as usual? Marilyn said she would be delighted to come to the Lawfords for dinner. Then she visited Dr. Hyman Engelberg, the doctor who treated her physical ills. From him she obtained a prescription for twenty-five sleeping pills. Then she drove to the office of her psychiatrist, Dr. Greenson, talked awhile, and afterward went to a pharmacy, where the prescription was filled.

On that same day, August 3, 1962, that nineteen-page report on "Albert Francis Sinatra, aka Frankie Sinatra" was completed in Washington. Given Kennedy's interest in the subject, it is safe to assume that a copy went to him the same day — before he left for California. His staffers knew he had personally ordered the investigation. Saturday, August 4, arrived. Pat Newcomb, Marilyn's press agent, who had a background of Washington, D.C., society, had spent the previous night with Marilyn. They were good friends as well as professional associates, and Marilyn didn't like to be alone at night. After Pat left Saturday afternoon and as darkness fell, Marilyn was seen playing in the yard with Maf, the white poodle Sinatra has given her. As she came into the house the phone was ringing. It was, as expected, Robert Kennedy, reminding her to come to dinner at Lawford's home. Marilyn told him she would come, but she didn't go. Instead she went to her bedroom and began playing records on her phonograph. Ironically, she selected Frank Sinatra albums. She was nervous and excited as she began taking her pills.

When Marilyn did not appear at the Lawford home an hour or so later, a call was made to her. Dazed, on the verge of unconsciousness, she still remembered her part. Over the sounds of the phonograph she begged Kennedy to come to her. She said she couldn't live without him. She had taken a lethal dose of sleeping pills. She was dying. If he wouldn't come, then this was goodbye. And the phone went dead. Marilyn had delivered her lines. The rest was up to Kennedy.

Kennedy never went. Whatever the reason, he did not go to Marilyn. All his courage and self-discipline were necessary that night as out in the dark a beautiful woman died.

Lawford, without acknowledging his brother-in-law's presence that night, has admitted conversing with Marilyn and becoming alarmed. He called his manager, Milton Ebbins, he said, and urged Ebbins to accompany him to Marilyn's house. Ebbins allegedly suggested that such a visit would be improper for the brother-in-law of the President and offered as an alternative to contact Marilyn's attorney, Mickey Rudin.

Rudin was hard to locate. According to the official version of events, when found at last he called *his* brother-in-law, Dr. Greenson. Either the lawyer or the doctor — accounts vary — then called Dr. Greenson's friend, Mrs. Murray, the housekeeper. She reported that everything was all right. A light was showing under Marilyn's bedroom door, and the record player was filling the air with Sinatra's voice.

This "comforting" information was reported to Rudin, who reported it to Ebbins, who reported it to Lawford. Still worried, Lawford demanded that Rudin talk to him in person. Ebbins relayed his request, and Rudin called to repeat Mrs. Murray's assurances to Robert Kennedy's brother-in-law. There was nothing more Lawford could safely do. If the conspiracy theory is to be accepted, organized crime had underestimated Kennedy, and Marilyn Monroe was dead as a result.

Mrs. Murray later reported that she awoke from a troubled sleep about 3:00 A.M. and decided to check on her patient. The light still shone under the locked door. She went outside, and through the French windows she could see Marilyn's arm clutching a telephone. The scene seemed "peculiar," so the faithful housekeeper called Dr. Greenson at his home. To do so, she said, she used a second telephone line to the house. Dr. Greenson drove to Marilyn's house, peeped in, and agreed the situation was indeed peculiar. He used the second phone to call Dr. Engelberg. A window was broken, the room entered, and Marilyn was officially pronounced dead. Dr. Engelberg estimated she had died between 10:00 P.M. and 1:00 A.M.

The coroner's report described the death as "probably suicide." Not as "suicide."

On August 5, 1962, Marilyn in death was more alone than she had been in life. She had no family to claim her body or make arrangements for her funeral. Into this vacuum stepped Joe DiMaggio, who wasn't her last husband or even her last lover. Much had happened since he and Sinatra had sallied forth with a private eye and a photographer in an attempt to catch Marilyn in bed with another man. DiMaggio, at least, had learned from the experience.

Heartbroken and angry, DiMaggio knew much about Marilyn's last days and suspected more. Ruthlessly he ignored the rich and the famous in planning the funeral. Only thirty-five persons were allowed in the chapel. Among those barred were Sinatra, Dean Martin, and Mr. and Mrs. Peter Lawford. Mrs. Lawford, sister of the President, flew to Los Angeles for the funeral and was bewildered to be treated so coldly. DiMaggio told an attorney: "If it wasn't for some of her friends she wouldn't be where she is."

Of all the double-talk to come out of Hollywood about Marilyn's death, that statement alone rings true. In fourteen words the Pride of the Yankees spoke volumes.

Dressed in a green sheath with a green silk scarf about her neck, Marilyn in her coffin was as lovely as the pink roses in her hand. In the months that followed the legend began to grow. Evidence of intellectual resources in the form of verses written by her was published. One of the verses could easily have been penned in those last days as hope struggled with fear within her mind and heart:

> Help Help
> Help I feel life coming closer
> When all I want is to die

PART III
The New Breed

The danger in this country is the private seizure of power. It is subject to no checks and balances, it is subject to no elections every four years, it is subject to no criticism and no attacks because no one even knows about it.
                                                    —THURMAN ARNOLD, 1940

I wonder if this business will ever turn honest.
                                                    —HAL B. WALLIS

10

George Raft's Last Score

The murder of President John F. Kennedy in 1963, and the subsequent loss of power by Robert F. Kennedy, did not automatically bring a cease-fire in the war on crime. Some investigations begun under Attorney General Kennedy were so far along they couldn't be stopped.

So it was that on August 31, 1965, George Raft was indicted on six counts of tax evasion. The indictment specified he had understated his income from 1958 through 1963 by $85,128.94. The IRS special agent in his final report listed the understatement as $143,651.85. The difference was largely a disputed $50,000 item relating to a gambling casino in Cuba.

Raft and his wife, Grayce, had been separated for almost forty years, but they filed joint income-tax returns during all that period. George could have well-publicized "love affairs" with Norma Shearer, Carole Lombard, and Betty Grable, and scores of "friendships" with lesser starlets, but he always had an excuse when the subject of matrimony came up — he was already married.

The Casino de Capri in Havana was one of those which flowered during President Batista's second tenure as dictator of Cuba. Meyer Lansky was the architect of the new gambling empire, "the Las Vegas of the Caribbean," and as usual he kept almost everyone happy by sharing the profits. His old allies of the Cleveland syndicate — Moe Dalitz and company — got the famous Casino Nacional. As previously noted, they held it until just three months before Castro cut down the money tree. For himself, Lansky built the Habana Riviera. His allies in the Mafia were awarded the Capri and given George Raft to serve as "greeter," host, and all-around shill. As usual, the Mafia wasn't satisfied, and an attempt by Albert Anastasia to take the new Habana Hilton, with Joe DiMaggio as "front," ended with DiMaggio walking out and Anastasia getting bumped off, rubbed out, or "hit" — depending on which gangster movie educated you.

The operating company of the Capri was the Maryland Re-insurance Company, Inc. It had nothing to do with Maryland or insurance, since it was a Panamanian corporation which was not subject to the supervision of the Securities and Exchange Commission or the Internal Revenue Service. The secretary of the corporation was Dr. Guillermo Belt, former Cuban Ambassador to the United States. Also on the scene was Stewart's Investment Corporation, formed in Florida by Benjamin Berkowitz, treasurer of the Casino de Capri. The purpose of Stewart's Investment was to clear checks issued to the casino and drawn on United States bank accounts. There was also muscle available if some sucker had second thoughts and stopped payment on his check upon returning home from Cuba.

The investigation of Raft by Kennedy's Organized Crime Section of the Justice Department began when intelligence information was received to the effect that "George Raft had taken a Texas oil man for $50,000.00 in connection with purchasing some 'points' in the Casino de Capri. Raft had to give Charlie 'the Blade' Tourine $40,000.00, and split the remaining $10,000.00 with another unidentified person."

Ralph Lowe was identified as the "Texas oil man," and, when questioned, he admitted he gave Raft a $50,000 check in March 1958 for "two points" — percentage points — in the casino. He received no stock certificates, he said, but did get a copy of a letter from Raft to Dr. Belt stating that in the event of Raft's death, Certificate No. 30 should be transferred to Lowe. When Castro took over in 1959, Lowe added, he wrote off his fifty grand as lost and never asked Raft for the money.

Raft, still playing the tough guy, tried to brush it off. Yes, he had purchased shares in the Casino de Capri for Lowe since Lowe, for personal reasons, did not want to be publicly identified with a gambling casino — even a legal one. He then wrote the letter to Dr. Belt. When asked, he produced "Certificate No. 30," which proved to be for eight shares in the Maryland Reinsurance Company. But, according to Raft, it was all one and the same. Eight shares in Maryland equalled two "points" in the casino.

But since he had purchased the shares for Lowe, he, of course, didn't keep the money. He endorsed Lowe's check over to Maryland Reinsurance. Berkowitz, the casino treasurer, endorsed it again for Maryland Reinsurance, cashed it, and bought two $25,000 cashier's checks made payable to — George Raft.

To further complicate this rather typical example of international syndicate financial dealings, the cashier's checks were endorsed in turn by someone — investigators could only say "the signature does not appear to be that of George Raft" — and sold to a Cuban, Albert Alejo. Alejo, who was dealing in the black market in pesos, said he bought the cashier's checks for his father-in-law, Nicholas Sierra, whose name appeared beneath the unidentified endorser. The purpose was to enable Sierra and Alejo to get cash out of the country, which, in view of the impending fall of Batista, was a good idea. The casino, of course, could use pesos it bought in its operations and was willing to exchange American dollars for them, since the difference in the black-market price and the official exchange rate gave it a tidy profit. In this affair, however, it would appear that the Cubans got the better of the deal.

Unhappily for Raft's story, however, his 1961 tax return contradicted it. In that 1961 return he had reported a capital gain of $137,733.30 as his share of the sale of the Flamingo, Bugsy Siegel's old dream in Las Vegas. The sale was to a group headed by Miami Beach hotelmen Sam Cohen and Morris Lansburgh. Meyer Lansky received a $200,000 "finder's fee" for arranging — permitting would be a better word — the transaction. Eleven years later Cohen, Lansburgh, and Lansky would be indicted for failing to pay taxes on an alleged $36 million skimmed "off the top" from the Flamingo.

To offset his 1960 windfall, Raft reported on his return a loss of $25,000 on stock of "El Casino de Capri S.A." Raft's accountants explained that while Mr. Raft had fifty grand invested in the casino and lost it all when Castro came along, they decided to claim only half that amount as a loss since he had no evidence to prove he owned anything.

So, in effect, Raft was trying to deny he had owned any stock in the Capri while, at the same time, claiming a tax loss for it. Moreover, he has sworn to the Nevada Gaming Commission that he owned no interest in the Cuban casino. The possibility that the original tip was correct, that Raft conned Lowe into giving him $50,000, was considered a logical explanation. Still, it would be hard to prove. There were other allegations of tax evasion closer to home, and the probers moved on to them.

Raft, for example, had neglected to report payments of $7,500 made to him in 1958, 1959, 1960 and a bonus of $5,000 in 1961 for motion-picture rights to *The George Raft Story*. It was a lousy picture about a louse. Raft admitted he failed to report the income but claimed he was entitled to reduce the amount by the 10 percent of his agent's fee. Investigation revealed that the agent was paid separately by the studio. George, never giving up, then claimed the right to deduct a thousand-dollar lawyer's fee he paid to defend against a suit by author Dean Jennings, who had written the story. The suit was settled out of court for $2,000, and Raft wanted to claim that as well.

There was other income from various sources such as the Hercules Container Corporation, a distributor to the rubbish industry. Raft was president, but his job was "entertaining important customers." In 1963, for example, he received $13,000. Yet he claimed that the money was a loan and didn't report it. In the same year he received $14,050 from the Consumer's Mart of America, a chain of discount houses. The money was for "expenses," he said. A one-thousand-dollar deduction was claimed on the grounds that he paid that amount to actress Jayne Mansfield to appear with him at the opening of a store in Phoenix. There was also a matter of two pairs of "platinum cuff-links with sapphires" and a pair of "14K white gold cuff-links set with 50 diamonds." Allegedly they were given to Raft by the CMA, but he claimed he didn't get them. That was in 1960. On his income-tax return of 1961 he deducted $5,845 for a "theft loss not compensated by insurance – jewelry, etc., at residence." A similar claim totaling $6,810 was listed in 1963. Among the items of jewelry alleged stolen were some expensive cuff-links.

As investigators zeroed in on the fifty grand from the Capri, the mysterious death of Benjamin Berkowitz, treasurer of the casino, eliminated a vital witness. The syndicate had reason to believe that Berkowitz was not reliable. The affair that made it suspicious began in 1959 when Special Agent Richard Jaffee, an IRS intelligence-division ace, spotted the white Cadillac of Charles "the Blade" Tourine. It contained Tourine, a feared if illiterate Mafia figure, his son, and another man. Jaffee followed. Tourine got out at a syndicate-owned hotel off Miami's 79th Street causeway, but the Caddy went on across the causeway to a nearby bank. Tourine's son, known as Charles Delmonico, rented a safety-deposit box, using a $100 bill, and apparently stored a large sum of money in it.

Special Agent Jaffee, who had followed the men into the bank, had no legal excuse to do more. Later, however, when another agent mentioned he was trying to collect a delinquent tax account from Delmonico but couldn't find any assets, Jaffee remembered that safety-deposit box. The box was rented under an assumed name, Sam Kay, and had not Jaffee been alert that day no one would ever have identified the money therein with Tourine's son.

It took the agent an hour to serve a lien against the contents of the box. Before the formalities were completed, Delmonico's attorney called and asked what was going on. Told the lien was to collect $8,000 in delinquent taxes, he promised to bring in a certified check the next morning. And he did. Delmonico came too, and when all was settled he left in a hurry, went to the bank, and cleaned out the box. With him at the bank was Berkowitz. It was easy to assume Berkowitz had been the unidentified man with Delmonico when the box was rented, and it was also easy to assume that the cash in the box came from the Capri. In the next few weeks informants reported great concern in syndicate circles. How did the IRS know that "Sam Kay" was Delmonico? Had someone squealed?

Suspicion gradually centered on Berkowitz as Raft's former

associates came up with a theory that to them seemed logical. When Castro forced the Capri to close, Berkowitz, as treasurer, was responsible for getting the bankroll out of Cuba. Aware that Tourine was illiterate, Berkowitz allegedly used some of the funds in the box for personal investments. To conceal the loss — so went the theory — he tipped the IRS, hoping the box and its contents would be seized.

Berkowitz apparently convinced someone that this assumption was wrong, but question marks remained. And when the IRS, as part of Kennedy's coordinated war on crime, began questioning Raft's alleged sale to, or purchase for, Lowe, it was decided to take no chances. The body of the ex-treasurer of the Capri was found slumped at a desk in a plush office near the 79th Street causeway. Local police, who had a cooperative attitude toward vice, called it suicide. Berkowitz had been shot through the heart. With his death, and the subsequent death of Lowe from natural causes, the Capri item was dropped and the indictment of Raft made no mention of it.

In 1965 the steam had gone out of the organized-crime drive, and Raft was permitted to plead guilty to one count. On September 28 he came into court to be sentenced. Pale and shaking, the 70-year old "tough guy" cried with relief when a kindly federal judge refused to send him to prison or put him on probation. Instead, the actor was fined $2,500. Reporters followed Raft from the courtroom. When his tears ceased, he thanked those actors who had written letters to the judge extolling his sterling character. They included Red Skelton, Bob Hope, Jimmy Durante, Bing Crosby, and Lucille Ball. But Raft wasn't through. He added, "I especially want to thank Frank Sinatra, who was first to call me to say he would do anything in the world to help me."

One year later Raft was living in the swank Belton Towers in London. Each evening a liveried chauffeur would drive him in a limousine to Berkeley Square and "George Raft's Colony

Sporting Club," a major syndicate gambling casino to which thousands of American were flown in chartered "junket" flights. Raft owned no part of the club. His duties were those of a shill, as they had been in Havana. Briefly, however, he had regained the Hollywood style of living he had known in the glory days of Bugsy Siegel. Then, in 1967, the British began waking up to the realities of legalized gambling, and, in a belated effort to clean house, they declared Raft an "undesirable" and booted him out of the country.

Raft was reduced in the final years of his career to living off the income from a television commercial made for Alka-Seltzer. The scene is a prison mess hall, and an aging Raft, looking more battered than tough, is dressed in convict attire. The food gives him heartburn, and he begins pounding on the table. Other prisoners join in the protest, the noise grows deafening.

Somehow it all looks very natural.

11

Calling Dr. Semenenko

An industry such as show business needs and perhaps deserves a Serge Semenenko. Like many of Hollywood's moguls, he was born in Russia, where his family apparently accumulated considerable wealth before fleeing to Istanbul during the Russian Revolution. Serge graduated from two colleges in Turkey and was sent to Boston, where he obtained a master's degree from the Harvard Business School. Shortly thereafter, in 1926, at age twenty-three, he went to work with the First National Bank of Boston. Soon he achieved a certain autonomy and was reputed to be operating "a bank within a bank."

Semenenko also became something of a swinger long before the term became popular in corrupt Boston. As his wealth increased, he bought a home overlooking the Charles River, next door to one later owned by Edward Kennedy. He also had a "cottage" on Cape Cod, a winter home above the bay

at Acapulco, and a hotel suite in New York City. Two
months of each year were usually devoted to cruising the
Mediterranean in a chartered yacht. A jet-setter, he was as
likely to pop up unexpectedly in Paris or Tokyo as Las Vegas
or Hollywood.

According to the New York *Times*, Semenenko became
best known in financial circles as the "financial doctor of the
entertainment industry." In the process of curing his patients
he also made a lot of money for First National and a lot for
himself. Unlike most bankers, he never hesitated to make
major personal investments in the stocks of companies he was
lending his bank's money. Such investments, he was wont to
explain, were proof of his faith in the borrowers.

It was inevitable, of course, that in dealing with the entertainment industry Semenenko became acquainted with some
of the shadowy men in the background. One such was Louis
A. Chesler, the man who was to bring big-name entertainment and, of course, big-time gambling to the Bahamas as a
front for Meyer Lansky.

A Canadian, Chesler was a big man physically. Six feet tall,
he scaled more than three hundred pounds. Tight curls
covered his head, and his big mouth — if he had a fault it was
talking too much — could stretch into a friendly grin. By the
time he was thirty-three, in 1946, Chesler made a million in
the Canadian stock market. Deciding he needed a vacation,
he came to Miami Beach and in those wide-open days got
acquainted with a variety of gangsters from Trigger Mike
Coppola to Meyer Lansky. Someone passed along a hot tip to
Chesler — that Serge Semenenko was coming to the rescue of
a sick company, International Paper, and its stock would
soar. A compulsive gambler, Chesler invested heavily in International Paper, but before Dr. Semenenko's miracles began to
work Chesler was wiped out. Undiscouraged, he went back to
Canada and built a new fortune. The technique was the
classic one of buying a corporate shell that happened to have

some convertible assets, convert them and use the money to repeat the process. In this fashion Chesler ended up in control of three important corporations.

Universal Controls manufactured pari-mutuel machines used at horse and dog tracks for betting. As long as gambling remained popular there would be a demand for the product. General Development became a land-development company in Florida, build:ng new cities where swamplands had been and selling the h uses for $10 down and $10 a month. Seven Arts was a Canadian TV-production outfit which ultimately would gobble up Warner Brothers in Hollywood — with a lot of help from Serge Semenenko.

Needless to say, Lou Chesler cut in his gangster friends whenever he had a good thing going. As had been the case since Prohibition, they had plenty of cash to invest. Coppola, a Mafia gangster so notorious he was even barred from Las Vegas, was one of the big investors in General Development. Stock promotion was also a major part of the deal as every method known was used to push up the value of the stock after the insiders were aboard. General Development went from $3 a share in 1956 to more than $77 in a few months. Chesler was able to sell 250,000 shares to Gardner Cowles and still remain the largest stockholder. By 1959 his stock in General Developm nt alone was worth $50 million.

Max Orovitz, a Miami Beach businessman and civic leader, was associated wit' Chesler in General Development. Moreover, as part of tl so-called "Miami Group" he had built hotels in Israel. By no coincidence, Orovitz and Lansky were well acquainted. C esler was also on good terms with John Pullman, Lansky's international courier, and was a partner in a nightclub with Pullman's brother-in-law, A.C. Cowan. These and other relationships were to be important in the months to come.

The Seven Arts story began in 1958 when Globe Film Productions, Ltd., a Canadian company, made a deal with Seven

Arts. In exchange for 325,000 shares of Seven Arts stock, Globe gave Seven Arts the rights to distribute on Canadian television Popeye cartoons and some feature films. Four months later Chesler and his associates bought the Seven Arts stock from Globe and assumed control of the company.

Meanwhile, Lansky's plans to build a new empire in the Bahamas to replace the one crushed by Castro were proceeding as fast as certain obstacles permitted. Gambling was illegal in the Bahamas, but, thanks to Stafford Sands, a huge and powerful leader of the white minority known as the Bay Street Boys, machinery for granting "Certificate of Exemption" existed. Nevertheless, absolute silence was required in order to corrupt the necessary Bahamian officials and get a "certificate" issued. Needed was a front man who could in all logic proceed to build a luxury hotel which ultimately would house the casino.

The site of the hotel-casino would be Grand Bahama Island, a long, narrow sandbar covered with pine trees and little else. It had last known prosperity in Prohibition days when its beaches were piled high with cases of booze awaiting shipment by rumrunners to the United States. In 1955 control of the island had been largely given to Wallace Groves, an ex-convict from New York who planned to develop a "free port" on the island and establish a tax haven for American companies. Sands masterminded the deal, of course, and was well paid, but the project had come to the verge of ruin. Groves was willing to change his target from industry to tourists and cooperate willingly with anyone Lansky designated to build a resort hotel on his island.

Chesler was selected. On July 11, 1960, a new agreement between the Bahamian government and the Grand Bahama Port Authority, which was controlled by Groves, was signed. It trebled the size of the area given Groves and authorized him to sell for residential purpose land originally designated for industry. In return Groves's Port Authority agreed to build at least one first-class hotel of two hundred bedrooms by December 1, 1963. That was Chesler's job.

Money was needed. Chesler invested $5 million of Seven Arts' funds. From other companies he secured another $5 million. Still more was needed. Chesler got the funds by a complicated series of manipulations involving $15 million of 5½ percent convertible subordinated debentures issued by Seven Arts to a group headed by Chesler. The financial paper was used to secure a $3.5 million loan to Chesler from a Long Island bank. As it turned out, Seven Arts loaned the money to the bank to loan it to Chesler. Assisting behind the scenes was good old Dr. Semenenko of the First National Bank of Boston.

Chesler set up the Grand Bahama Development Company to handle the building of the hotel as well as to sell lots to thousands of Americans who would naturally want to live near a gambling casino. The company, called Devco, gave the Port Authority (Groves) 50 percent of its stock, with Seven Arts and other Chesler companies getting 41½ percent. Chesler kept only 8½ percent in his own name, yet so long as he could control Seven Arts and his other companies he could deal equally with Groves.

In the next three years roads were built, sewers installed, stores constructed, and, in short, the city of Freeport was created from the ground up on Grand Bahama. At the same time the Lucayan Beach Hotel was under construction on the shoreline. Plans for the hotel included a large space, 76 by 120 feet, which was labeled "Handball Court." Only a select few knew it was the future home of the casino.

As the building progressed, so did the corruption of the Bahamian government. And by March 1963, with a hundred factors juggled, the "Certificate of Exemption" was secretly approved. Gambling could now begin as soon as the hotel was completed. It was time for Stafford Sands to receive his *big* payoff, or one of them. And Sands, who as virtual director of the Bahamas had life and death powers over the casino, wanted $519,000 this time around. Much later it was established that Sands received *at least* one million dollars in all, and there was strong reason to believe the total was a half million more.

To get the cash, a telephone call was made to Semenenko in Boston and a formal letter written:

> First National Bank of Boston
> Milk Street
> Boston, Massachusetts
>
> Gentlemen:
>
> This will confirm our telephone request that you telegraph $519,900.00 to our account at Irving Trust Company, New York City, this day.
> This amount is to be charged to our regular account at your bank.
>
> Very truly yours,
>
> THE GRAND BAHAMA
> DEVELOPMENT COMPANY LIMITED
>
> (Signed) Louis Chesler
> (Signed) C. Gerald Goldsmith

The money was transferred to Irving Trust, and a letter was written authorizing it to be shifted to Sands' account there. Why was this method used? Much later, the Devco treasurer explained cryptically that First National "were payee and payer."

With Sands happily counting his cash and the "Certificate of Exemption" signed, it was time to convert that "Handball Court" into a casino. In his office Max Orovitz, that Miami

Beach civic servant, met with the architect, A. Herbert Mathes, and Chesler. Also present was Meyer Lansky, one of the few times Lansky surfaced during the entire affair. Designing a casino, determining the layout of the tables and security devices, required specialized knowledge, and of all experts in the field none was greater than Lansky. A second meeting followed — this time to select top casino personnel. Those chosen were trusted Lansky lieutenants who had worked for him either in Havana or in Las Vegas. Rank-and-file dealers were another matter. To give an impression of purity and to quiet opposition in the Bahamas, the "Certificate of Exemption" provided that all casino personnel except the supervisors should have been born in Western Europe and resided there for three years prior to their employment in the Bahamas. To meet this requirement Lansky arranged to have a number of Sicilians then working in a new casino on the Isle of Man in the Irish Sea transferred to Grand Bahama. And to provide for future needs as more casinos were built, a school was set up in London with Dino Cellini, a native of Steubenville, Ohio, in charge.

The "Grand Opening" of the casino came off on schedule, January 22, 1964. It was a glittering occasion, and, logically enough, it had more of a Palm Beach than Hollywood flavor. Jet-setters filled the hotel, free-loading in honor of the *S.S. Hope* Charity Ball, which had been transferred from the mainland for the occasion. Society columnists had a great time describing the clothes, the jewels, and the gay abandon of the cream of society, while saving a few adjectives for the casino, its painting of Queen Elizabeth, and its crystal chandeliers.

But lest anyone feel that show business was neglected, there were a number of beautiful and apparently unattached young ladies who had been flown in by helicopter to entertain any male thoughtless enough to come stag. Most of the girls were collected in the Miami area, where they were serving during the tourist season, but some were brought all the way from New York and Los Angeles. The emphasis, however, was on "European gambling" rather than the Vegas variety, and it would be several weeks before they dropped the pretense and moved in the one-armed bandits.

Helping to destroy illusions was a story next day in the Miami *Herald.* Reporter Jim Buchanan listed the operators of the casino by name, described their arrests records in the United States and their association with Lansky-controlled casinos in Las Vegas and Havana.

It was the first shock in a series which would ultimately cause sufficient stink to bring about the overthrow of the Bay Steet Boys and the formation of a "black" government under Premier Lynden O. Pindling. That change caused Lansky no distress. He had learned in Havana the folly of basing a gambling empire on the power of one man. In the Bahamas he planned that gambling would become as necessary to the economic life of the islands as it had become to the barren state of Nevada. Nevertheless, Lansky began a program to cut all obvious ties with anyone in the Bahamas. That meant, first of all, cheerful Lou Chesler. Chesler had served his purpose in attracting non-syndicate capital to the islands, and he had succeeded in building a casino. There was nothing left for him to do.

Chesler's power in Devco, the company controlling the company which controlled the casino, depended, it will be remembered, on his retaining control of Seven Arts, which held some 20 percent of Devco's stock. If Seven Arts decided to dump Chesler and sell its stock to Groves — who through the Port Authority already held 50 percent — then control would pass to Groves.

And that's exactly what happened.

Suddenly things began going sour for Chesler. He tried to borrow money from Semenenko's "bank within a bank" to buy enough Seven Arts stock to retain control of that company. Semenenko was not interested. But he was interested in lending money to dissident shareholders in Seven Arts to buy Chesler's holdings in the company. Whereupon Seven Arts put its Devco stock on the market. Chesler tried to find enough money to buy it all — for he needed all of it if he was to stay on equal terms with Groves. He got no help. Someone, and subsequent events leave no doubt It was Lansky, passed the word, and abruptly Chesler was a bad risk. Groves, the ex-convict, on the other hand, had no trouble buying enough of the Seven Arts Devco stock to get absolute control of Devco.

A board-of-directors meeting followed. Chesler was replaced as president of Devco. His directorship was handed to Max Orovitz, in whose Miami Beach office Lansky had designed the casino. Chesler was at Durham, N.C., at the time, trying Duke Hospital's famous "rice diet." When he came back to Grand Bahama he found he had been evicted from the hotel for non-payment of rent.

Years later when Steve Allen, a television funny man who, however, is quite serious about organized crime, was asked by the General Development Company to film a commercial for the land company, he remembered Chesler. Before accepting the assignment he submitted a list of pointed questions in writing. He was told in reply that "In 1963, General Development was completely reorganized with a new management. Mr. Louis A. Chesler resigned from the board of directors in December, 1965. In 1966, Mr. Chesler's interests in General Development ceased. From this point on, we have endeavored to build a corporation of the highest ideals."

With Chesler's departure from the stage, Lansky went on to put gambling in the Bahamas on the same broad base it enjoyed in Nevada. Gambling taxes became the chief source of revenue for a new government pledged to end centuries of neglect by building roads, schools, and sewer lines for the black majority. As in Nevada, it is a story without an ending. Only the beginning is clear.

Semenenko, the financial doctor of show business, who had

helped pay off Sands to start the Bahamian project and who had pulled the rug out from under Chesler when he became a liability, had more in store for Seven Arts. In 1967 he arranged for that little Canadian company to buy Jack L. Warner's stock in Warner Brothers for $32 million. Then Seven Arts and Warner Brothers merged. Semenenko made the deal possible by helping Seven Arts get a $19.5 million loan, with First National putting up $3.8 million of the total.

For his services in the various deals Semenenko received a $1 million "personal fee" from Warner Brothers for work done as vice-chairman of the First National Bank of Boston. When this fact became news some bank officials were a trifle disturbed. Serge had been pulling similar deals for years, but this was a little too much. On July 17, 1967, Semenenko resigned from the bank a year ahead of his scheduled retirement. Nevertheless, criticism continued, and on August 10 Semenenko agreed to return the one million bucks to the bank.

After the merger with Seven Arts Warner Brothers continued to be a football. It was taken over by Kinney National Services, Inc., which listed its value at $59 million for tax purposes. Kinney is an unusual company which started as a parking lot on Kinney Street in Newark, New Jersey, and diversified into funeral homes, building maintenance, banking, and other fields. It even became the owner of a company publishing *Mad* magazine. The executive vice-president and one of the biggest stockholders of Kinney is at the time of this writing a gentleman named Caesar P. Kimmel. His father, Emmanuel Kimmel, was a syndicate gambler who gave his son some parking lots and said, "See what you can do with them." It developed, however, that the older Kimmel had some ideas of his own. As his son told it: "My dad came to us with a business proposition to let limousines use our lots at night. I was so young and inexperienced. We had so little to gain and it left us open to trouble."

The limousines were carrying suckers from Manhattan to the syndicate-controlled casino that operated for many years in New Jersey. It was perhaps the original Riviera and became so famous the name was used in Las Vegas and Havana and points in between. The New Jersey Riviera featured some of the biggest names in show business during its long and illegal run: Durante, Sinatra, Raft, Joe E. Lewis, and the rest.

An official investigation confirmed the use of Kinney parking lots by the syndicate and cast a cloud over the company. Shortly after taking over Warner Brothers Caesar Kimmel made a public denial of what he said was "the charge that we are run by the Mafia." It just wasn't so, he repeated. As to his father, he commented: "To put it bluntly, I am not my father's keeper. He has his world — he was born about 1898 — and I have mine."

Times were changing. Even Serge Semenenko knew that.

According to my best recollection,
I don't remember.
—VINCENT ALO

12

Jimmy Blue Eyes
Lends a Hand

Vincent Alo, affectionately known to the underworld as "Jimmy Blue Eyes," was once asked what he thought of Joseph Valachi, the celebrated Mafia songbird. With characteristic modesty Alo replied; "I'm only a two-dollar bum and Valachi is dirt under *my* feet."

As a close associate of Meyer Lansky, Alo well knew the importance of taking the cash and letting someone else get the credit — or the publicity. Two years younger than Lansky, he grew up with him in New York and followed him to Florida. In the 1940s he was a junior partner in several of Lansky's casinos. Following the deportation of Joe Adonis in the 1950s Alo became the official liaison man between Lansky, as chairman of the board of the syndicate, and the Mafia. As such he fell heir to a small but plush casino, the

219

Sans Souci, in Havana. Once it had been owned by Lucky
Luciano — at the time Frank Sinatra visited Lucky with the
Fischetti brothers.

Small in comparison to those Lansky built later, the Sans
Souci was still quite famous. In April 1952 Senator Richard
M. Nixon and a friend, Dana C. Smith, visited the casino.
Smith paid for his gambling losses with a check. On returning
home he had second thoughts and stopped payment. Norman
"Roughhouse" Rothman, who was the casino manager,
threatened to sue, and it was necessary for Senator Nixon to
write to the State Department and ask it formally to intervene and stop the suit. Smith later achieved fame as the
organizer of the controversial "Nixon Fund" during the 1952
campaign.

Another dispute over gambling debts ended more happily
for the casino. Louis Chesler wandered in one night and
started shooting dice. He said later he told the dealer to stop
him when his losses hit ten grand. If so, the dealer did not
obey. Carried away by the excitement, Chesler kept going
until he was one hundred thousand in the hole. Blaming the
dealer for allegedly ignoring his instructions, Big Lou said he
would pay $10,000 and no more. Since Chesler was con-
sidered fairly important in syndicate circles, Roughhouse
treated him with respect. He told Lou to work it out with the
boss, Alo. Jimmy Blue Eyes in Hollywood, Florida, was reasonable — he offered to compromise at $75,000. Indignantly,
Chesler said he would pay ten or a hundred, but nothing in
between. He paid $100,000.

Testimony to Alo's and Lansky's wide-ranging interests was
given on December 4, 1956, when an investigator for the
New York State Crime Commission reported a meeting between the two men and George Wood, an official of the
William Morris Agency, which for generations had represented top stars of stage, screen, and nightclub. George
Wood, it will be remembered, was the employee assigned by
the agency to keep Frank Sinatra from slashing his wrists

when he was mooning over Ava Gardner. The purpose of the meeting in 1955 was to arrange for Alo, as a representative of the syndicate, to become a part owner of the talent agency.

The value of such ownership in controlling stars and pressuring studios cannot be overestimated. The entertainment star of the past had been largely dependent upon the whims of studio executives who could force a Jean Harlow to work when she was ill or suspend a Marilyn Monroe when she arrived late. Gradually, however, the star attained a measure of freedom when talent agencies signed up enough of his colleagues to be able to exert pressure on his behalf. Myron Selznick, son of movie pioneer Lewis Selznick, got the whole idea going, and part of his motivation was to revenge himself on the Hollywood which had driven his father into bankruptcy. By the middle of the 1930s his list of stars included Billie Burke, Richard Arlen, Ruth Chatterton, Fred Astaire, Constance Cummings, Charles Bickford, Kay Francis, Gary Cooper, Helen Hayes, Jackie Cooper, Katherine Hepburn, Henry Fonda, Miriam Hopkins, Cedric Hardwicke, Carole Lombard, Boris Karloff, Myrna Loy, Ida Lupino, Charles Laughton, Merle Oberon, Maureen O'Sullivan, Victor McLaglen, Fredric March, Pat O'Brien, Ginger Rogers, Fay Wray, Laurence Olivier, Lupe Velez, William Powell, and George Raft.

Inevitably, just as the mob moved in on the studios, on the unions, and on the stars, it also sought to control the talent agencies. By determining which actor played what part, and by controlling nightclub appearances in Las Vegas and elsewhere, the crime syndicate could make or break stars as it wished. Control of an agency was but another weapon in the continuing effort to dominate the entertainment industry, but it was an effective one. The William Morris Agency continues today to be a leading representative of talent. Mark Spitz, the handsome American who won seven gold medals at the 1972 Olympic Games, signed up with the William Morris Agency almost before he got out of his swimsuit. So the

glimpse into the behind-the-scenes activity provided by
Jimmy Blue Eyes is rare indeed. Among other things we learn
that the William Morris Agency heard that Cameca, a sub-
sidiary of a large French electronics firm, had developed an
interesting new device called "Scopitone." It was a jukebox
with movies, having a screen capable of showing any of
thirty-six color films of 210 seconds' duration every time a
quarter was inserted in a slot.

Some fifteen years had passed since Lansky, Dalitz,
Costello, Zwillman, and the rest had created Consolidated
Television in the belief that bars and taverns — not home-
owners — would be the big buyers of television sets. As
Lansky admitted, they had been thinking in terms of jukeboxes which had developed into an industry largely dominated by the syndicate. They had been wrong then, as
Lansky also admitted, but they had continued to seek a
device to get TV viewers away from their homes and down to
the local taverns. And when Wood told Alo about Scopitone,
he hustled over for a look at one of the machines William
Morris had managed to obtain in France.

Some years later the Securities and Exchange Commission
sought information on some of the complicated stock deals
centering around Scopitone and asked Alo about them. He
proved very evasive — a fact that ultimately caused him to
go to prison briefly — but he left no doubt about his "friendship" with Wood. The "Q and A" went like this:

Q: Where did you first see the machine?
A: William Morris office.
Q: Which office of the William Morris Agency?
A: New York City.
Q: Who was present when you saw this machine in the
    William Morris Agency?
A: Well, I had a friend at William Morris and he asked me to
    look at it.
Q: Would you identify that friend?

A: George Wood.

Q: Why did you think Mr. Wood thought you might be interested?

A: He was a personal friend of mine and he was very enthusiastic about this machine, and he asked me if I wanted to do anything about it, and I turned him down and never spoke about it again.

That Alo was lying about never having spoken of Scopitone again the record makes clear. One of those to whom he spoke was Alvin Ira Malnik, the young Miami Beach attorney previously mentioned as the author of a rhyming telegram to Sam Ford Fishbine which mentioned a "house on the hill."

Alo was impressed with Malnik, who gave promise of rising high in the world of international deals. Malnik had helped create the "Bank of World Commerce" in Nassau, which was used by the syndicate to "dry-clean" money without sending it all the way to Swiss banks. In Las Vegas he became chummy with such personalities as George Raft, who presented him with — what else? — an expensive set of cuff links. Malnik was also on good terms with John Pullman, Lansky's representative in Switzerland, and other syndicate figures such as Al Mones and Ed Levinson. But it was Jimmy Blue Eyes who remained his special friend, so much so that some cynical gangsters referred to Alo as "Malnik's new rabbi."

Malnik got the job of pushing through the Scopitone project. Success was signaled on October 22, 1963, when a jubilant Malnik sent this telegram to a friend in London: DEAL CLOSED FUNDS REC'D WILL FWD THIS DAY. HALLELUJAH REGARDS.

The American rights to Scopitone were then sold to Tel-A-Sign, Inc., a Chicago manufacturer of plastic electric signs. The 1964 sale was profitable. Malnik alone got stock in his name worth $2,060,437, and others in his "group" received equally large amounts. Mrs. Lois Wood, widow of George Wood, was cut in for stock worth $20,625. Her husband had died in November 1963, following Malnik's success in acquiring the American rights. The agency where Wood had worked so long and risen to the position of vice-president was not neglected either. It was to receive a "finder's fee" amounting to 10 percent of the costs of films prepared by Scopitone, Inc., for use in the machines and 10 percent of the revenue from advertising carried on such films. A lot of years had passed since Moe Dalitz consulted with Robert Goldstein of Universal Pictures about making "soundies" for use on tavern television, but the principle was the same.

Not everyone was satisfied with the proceeds of the split when Scopitone, Inc., sold out to Tel-A-Sign. One dissident was Alfred Miniaci, who had dined with Frank Costello the night someone blasted Frank back in 1957. With three others, Miniaci threatened to make trouble for Malnik, who they considered something of a young upstart. To save the situation Malnik called upon Jimmy Blue Eyes, who had two meetings with Miniaci and his friends at the Warwick Hotel in New York. Apparently Alo was convincing, for the rebel group settled for a lot less than they had demanded. When Alo suffered a memory lapse in court and could remember nothing about what he said to the four men, he was indicted on obstruction-of-justice charges and sent to prison. Assistant Attorney General Gary Naftalis told the presiding judge that "Alo is considered one of the most significant organized crime figures in the United States. He is closely associated with Meyer Lansky, who is the apex of organized crime."

Not bad for a "two-dollar bum."

13

The Wonderful Wizard

July 2, 1969, and everything was ready for the grand opening of Las Vegas' latest refinement of Bugsy Siegel's dream — the International Hotel. A last-day crisis had threatened to dampen the happy excitement. The largest swimming pool in the state, containing 350,000 gallons of water, had leaked into the largest casino in the world. But the pool had been drained, the water mopped up, and the 850 slot machines remained in perfect working order. To assure heavy action in the casino, hundreds of suckers had been flown in from all parts of the country. For them everything was "comped" — complimentary — except the chips at the tables.

Heading the entertainment was Barbra Streisand, who had been given a $250,000-a-week contract for a four-week run. Publicity flacks said that made her the highest-paid performer in entertainment history. Cary Grant was master of ceremonies. Celebrities ranged from Natalie Wood to Wilt "the

Stilt" Chamberlain. Drinks in the Showroom were five dollars each.

Kirk Kerkorian, a tanned, athletic son of an Armenian fruit peddler, was introduced by Grant "as the guy who's made this spectacular hotel possible." An eighth-grade dropout — he quit to go to work — and former used-car dealer, Kerkorian had come a long way fast since starting his own airline in 1947 with one well-used plane. But 1947 was the year Bugsy Siegel opened the Flamingo in Las Vegas, and there were plenty of suckers who preferred flying over Death Valley to driving through it. Kerkorian's airline prospered.

Shift the scene, however, from the glittering thirty-story, $60 million International Hotel to a small hearing room at 14 Vesey Street, New York City. The Joint Legislative Committee on Crime is meeting and the witness is Charles "the Blade" Tourine. The aging Mafia leader testifies he keeps his money in a can "under the bricks" where the "rats can't get it." On a December day in 1969 Tourine is asked:

Q: Do you know a person by the name of Kerkorian?
A: Yes.
Q: How long have you known Mr. Kerkorian?
A: Several years.
Q: When you say several years, about how far back would that go?
A: Fifteen years.
Q: Have you ever received money from Mr. Kerkorian?
A: No, I have not.
Q: Have you ever given money to Mr. Kerkorian?
A: No, sir.
Q: Have you ever received money from a person named George Raft which came from Mr. Kerkorian?
A: No, sir.
Q: Have you ever given money to George Raft?
A: George Raft received money from the casino in Havana, Cuba, which I was the manager of.

On January 16, 1970, a month later, Tourine was recalled. This time he brought along an attorney, and in response to all questions he claimed the privilege of the Fifth Amendment. The questions began with Kerkorian: "Have you ever received a check in excess of $20,000 from a person named Kirk Kerkorian?"

When the angry gangster refused to answer on the grounds that to do so might incriminate him, a tape recording of a telephone conversation between Tourine and Kerkorian was played.

The tape was said to contain the conversation when Tourine called Kerkorian at his home in Beverly Hills on October 5, 1961. The conversation indicated that Kerkorian was sending Tourine a check for $21,300, by George Raft, and he didn't want Tourine's name on it as endorser because there was "a lot of heat around." (The Robert Kennedy war on crime was getting in high gear at that time.) Tourine assured Kerkorian, according to the tape, that he could have the check cashed without his endorsement appearing on it.

While Tourine steadfastly refused to answer any questions about the recorded conversation — one of several played that day — Kerkorian in Los Angeles issued a denial that he had ever associated with underworld figures. He did not volunteer, however, to appear in person and answer questions under oath. The New York committee, of course, couldn't subpoena him outside the state.

Some twenty months later the Joint Legislative Committee held another session on Vesey Street. This time the witness was Harold Roth, former head of Continental Vending Machine Corporation and an ex-convict. Describing himself as a good friend of Charles the Blade, Roth said Tourine introduced him to Kerkorian "about twelve years ago." A meeting was held at Tourine's plush apartment at 40 Central Park South. The purpose of the meeting, Roth continued, was to arrange for a company controlled by Roth to finance the purchase by Kerkorian of a DC-8, a plane valued at $8 million.

The deal didn't come off, Roth said, and added that Tourine had described Kerkorian "as a very good friend of his."

In Las Vegas, a spokesman for Kerkorian repeated that his boss had never associated with underworld figures. And there the matter rested.

Kerkorian, however, was only getting his second wind. In 1968 he sold his airline to Transamerica Corporation for $78 million after taxes. He then borrowed $73 million unsecured from the Bank of America. With a combined bankroll he picked up the Bonanza, a bankrupt casino in downtown Las Vegas, some forty acres of land where soon a hamburger chain called Lum's would build Caesar's Palace and the good old Flamingo from which Meyer Lansky had skimmed an officially estimated $36 million during the years Siegel's monument was owned by Morris Lansburgh and Sam Cohen. Kerkorian had enough left to build the International Hotel and combine it with the Flamingo to form International Leisure Corporation.

Stock in International Leisure shot up from an opening price of $12 a share to $66.50, enabling Kerkorian to use about one-third of his shares as collateral for a $72 million loan from two European banks. And with that cash in his pocket he proceeded to buy control of Metro-Goldwyn-Mayer, Louis B. Mayer's former domain.

The Nixon recession of 1970 and the falling stock market created some problems for Kerkorian. He had planned a secondary offer of International Leisure stock to raise needed cash, but the Securities and Exchange Commission blocked the move because Kerkorian could not produce the required three-year financial statement for the Flamingo. The previous owners, Lansburgh and Cohen, had refused to supply it. Kerkorian said he was puzzled; he thought the two were "the most honest men in America." Some months later both were indicted along with Lansky for failing to pay taxes on the money they allegedly skimmed from the Flamingo.

Somehow Kerkorian kept climbing. MGM became an important tool. That Las Vegas casinos controlled Hollywood had been suspected by many, but Kerkorian brought it into the open. If anyone had doubts, he soon resolved them when he began selling MGM's assets — everything from its London studio, which fetched $4.3 million, to the magic shoes of Dorothy, worn by Judy Garland in *The Wizard of Oz*. Each shoe brought $7,500. And what did Kerkorian intend to do with the money? MGM would build a huge new hotel-casino in Las Vegas and three gambling ships to cruise the seas.

In late 1972 the *Wall Street Journal* carried a little story which told it all. The story began:

> CARSON CITY, NEV. — The Nevada Gaming Control Board recommended approval of a $90 million financing package by Metro-Goldwyn-Mayer, Inc. to build the 2,000-room Grand Hotel in Las Vegas. . . .

Earlier, Kerkorian had been blunt. "We are not going to look to movies for the bulk of MGM's profits anymore," he said.

The Grand Hotel and Casino was to be built on twenty-six acres of land purchased from Moe Dalitz for $1.8 million. Doing business with the old rumrunner and syndicate leader apparently didn't bother Kerkorian. He asked, "What's wrong with Moe?"

14

Up the Hill
with Sid and Jill

Jill St. John, born Jill Oppenheim in 1941, was a late-bloomer on the Hollywood scene, but her beauty and intelligence have given her active associations that effectively make her a bridge between the sordid past and the sophisticated future.

The daughter of a Beverly Hills restauranteur, Jill began toddling in a town where almost every mother remembered the success of Shirley Temple and was certain their own little darling could duplicate it. At five Jill was performing in a little-theater production of *Pigtails*. A year later she was starring on the *Red Rider* radio serial and, according to her press agents, standing on a box in order to reach the microphone. By age seven she had graduated to that long-running soap opera *One Man's Family,* and there she stayed for six years. Between shows she modeled children's clothes.

When Jill was eleven her mother changed the budding starlet's name to St. John, because it was "musical" and would fit better on a theater marquee. Other preparations for the future included plastic surgery to reduce the size of her nose. Nothing more was needed, for her body was reaching the right size in the most pleasing proportions. In fact *Time* was later to comment on her auburn hair, sparkling brown eyes, and "gothic chest."

In the pattern of previous sex queens, Jean Harlow and Marilyn Monroe, Jill sought escape by an early marriage. Unlike the others, however, she displayed a certain maturity of judgment in her choice — Neil Dubin, the heir to a laundry fortune. Jill was only sixteen and lied about her age to the justice of peace who married them. "I wanted to get away," she said. Although the marriage ended in divorce a year later, the young couple had lived together for only a month. "I realized I had made a bad mistake," said Jill.

Two years after her divorce she tried again. And once more, finance was at least as important as romance. Her second husband was Lance Reventlow, described as a "millionaire playboy," the sole child born to Woolworth heiress Barbara Hutton in seven marriages. The now nineteen-year old Jill set up housekeeping in a $350,000 home in Beverly Hills. Given to Lance by his mother on his twenty-first birthday, it was located high above Sunset Boulevard. Its most notable feature was the indoor-outdoor swimming pool which ran from deep inside the living room out onto a wide patio.

While Lance played with his Scarab, a Grand Prix racing car he had spent a large fortune developing, Jill fed the wild animals on the three-acre estate, rode her horses, and shopped for clothes. "I love to spend money," she once told an interviewer. "It's fun." Eventually even the pleasures of unlimited charge accounts were insufficient compensation for a girl with an IQ of 162. Nineteen months of this marriage was enough. She moved out. Later, in an uncontested hearing, she was awarded a $100,000 settlement.

Two men were primarily responsible for Jill's decision to quit marriage and resume her career: Frank Sinatra and Sidney Korshak.

Sinatra was the man out front, the lightning rod to attract publicity. He co-starred with Jill in the movie *Come Blow Your Horn* and became her close friend and escort. As usual there was much talk of marriage, but apparently both parties decided there was no need to tie each other down. Yet Jill, as one of Sinatra's girlfriends, was automatically entitled to inner-circle privileges. As she once put it, "Fortunately, all Frank's friends happen to be very influential." Less conspicuous than Frank but very much behind the scenes was Korshak, a man of even greater influence who had been around much longer.

Sidney Korshak is a mystery man. Not too much of his background has reached the public record. He apparently was born about 1907 and grew up on the West Side of Chicago. Charles "Cherry Nose" Gioe told the Kefauver Committee in 1950 he had known Korshak "maybe sixteen or seventeen years." When asked how he met the lawyer, Gioe replied, "Through some fellows on the West Side when he opened his office. He had just finished school and opened an office, I believe, at that time."

"What fellows?"

"Oh, some kids he knew around there that I just happened to know. It was just a casual acquaintance at the time when I met him."

Gioe knew a lot of people. He went to school with Tony Accardo — a modern successor to Al Capone — and even had the honor of once being arrested with him. They were charged with concealing the weapons they allegedly were carrying. Gioe also was arrested with "Machinegun Jack" McGurn, the Chicago killer who ordered Joe E. Lewis' throat cut back in the Twenties. But Cherry Nose didn't really know McGurn very well. He was "just riding with him" when the

cops picked them up. Gioe admitted he had done a little
bootlegging in his time and said he had been in a handbook
business.

At the time Gioe was questioned he owned an interest in
Chicago's Seneca Hotel, at 200 East Chestnut Street. His
partner was Alex Greenberg, who got acquainted with Frank
"the Enforcer" Nitti because Frank was a good barber. Both
Gioe and Greenberg lived at the Seneca in 1950 and so did
Sidney Korshak, By then they all were good friends. Yet the
lawyer and the gangster had more in common than residence
at the same hotel.

Gioe, it will be remembered, was one of those gangsters
involved with Willie Bioff in the Movie Extortion Plot. Along
with Nitti and some others, he had been indicted after Bioff
squealed. Nitti had killed himself, but Gioe had gone to
prison.

And what was Attorney Korshak doing at the time? An
official fifty-five-page report by two special agents of IRS
Intelligence, dated July 25, 1942, gives an answer in the
course of a thorough review of the then still developing
investigation. It notes:

> Our informers have stated that Sidney Korshak, a
> lawyer in Chicago, Illinois, is often delegated to represent
> the Chicago gang, usually in some secret capacity. Since
> the conviction of Browne and Bioff on charges of racket-
> eering, Korshak acts as Browne's attorney. He paid
> Browne's $10,000 fine and we are reliably informed that
> the gang, and not Browne, produced that money.

This, of course, was before Bioff and Browne talked, and it
was good policy to provide them with an attorney and pay
their fines. The memo continues:

> John Smith testified that about one year and a half ago,
> Frank Olsen telephoned him that George Browne had

expressed the opinion that Local 110 should employ an attorney. Korshak subsequently appeared on the scene. Smith states that he was not employed or paid any money. He [Smith] did testify, however, with respect to the election of union officials on March 4, 1942:

Q: How much money did you draw to pay off the policemen?

A: About $1,000; made out a check for them.

Q: Made it out to cash?

A: I don't know whether Pete cashed the check or I cashed the check.

Q: Did the police get the entire $1,000?

A: Yes.

Q: Was Sidney Korshak in the picture?

A: Well, he asked me if I want protection and I said No. At that time he thought I was going to hire him as attorney for the local and since there is trouble here I don't want no part of Korshak.

On August 28, 1942, another memo by IRS Special Agent A. P. Madden made mention of Alex Greenberg, Gioe's partner in the Seneca:

Alex Greenberg has commonly been regarded as the "fiscal agent" for the Capone group. He formerly operated a business known as the Roosevelt Finance Company. Some years ago, in the midst of the Capone investigation, an effort was made to examine the records of that company. The examination had barely gotten under way when the records disappeared over night. Interrogations of Greenberg and others, before the grand jury and elsewhere, failed to produce the records. Greenberg stated that they had been taken in a robbery and, while no one representing the Government believed him, they were never found.

The following year, when the Chicago gangsters came to trial, Bioff testified that it was Cherry Nose Gioe who introduced him to Korshak in 1939. According to Willie, Gioe laid it on the line in these words: "Sidney is our man and I want you to do what he tells you. . . Any message he may deliver to you is a message from us." To help Gioe win his parole as quickly as he was eligible, Korshak persuaded Harry A. Ash, Illinois superintendent of crime prevention, to write a favorable letter to the federal parole board on behalf of Cherry Nose.

Old associations are sometimes hard to shake. In 1962, three decades after Willie Bioff set up a soup kitchen in Chicago, Korshak became part of a consortium to bid on the parking franchise at the new home of the Los Angeles Dodgers. Associated in the deal was Ben Teitelbaum, a Hollywood film supplier. Five years later, in 1968, Teitelbaum was one of several men convicted of crooked and illegal gambling at the Friars Club in Los Angeles. One of the other men convicted was John Roselli, who had gone to prison with Gioe and the rest in the movie extortion case.

As previously noted, Bioff died when his booby-trapped car blew up in Phoenix, Arizona, in 1955. Gioe's body was found stuffed in a car trunk in 1953, and Greenberg was burned down with four bullets in 1955. But Korshak survived and prospered.

Somehow out of the Bioff—Browne era and the bloody excesses of Chicago gangsters, Korshak emerged as a suave, sophisticated "consultant" — numbering among his clients all sorts of people, from movie stars to union executives. As counsel for a talent agency, Associated Booking Corporation, Korshak personally represented many top stars in their dealings with Las Vegas hotel-casinos and other institutions with mob connections. It was Korshak who arranged a $1 million contract for the nightclub debut of Debbie Reynolds in Las Vegas. He was helpful to Barbra Streisand and to such Sinatra pals as Dean Martin. But prior to Jill St. John he was perhaps most famous for his assistance to Dinah Shore.

Dinah once described Korshak as "a friendly man, sweet and sort of shy," with the irritating habit of getting telephone calls at parties and "disappearing" for the evening. Dinah was partly responsible for some information about Korshak's income becoming public knowledge. It seems Sidney listed $5,612 allegedly spent on her 1963 wedding as a business expense. In 1971 the IRS sought to collect an additional $149,153 in taxes and penalties for the four years from 1963 through 1966 on the grounds the Korshaks had improperly deducted $38,767 for travel and entertainment, $64,686 for use of their twelve-room home as "branch office," and $8,510 as business gifts. Even with these deductions their net taxable income listed averaged about a half million dollars a year for the period.

While his associations with Dinah Shore may have been more publicized, Korshak's arrangements with Jill St. John have capitalized on her brain as well as her body. While starring in a series of "dumb broad" movies, she has been involved by Korshak in multimillion-dollar financial deals so complicated only a Meyer Lansky could easily understand them. A key individual in many of these deals is another figure from Chicago, Delbert W. Coleman.

The Seeburg Corporation, founded in 1902, was for many years an exception to the rule that gangsters dominated any business involving coin-operated machines. As late as 1954 Seeburg was given a clean bill of health by Virgil Peterson, head of the Chicago Crime Commission. Two years later Coleman became chairman of the board. Exclusive distribution rights to Seeburg's "jukeboxes" was granted to Worldwide Distributors, Inc.

Insight into the manner in which Coleman got control of Seeburg came from Robert Sunshine, a Denver attorney.

Forced to embezzle to pay back "black money" taken "off the top" at the Desert Inn, Sunshine talked to federal officials before going to prison. Among other things he disclosed that the syndicate invested "considerable" black money in the Seeburg Corporation. And when the new management, headed by Coleman, apparently encountered opposition, it brought in George Gordon, a veteran syndicate courier and enforcer, to straighten things out. Korshak, an old friend of Coleman, was labor consultant to Seeburg during this period.

Delbert W. Coleman, of course, had no intention of sticking with this company and developing it over a period of years. Like other modern money men who wheel and deal in this age of conglomerates, he wanted in and out. A proposed merger with General Time was almost achieved early in 1968, but the larger company investigated Coleman's past and backed out at the last minute. Later that year, however, Coleman and a partner sold their stock in Seeburg to Commonwealth-United, a company largely financed by Bernie Cornfeld's Investors Overseas Service. Commonwealth-United then tried to buy control of Warner Brothers but lost out to Kinney National. Left with millions in cash to play with as a result of his sale of Seeburg stock, Coleman looked about for a new project.

In late October 1968 Coleman found just what he wanted: Parvin—Dohrmann, Inc. The first president of Parvin—Dohrmann was Albert Parvin, the man who briefly owned the Flamingo in Las Vegas before selling it to Sam Cohen and Morris Lansburgh. In lieu of Siegel's monument, he secured for Parvin—Dohrmann the Fremont and the Aladdin in downtown Las Vegas. But Parvin was willing to sell out, the more so since the Fremont manager, Edward Torres, and the previous owner, Ed Levinson, had been indicted on "skimming" charges. There was much bad publicity when they beat the rap by charging the FBI had illegally "bugged" the casino executive suite.

So Coleman and Korshak put together a deal to buy 300,000 shares of Parvin—Dohrmann and thus obtain effective control. Associated with them were a rather typical group of investors: Allen & Company, a New York investment firm which poured millions into the development of the casino on Grand Bahama; the Fund of Funds, one of many companies formed by Bernie Cornfeld as part of the IOS complex, which had purchased a huge piece of Resorts International, operators of the Paradise Island Casino at Nassau; the Stephen Leedom Carpet Company, owned by Gerald Saul and Nathan Herzfeld; and Jill St. John. The stock was purchased for $35 a share. Seven months later it was selling at $141 a share. The Securities and Exchange Commission suspected a little stock manipulation and began an investigation.

Coleman took over as chairman of the board on January 10, 1969. Thirteen days later, with Korshak pulling the strings, Parvin—Dohrmann bought the Stardust Hotel and Casino in Las Vegas from the Cleveland syndicate headed by Moe Dalitz. The Stardust, it will be remembered, was begun by Tony Cornero, the gambling-ship operator, and finished by Jake "the Barber" Factor. On completion the casino was taken over by the Cleveland group. But in 1969, having sold the Desert Inn to Howard Hughes, the old rumrunners from Lake Erie were cashing in their chips. They knew Coleman, of course, having allowed Ruby Kolod and George Gordon to assist him in getting control of Seeburg. And Korshak was an old friend. Back when Dalitz and Company took over the Riviera in Las Vegas on an unofficial basis, after the murders of Willie Bioff and Gus Greenbaum, Korshak had arranged for Dinah Shore to make her Las Vegas debut there.

(Dalitz, it should be noted, was not ready to retire when he sold his official interests in his Las Vegas casinos. Not only did he continue to serve as a consultant to the Howard Hughes organization in gaming matters, but he was the principal investor in the fantastic La Costa Country Club near

San Diego. Financed with Teamster pension funds, La Costa surpasses Las Vegas in magnificence and is the social head-quarters of the syndicate on the West Coast.)

Just before Parvin–Dohrmann stock reached its peak, the Nevada Gaming Control Board made a belated discovery like the one in 1958 which enabled Moe Dalitz and his Cleveland friends to pull out of the Nacional in Cuba without alarming anyone. The board ruled that the IOS company, the Fund of Funds, had to sell its 81,000 shares of Parvin–Dohrmann stock because it also owned stock in Resorts International in the Bahamas. The forced sale brought a $4,450,000 profit without disturbing in the slightest the upward climb of Parvin–Dohrmann stock.

Meanwhile the Securities and Exchange investigation had begun. In May 1969, when the SEC suspended Parvin–Dohrmann, Korshak rushed into the fray. The SEC later charged he persuaded Coleman to hire Nathan Voloshen – a Washington "fixer" – for $50,000. Voloshen tried, using Martin Sweig, the principal aide to House Speaker John McCormick, to get the suspension lifted. Both Voloshen and Sweig were convicted on influence-peddling charges the following year and sent to prison. Speaker McCormick, who denied knowing what his aide was up to, retired.

The suspension in trading was lifted after a week, although the SEC denied that Voloshen had anything to do with it. The boom was over, however, and the stock started moving down as fast as it had gone up. When it reached $65 a share, the SEC suspended trading again and this time filed formal charges of manipulation.

Before the second SEC suspension, however, there had been another amazing development. Korshak had worked out a deal to merge Parvin–Dohrmann with Denny's Restaurants, a chain of small franchised eat-and-run type spots. Abruptly Harold Butler, president of Denny's, canceled the merger and announced he personally had bought out the holdings of five of the company's stockholders: Korshak; his brother, Marshall, city treasurer of Chicago; the carpet company; Edward Torres, the Las Vegas gambler and former partner of Bobby Baker; and Jill St. John.

Although the stock was selling at only $96.75 on the day of the announcement and was obviously heading for the basement, Butler said he would pay $150 a share to the favored group. This worked out to a neat profit of $10,120,000 for the favored five — or at least for the people they represented

This fascinating deal formed the basis of one of five charges the SEC brought in connection with the second suspension. Others included the allegation that Coleman had failed to disclose the payments of various fees. It specified the one to Voloshen and a $500,000 payment to Sidney Korshak for his help in purchasing the Stardust for $15 million. In the end, the SEC action amounted to locking the barn door after the horse had been stolen. It produced a "consent injunction" forbidding all concerned to continue violating the securities laws. Early in 1970 Coleman resigned, and new management took over Parvin–Dohrmann.

It was the old pattern: get in, make a killing, get out, move on.

Jill St. John, following her divorce from Lance Reventlow, was presented as "Hollywood's Carefree Child." Stories had her playing with toy railroad trains, riding elephants, and swimming with porpoises. The theory behind this frantic activity was said to be her desire to enjoy the childhood she never had. Those days, if they ever existed outside a PR man's imagination, are long gone. Today the still curvy redhead is one of Hollywood's richest women, thanks to her friendship with Sidney Korshak. If she plays today, it is not with toys or animals but with real railroads, resort hotels, and a chain of jewelry-boutique shops.

A businesswoman Jill may be, but a woman she still is too.

Her combination of brains and beauty enabled her in 1972 to visit the California White House on the arm of Henry Kissinger, President Nixon's confidential agent in international intrigue.

Considered a "swinger" as well as an intellectual, Kissinger and St. John were as perfectly matched as vodka and caviar. So what if some of her associates were friends of gangsters?

After dating Jill, Kissinger was also looking ahead. Asked about his post-government plans, he smiled and commented, "I'm thinking of going into the movies. I've got the connections now."

Which may very well be the understatement of show-business history.

Afterword

The history of the gangster in show business teaches one the value of entertainers in those other worlds where their names are not the ones in lights.

In the beginning, the bootlegger enjoyed nightclub stars because they enjoyed the nightclubs the bootleggers owned — the clubs were places to throw around easily earned cash, to play the big shot, to enjoy the entertainment. The more astute soon recognized there was economic profit in owning both the clubs and the stars who performed in them — a way, in other words, to combine pleasure with business. Similarly the movies were first a toy, a means of gratifying the ego. Soon the businessmen of the developing syndicate saw the vast potential for profit. Every method that came to hand was used to control the studios, the theaters, the stars. By the time Las Vegas and plush regional gambling centers came along, the star had become largely a shill for gangsters. And at mid-century Las Vegas was the capital of organized crime *and* of show business.

Las Vegas had survived repeated scandals and economic recessions. In the summer of 1972 the suckers were standing in line to see the high-priced "name" drawing cards: Elvis Presley, Liberace, Englebert Humperdinck, Sammy Davis, Jr.,

Perry Como, Andy Williams, Barbra Streisand, Don Rickles, Debbie Reynolds, Johnny Carson, and Rowan and Martin. The gambling handle for the year was up 17.2 percent above 1971, and 1971 had been 10 percent above 1970. The city had grown to 300,000 permanent residents, almost all of them dependent one way or another upon gambling. The tourist population was estimated at eighteen million per year, most of them traveling on the 250 airline flights daily. In every major city the syndicate had "junket organizers" whose duty it was to arrange chartered flights of high-rollers and to collect gambling debts. And John Reible of the Las Vegas News Bureau issued the same old statement in 1972 that had been put forth regularly since the murder of Bugsy Siegel: "The skimming scandals are behind us. Gamblers and tourist alike feel that they are getting a fair shake now. Some people, though, miss the aura of the criminal element."

Since the gangster owners of some Las Vegas casinos were patterning themselves after so-called legitimate businessmen – and vice versa – it isn't surprising that eventually the show-business personality should become a leverage for political influence. The Watergate scandal has brought home the realization that the cowboy with the white hat may be just as big a crook as the villain in the black hat. But Watergate is, in fact, a logical development. It flows naturally from individual actions which have gone largely unheeded and unreported. Why is it surprising that ex-FBI agents should use electronic devices illegally when for a decade the FBI had engaged in a massive illegal campaign of electronic snooping against gangsters, newspaper reporters, and liberals? Why should anyone be astonished to learn that ex-CIA agents violated the law when for decades the CIA allied itself with gangsters and followers of Caribbean dictators in a no-holds-barred battle against Red spies and Rad-Libs? And lastly, why should it shock anyone to learn that corrupt businessmen contributed millions to help re-elect a politician known since his career began as "Tricky Dick"? Only naive people who allow their choice for high office to be influenced by such astute political observers as Shirley Temple Black, John Wayne, Ronald Reagan, and Frank Sinatra would be bewildered by Watergate. Unfortunately, a majority of Americans were in that group.

Much of show business had been thoroughly corrupted over the decades by organized crime and its allies — those businessmen who believe that money and power are the twin goals of free enterprise and that the freer one is with his enterprise the more of both he will achieve. Show business isn't unique in being corrupted, but show business has been a key conquest of the fast-buck boys. Not only did it influence the way the public dressed, the way the public talked, the way women shaved their eyebrows, but it proved a bland, unrealistic concept of life itself. Put bluntly, show business helped create the illusions which blinded Americans as to what was really happening and why.

While there are exceptions to the rule, the men and women of show business have as a class deliberately denied their additional roles as human beings and citizens. For themselves they have claimed the extra-legal, extra-moral status of neutrality. In return for high salaries and ego-satisfying publicity, they too often became shills, prostitutes, pimps. They sold themselves to the highest bidder and, by doing so, they sold out the American public. More than anyone else they contributed to the cynicism of the corrupt, the belief that success justifies any means or methods, the decline in private morality. For they were the heroes of this country and, despite the protective insulation, the country sensed they were amoral. Instead of rejecting the heroes, however, the country — by and large — either rejected morality or, in lieu of that, refused to think about it at all. As a result this nation came very close to losing its freedom to a right-wing dictatorship.

Until we shed our illusions, until we look at movie stars and public officials with what might be termed skeptical compassion, the danger remains. And next time chance may not be our friend, and we may by a large majority elect a President for Life. While we must never assume that *everyone* is a crook, we must never conclude that *anyone* is a saint. Above all, we must stop confusing illusion with reality — on screen or off.

And so it might be well to remember one moment at the Republican National Convention at Miami Beach in 1972. When the President of the United States spoke of the fight for "law and order," all the TV cameras naturally focused on him. But one network turned its camera briefly from the President and panned to the box occupied by the family of Vice President Spiro Agnew where Frank Sinatra sat as a special guest. No comment was made, and, for the informed, none was necessary.

Index

247